STUDY GUIDE TO ACCOMPANY
WHITMAN / GERGACZ

The Legal and Social Environment of Business

FOURTH EDITION

SUSAN E. GRADY
University of Massachusetts at Amherst

McGraw-Hill, Inc.

New York   St. Louis   San Francisco   Auckland   Bogotá   Caracas
Lisbon   London   Madrid   Mexico City   Milan   Montreal   New Delhi
San Juan   Singapore   Sydney   Tokyo   Toronto

Study Guide to accompany Whitman/Gergacz
THE LEGAL AND SOCIAL ENVIRONMENT OF BUSINESS, Fourth Edition

 This book is printed on recycled paper containing a minimum of 50% total recycled fiber with
10% postconsumer de-inked fiber.

1 2 3 4 5 6 7 8 9 0 SEM SEM 9 0 9 8 7 6 5 4 3

ISBN 0-07-070008-7

The editors were Kenneth MacLeod and Peitr Bohen;
the production supervisor was Paula Flores.
Semline, Inc., was printer and binder.

Contents

To the Student

Although the law is often complex, you will be well rewarded by studying it. On one level, as a citizen of the United States, it is important for you to be aware of the goals and impacts of the law. And as a future member of the business community, a knowledge of the legal environment of business will be of great benefit to you in making sound and informed decisions.

As a supplement to your textbook, *The Legal and Social Environment of Business*, Fourth Edition, this Study Guide will simplify and assist you in your study of the law. Note, of course, that reading the material in the study guide is not a substitute for going to class or reading the text, which offers more complete treatment of each subject area and case. However, the Study Guide will help you to identify the key concepts you should become familiar with, will help you review those concepts, and will test your understanding of them.

Each chapter of the Study Guide contains features that will help you review and study the materials:

1. **Synopsis,** which gives you a brief overview of what the chapter is about

2. **Chapter Objectives,** to make you aware of the key points of the chapter

3. **Major Points to Remember** section, which sets forth in greater detail the major legal principles in each chapter

4. **Major Points of Cases** section, which provides notes on the major legal principles in each case

5. **Self-Test Questions,** which give you the opportunity to check on your mastery of key terms and concepts

The aim of both the text and the Study Guide is to provide you with *an understanding* of the law and the legal environment of business. Avoid simply memorizing rules or terms, for that technique often actually limits rather than increases how much you understand. If you try to understand the information covered in your course, you are much more likely to be able to remember it and to see how the general legal principles can apply to situations not covered in the examples in your text, situations you may have to manage in your future career.

The advice of Douglas Whitman and John William Gergacz in the preparation of this study guide is gratefully acknowledged.

Susan E. Grady

How to Read a Case

All of the cases in this textbook are decisions of appeals courts as opposed to decisions of trial courts. As these decisions are often quite long and involve several issues of law, the authors of the text have done several things to assist you. They have edited the cases to eliminate portions of the opinions they feel are unnecessary. The cases, as edited, focus on the basic reasoning of the court in each case. Citations by the judges to cases, statutes, and other such matters have generally been removed -- except where such a reference is essential to understanding the case. When cases discuss two or more issues of law, they usually have been edited so as to deal with only a single point of law.

Appeals courts typically have a number of judges -- for example, the U.S. Supreme Court is composed of nine justices. In order to win a case, at least five of the nine must rule for the prevailing party. Although five or more justices may believe a given party to a suit should win, they may nonetheless disagree as to the reasons why. In such cases, the justices may write several opinions, each ruling for the same party, but for different reasons. In other cases, when justices may feel the majority has ruled for the wrong party, the justices may write a dissenting opinion. What counts, as far as the litigants are concerned, is the opinion of the majority. The majority's opinion also serves as precedent for later cases dealing with the same issue. Generally, the cases in this text have been taken from cases in which a majority of the justices all agree on the same result and reasoning. On occasion, very good dissenting opinions also appear.

A special effort has been made to simplify the major facts of each case. The first material that appears after the name of the case is the *authors'*--not the court's--summary of the major facts and the decisions of the lower courts, as well as the decision of the court whose opinion is reproduced following the summary of facts. The judge's name follows the summary, followed by an edited version of his or her opinion.

Your first task when reading a case is to determine the *facts*, that is, what happened between the parties that caused the case to be filed. Once you have determined what the basic facts in the case are, your next major consideration is to determine what the judge is being asked to decide. In other words, with what *issue* of the law is the case concerned? Sometimes the issue is clearly stated or identified in the case; at other times you must read the case more carefully. In trying to determine what the issue is, first look to see if the court (the judge) has identified it for you by using such language as "The court is asked to decide...." or "The issue in the case is ...." If the court has not specifically identified the issue, try to determine what the plaintiff hopes to accomplish by instituting the lawsuit, and why he or she wants to accomplish it. When you analyze the answers to those items, the issue in the case should become clear.

After you determine what the facts and the issues are, the next item that should be considered is the *decision*, that is, for whom the judge has ruled. Determining this is quite easy because it is specified in the authors' summary of the facts just prior to the judge's opinion. The judge also states in the opinion for whom he or she has ruled.

The final element in reading a case is determining *why* the court ruled (or decided) for the plaintiff or the defendant, in other words, the *reasoning* or *rationale*. The decision of the appeals court comprises the bulk of the case. It explains how the court arrived at its decision and the principles of law upon which it relied. When reading the case, you should first try to extract the principles of law from the language used by the court. After doing this, then try to understand how the court used the rules of law to justify its decision. It may be helpful to memorize the rules of law announced in the case for testing purposes.

Each chapter of this Study Guide states the main point of each case in the text. Looking at this material in the guide also will help you to understand a case.

The rule announced in each case may be used by your professor in class or on a test. You must understand this rule and how to apply it. Very often, professors present students with similar facts to cases in the book and ask students how the case should be decided.

The best way to answer such a question is to state for whom a court should decide, then state the applicable rule of law, and then apply the rule to the facts of the case.

For example, suppose a test question reads as follows: Jack posted a notice on a bulletin board offering his Corvette for sale. Elmo asked Jack if he would take $18,000 for it. Jack said yes. They both signed a piece of paper that stated, "I, Jack agree to sell to Elmo, who agrees to buy, my Corvette for $18,000." The next day when Elmo presented Jack with a check for $18,000, Jack refused to deliver the title to Elmo. Jack claimed he had been joking and no contract ever came into existence. Is Jack correct?

SAMPLE ANSWER: No. The court should rule that a contract was created when Elmo and Jack signed the paper. The applicable rule of law is that if a person's words or acts, judged by a reasonable standard, manifest an intention to agree, it is immaterial what may be the real but unexpressed state of his or her mind. While Jack may have in fact been joking, this fact is irrelevant to the decision in this case. If a person in Elmo's position could reasonably have thought Jack was making an offer to sell the Corvette for $18,000, an offer has been made. As Elmo accepted the offer, a contract was formed. Thus, the court should rule for Elmo.

Read the cases slowly and carefully, with the precision that the law requires. A judge's decision is a well reasoned piece of work that, when fully absorbed, can be very enlightening and informative. It must be analyzed and digested fully. When you do this, the case will open up a world of knowledge, and the concepts of the law will take on additional meaning. You will also be well prepared for class and for any tests administered during the semester.

Douglas Whitman

Chapter 1

Introduction to the Law and the Legal Environment of Business

Law can be defined as the rules that govern the social environment in which we live. The legal environment of business focuses on the rules under which business must operate. A major concept of this chapter and the chapters that follow is that these laws reflect American traditions and values. As values change, or as some laws are recognized as unjust, the law changes.

CHAPTER OBJECTIVES

After reading Chapter 1 of the text and studying the related materials in this chapter of the *Study Guide*, you will be able to fulfill the following objectives:

1.   To understand the limitations and goals of law in business and society.

2.   To understand the three premises that underlie this text:
     a.   The development of law is a reflection of historical and social movements.
     b.   The law endeavors to regulate large concentrations of power.
     c.   The law endeavors to regulate disputes involving rights.

MAJOR POINTS TO REMEMBER

Law in Business and Society

1.   Every aspect of business is governed by law. Although a business manager is not expected to be a lawyer, he or she must understand the legal environment in which business must function.

2.   Legal rules are not unalterable. The law changes as society's values change.

3.   There are limitations to the law. It cannot effectively regulate all aspects of human behavior. The law cannot regulate morality, for example.

4.   Most laws that endure contain the following elements:
     a.   Predictability - People must be able to anticipate the probable legal outcome of their actions. As an example, consider the concerns of property owners after the reunification of Germany.

b.   Flexibility - Laws made in the past must be adaptable enough to be applicable to modern problems. As an example, consider the application of copyright law to computer programs.

c.   Reasonable application and coverage - Individuals, business, and government must have access to the legal rules that regulate their conduct. The content of the law should be a reasonable reflection of society's beliefs.

How Law Affects Business

5.   Differing kinds of laws have various impacts upon business. The most common of these laws are:

a.   Those which generate new opportunities for business.

b.   Those which limit or forbid certain business practices.

c.   Those which ease the acquiring of certain business benefits.

d.   Those which formalize and acknowledge certain private business decisions.

Recurring Themes in the Study of the American Legal Environment of Business

6.   Three major concepts that underlie this text and that must be understood if one is to master the material are:

a.   The historical and social movements that are the background of legal rules.

b.   The attempt of the law to control concentrations of power.

c.   The attempt of the law to regulate disputes involving rights.

Historical and Social Movements and the Development of Law: From Slavery to Employment Discrimination

7.   The historical and social backgrounds reflect the context in which legal rules are made or changed. Racial discrimination is an example of a societal problem that was dealt with by the courts at varying times. Each historical period had different societal beliefs, which were reflected by the courts. Note not only the beliefs about racial equality, but the varying beliefs about the function of education.

The Law and Its Efforts to Control Concentrations of Power: Drug Testing in the Workplace

8.   The law carefully oversees groups that have large concentrations of power in order to prevent any abuse of such power. Two major groups with power are the government and business. The Constitution formed three separate branches of government in order to divide governmental authority. As business gained more dominance, antitrust laws, labor laws, and consumer laws were enacted to curb any ill use of power.

9.   Drug abuse has posed a problem to the government, business, and individuals. The Constitution protects individual freedoms, including a right to privacy. A major issue in today's society is the legitimacy of drug testing by both governmental and private employers. Those who argue for drug testing point out the duty an employer has to protect the safety of other workers and the public in general. They also point out that

drug use by employees results in lower worker productivity and higher absenteeism. Those who argue against drug testing for governmental employees cite the Fourth Amendment of the Constitution, which prohibits "unreasonable searches and seizures." They further argue that there should be self-restraint by private businesses' exercise of power over its employees. *Borse v. Piece Goods Shop, Inc.* focuses upon drug testing by a private employer.

The Law as a Means of Adjusting Claims of Rights

10. The law carefully oversees individual rights. One of the most difficult functions of the law is settling disputes between parties that involve a conflict of individual rights.

11. Legal rights are granted by the constitutions of federal and state governments, by statutes passed by the federal and state legislatures, and by judicial decisions made by federal and state judges. These rights reflect the philosophical beliefs of society.

12. There are limitations on legal rights. Since no individual, business, or government has absolute rights, courts must sometimes choose between differing values of society. Two cases that illustrate the conflicts between rights are *Schley v. Couch* and *Regina v. Dudley and Stephens*.

MAJOR POINTS OF CASES

Borse v. Piece Goods Shop, Inc. (p. 13)

Borse was an at-will employee which is an employee who is hired for an indeterminate time period. When she was fired for refusing to sign a consent form for urinalysis testing, she sued her employer for wrongful discharge claiming that testing violated her right to privacy. The trial court dismissed Borse's complaint and she appealed.

The appellate court stated that an employer can fire an at-will employee for any reason unless the reason violates public policy. Since Pennsylvania had a law against intrusion upon seclusion, the issue for the court to decide was if urinalysis testing could intrude on an employee's seclusion.

The court held that there were two ways that urinalysis testing could be against this law. The first was if the person giving a sample was monitored by another person. The second was if an employee was fired because of some other medical fact which was revealed by the test. The court held that if this urinalysis testing intruded upon the employee's seclusion it violated public policy. The appellate court therefore overturned the dismissal of the trial court.

Schley v. Couch (p. 17)

The issue in this case is who has the right to the money found buried in the garage. Two weeks after purchasing the house, the new owners hired Tomlinson and his workers to continue laying a concrete floor in the garage. This floor construction had been begun by a previous owner. When one of the workers was digging, he found $1,000. In your opinion does the money belong to the finder? To his boss who told him where to dig? To the present owners of the house who hired the workers? To the person who sold the house to the present owner? To the owner of the house at the time half the garage floor was covered in concrete?

Regina v. Dudley and Stephens (p. 18)

The issue in this important historical case is whether killing a person in order to ensure survival is to be considered murder. (Note that the issue of self-defense is not mentioned in this case; the situation, not the boy, was the threat to survival.)

The English court had to interpret and apply the Criminal Code, which provided no definitive answer to the question of killing by necessity.

The court balanced conflicting rights and ruled that under these circumstances, one's individual right to live did not justify infringing upon another's right to live.

SELF-TEST QUESTIONS

True/False

F   1.   All of society's desirable goals can be achieved by law. (p. 4)

T   2.   An effective law sets the minimum standards of conduct that society will tolerate. (p. 4)

T   3.   To a large extent, law reflects the moral and cultural values of society. (p. 4)

T   4.   The law attempts to be both predictable and flexible. (pp. 4-5)

F   5.   In order for law to have reasonable application, every citizen must know the law. (p. 6)

T   6.   Laws that most people find to be unreasonable soon become unenforceable. (p. 6)

F   7.   Every rule of law has the same general effect upon business. (p. 7)

T   8.   The development of law reflects historical and social movements. (p. 8)

F   9.   The Civil War Amendments to the Constitution were enacted so that every person regardless of race or sex has the right to vote. (p. 9)

T   10.   The separate but equal doctrine legalized segregation for many years after the Civil War. (p. 10)

T   11.   One way the Constitution limited governmental power was by creating three branches of government. (p. 11)

F   12.   Constitutional issues arise in drug testing by both private and public employers. (p. 12)

F   13.   Most of our legal rights are contained in the United States Constitution and change very little in response to changes in society. (p. 16)

_E_ 14. Some legal rights are considered to be so fundamental to a free society that they are subject to no limitation. (p. 16)

_T_ 15. A major function of the legal system is the settling of disputes. (pp. 16-17)

Multiple Choice

1. All of the following statements are true about law except:
   a. the existence of law ensures that a just society will exist.
   b. law embodies the history, values, and cultures of society.
   c. law is a series of concepts and rules which shift to meet social changes.
   d. legal rules and institutions are continually evolving. (p. 3)

2. In order to be effective, law must be:
   a. predictable.
   b. absolute.
   c. unchanging.
   d. moral. (p. 6)

3. Jerry was arrested for computer fraud. The state which arrested him had laws against fraud, but they did not specify computer fraud. Which of the characteristics of law apply to Jerry's case?
   a. Predictability.
   b. Flexibility.
   c. Reasonable application and coverage.
   d. Both b and c. (p. 6)

4. Reasonable application and coverage of the law means:
   a. if a person feels a law in unreasonable, he or she doesn't have to obey it.
   b. since it is unreasonable for any one person to know all the laws, only the known areas must be obeyed.
   c. laws which most people find unreasonable will become unenforceable.
   d. none of the above. (p. 6)

5. The effects of law on business include:
   a. creating new business opportunities.
   b. restricting certain business conduct.
   c. formalizing certain business decisions.
   d. all of the above. (p. 7)

6. Which of the following is *not* a major function of law?
   a. To balance conflicting rights.
   b. To control concentrations of power.
   c. To create a uniform system of law.
   d. To perpetuate past laws and regulations. (p. 8)

7. The change in the Supreme Court's interpretation of the Fourteenth Amendment between *Plessy v. Ferguson* and *Brown v. Board of Education* can best be explained by:
    a. changes in the United States Constitution.
    b. changes in social and cultural values.
    c. the Court's continuing efforts to control concentrations of power.
    d. the impracticability of the "separate but equal" doctrine.   (p. 10)

8. The law has become increasingly concerned with limiting concentrations of business power because:
    a. the Constitution places numerous restrictions on the exercise of such power.
    b. most corporations produce products that are sold directly by the manufacturer to the consumer.
    c. corporations have become large and their relationship with their customers has become impersonal.
    d. of a growing concern that too much power is in the hands of various consumer interest groups.   (p. 11)

9. Critics of drug testing in the workplace are concerned because:
    a. employee drug use has lessened in the past few years.
    b. tests are not one hundred percent accurate.
    c. the majority of states have enacted drug testing legislation.
    d. the Supreme Court has upheld the rights of corporations to conduct random drug tests.   (p. 11)

10. In the *Borse* case where the employee was fired because of her refusal to consent to a urinalysis testing, the court held the employee:
    a. could be fired for any reason because she was an at-will employee.
    b. could be fired because her employer had public policy reasons for testing for drugs.
    c. could possibly be fired if the employer had no reason to suspect she was using drugs.
    d. could possibly be fired if the drug testing was monitored.   (pp. 13-14)

11. Legal rights:
    a. have usually been created as a response to perceived injustices.
    b. protect individuals only from abuses of government power.
    c. are not subject to limitation by courts or legislatures.
    d. are well established and do not change as society changes.   (pp. 14-16)

12. Generally, for legal rights to exist:
    a. they must be stated in the Bill of Rights.
    b. they must be absolutely enforced.
    c. they must be recognized by society.
    d. both a and b.   (pp. 14-16)

13. In deciding a case involving the rights of an individual, the court is most concerned with:
    a. protecting the rights of the individual.
    b. limiting the rights of the individual.
    c. protecting society from certain behavior.
    d. balancing the rights of the individual and those of society.

    (pp. 16-17)

14. The burden of balancing conflicting rights falls mainly upon:
    a. legislatures.
    b. courts.
    c. voters.
    d. the United States Constitution.

    (pp. 16-17)

15. The *Regina* case involving the killing of the young boy best illustrates the rights of:
    a. one individual against the rights of another individual.
    b. an individual against the rights of society as a whole.
    c. an individual against government power.
    d. an individual against business power.

    (pp. 18-19)

Essay Questions

1. Discuss the two powerful groups whose power the law attempts to control. Give the reasons for the attempt.

2. Discuss the concept of absolute rights using the cases in this chapter as examples.

Chapter 2

Introduction to the Courts

This chapter discusses the dispute settling function of the courts. There are three classifications of judicial lawmaking. The first is the creation of new law, called common law, which is based upon these judicial decisions. The second is the interpretation of a statute and the third is the interpretation of the Constitution. All of these decisions affect not only the particular parties involved, but act as guidelines for others.

The chapter begins with a discussion of the court's power to hear cases and then analyzes the structures of both the federal and the state court systems. It is important to realize that the two systems are separate from each other.

The roles of judges and lawyers as principal figures in lawsuits are also focused upon. Because judges and lawyers are essential in the majority of lawsuits, it is of the utmost importance that they perform their functions both to the best of their ability and without bias. Courts police themselves; that is, they evaluate complaints and have the power to remove judges and disbar lawyers. Some common criticisms of the roles that both judges and lawyers play in court and their effects on society are stressed.

CHAPTER OBJECTIVES

After reading Chapter 2 of the text and studying the related materials in this chapter of the *Study Guide*, you will be able to fulfill the following objectives:

1. Understand the concepts of jurisdiction and venue.

2. Describe the structure of both the federal and the state court systems.

3. Identify the various functions of judges.

4. Identify the various functions of lawyers.

5. Debate both sides of some popular criticisms of judges and lawyers, including:
    a. Expanded judicial decisions and their effects on society.
    b. Independence and accountability of judges.
    c. Lawyers' duties to represent clients earnestly, including "guilty" ones.

MAJOR POINTS TO REMEMBER

The Power to Hear a Case

1. In order to have a case heard in court, the plaintiff, or party bringing the suit, must choose a court with proper jurisdiction. The court must have the right to hear petitions or cases of the type the plaintiff or petitioner is bringing. This is known as subject matter jurisdiction. Some courts have general jurisdiction, while others, like probate courts, have limited jurisdiction. The court must also have the right to judge the defendant or person against whom the suit is brought. This is known as in personam jurisdiction. A court has jurisdiction over the plaintiff when he or she files. If the defendant lives in the jurisdiction, the court automatically has the right to judge him or her. If a defendant does not live in the state, but is present when a summons and petition is served, the court has jurisdiction. *Burnham v. Superior Court of California* is a case in point.

2. If the defendant has had "minimum contacts" with the jurisdiction, the court may use the long-arm statute to gain jurisdiction. This concept was first developed in the case of *International Shoe Co. v. State of Washington*. As a result of the *International Shoe* case, the due process clause requires that a party have fair warning and establish some minimum contacts within the foreign state. This is done by looking at the intent and actions of the parties involved. Even so, a state will not have jurisdiction unless it is fair and just to do so.

3. *Venue* refers to the process of selecting the appropriate court in the particular jurisdiction. The defendant may ask for a change in venue if he or she feels that the plaintiff has chosen a court that is inconvenient or that may be biased. For example, residents of a college town may be biased against college students.

4. The United Kingdom developed equity courts to enable people who had no available legal remedies to get some relief. One equitable remedy is specific performance . It requires people to perform certain contractual promises when money damages are inadequate. The United States originally followed the practice of having separate law and equity courts. Today most states have combined the two courts. However, equitable principles still apply today.

Structure of the Court System

5. Courts are in either the federal court system or the state court system. Federal courts have limited jurisdiction. A lawsuit will be heard in the federal courts if it involves a federal question or if the parties reside in different states and are asking for a minimum of $50,000 in damages. Otherwise, the lawsuit is brought in state court.

6. There are three levels of federal courts:
   a. United States District Court--This is the trial court. There are special trial courts that hear only one type of case, such as bankruptcy courts. The general trial courts hear all other cases that the special trial courts do not hear.
   b. United States Court of Appeals--These courts hear cases appealed by a party who is dissatisfied with the results in the trial court.
   c. United States Supreme Court--This Court generally hears cases that are appealed from the United States Court of Appeals or that are appealed from appellate state courts and from state supreme courts. It also can serve as a trial court, but only in limited instances, such as in a lawsuit between two state governments.

7. All states have the following two levels of court systems.
   a. State trial courts.
   b. State appellate courts.
      Many states have special trial courts in which only one type of case is heard. Small claims courts are an example. Some more heavily populated states have intermediate appellate courts.

8. A trial court is the place where legal disputes are resolved at first. A judge is always present: a jury may or may not be. The facts of the case are determined and a verdict is given. Sometimes a jury is asked to answer specific questions in the verdict; this is called a *special verdict*.

9. An appellate court is one that reviews the decision of the trial court. Most often, this is done by reading the trial court transcripts. The appellate court reviews any legal errors or decisions that the judge made; it does not reconduct the trial.

10. The appellate court's decision is usually published. All of the cases in the text are appellate decisions. The decision reached is the majority decision; if a judge disagrees, he or she has the right to write a dissenting opinion. If a judge agrees with the result but not the reasoning, he or she has the right to write a concurring opinion.

Personnel in the Judicial System

11. One major figure in every court case is the judge, who must preside impartially throughout the case and apply the relevant law.

12. Often judges must make decisions about the actions of other branches of government. Modern judges have been handing down more decisions that involve the courts in a supervisory capacity in business and governmental activities. This involvement is known as judicial activism. *Missouri v. Jenkins* is an example of this concept.

13. Judges either are appointed or elected to their positions. Federal judges are appointed for life. Some states follow the Missouri Plan, by which judges may be appointed, with voter approval or disapproval after the judge has served for a time. Other states elect their judges for various terms. No matter what manner of selection is used, sometimes a judge behaves in an inappropriate manner. Note the improper remarks to the Robins Company, in which a judge did not remain impartial.

14. The role of judges has been criticized on two counts:
    a. Judges, especially those using judicial activism, are taking more power upon themselves.
    b. Judges who are appointed for life are not accountable to the public. All judges are immune from lawsuits, but those who are elected have to answer to the voters.

15. Advocates of maintaining the present role of judges argue:
    a. Citizens welcome a more active role by judges.
    b. Judges *are* accountable, because of:
       1. Peer and community pressure.
       2. Possibility of removal by the courts for misconduct.
       3. Judicial temperament or respect for the parties in court.

16. Judges have to balance being independent in their thinking and yet being accountable to the public. Judges are immune from lawsuits on the theory that they must have security in order to make some correct, but sometimes unpopular, decisions. However, judicial immunity does not mean that a judge cannot be removed from a case in which he or she clearly abused his or her power, as *Aetna Life Insurance Co. v. Lavoie et al.* demonstrates. As stated earlier, a judge who consistently abuses his or her power may be removed from the bench.

17. Lawyers are the other major figures in a lawsuit. Hiring the right lawyer is very important. A person seeking legal advice should make certain that the lawyer he or she selects is well versed in that particular area of law. Most lawyers do not go to court. They help their clients avoid potential problems. Those lawyers who are trial lawyers specialize in adversarial law. That is, they attack the opposing lawyer's theories and attempt to convince the court that their reasoning is more sound.

18. All lawyers owe their clients the duty of loyalty and good faith. While lawyers must act in the best interest of their clients, they also have a duty to the law and the legal system. For example, a lawyer cannot allow a client to lie on the witness stand, but under the attorney-client privilege the lawyer cannot testify against the client. *Nix v. Whiteside* is an example of an attorney who would not allow his client to perjure himself in court.

19. All attorneys must respect the historical attorney-client privilege. Anything that the client tells the attorney remains confidential between them. The rationale for this privilege is that in our adversial system, the attorney must have his or her client's complete trust in order to ensure the best representation possible.

20. A common criticism of lawyers is that they sometimes represent parties who are guilty. There are three responses to this criticism:
    a. Each person, under the Constitution, has the right to counsel.
    b. An attorney's job is to represent the client; the judge and jury decide the verdict.
    c. The legal definition of guilt is "proof beyond a reasonable doubt." If the state does not use proper procedures or cannot prove guilt, legally the client is not guilty.

MAJOR POINTS OF CASES

Burnham v. Superior Court of California (p. 25)

The issue in this case was whether the state court of California had in personam jurisdiction over Burnham. He argued that he did not have minimum contacts with the state as he was only in California infrequently on business and to see his children. He also alleged state service violated his due process rights under the Fourteenth Amendment of the Constitution. The state argued that since Burnham was personally in California when he was served, that it had jurisdiction.

The Supreme Court agreed with the state. The Court reviewed previous cases which had dealt with this issue. Cases dealing with minimum contacts have only considered jurisdiction over absent defendants. No decision has ever held that state service on a physically present person has violated their due process rights. The Supreme Court held there was no reason to break with this precedent.

Justice Brennan concurred in the holding, but argued that minimum contacts analysis should be used on defendants served personally in the state. He further argued that a person voluntarily in the state had minimum contacts because of their use of state facilities.

International Shoe Co. v. State of Washington (p. 27)

This important case defined the vague term "minimum contacts." The International Shoe Co. argued that the Washington court did not have jurisdiction over it, because it was a Missouri company and did not have minimum contacts with Washington.

The Supreme Court decided that the shoe company did have minimum contacts with the state, as its business in that state was "systematic and continuous." In addition, the shoe company did a "large volume of business" in that state.

If a company has minimum contacts with a state, the company must submit to the state's jurisdiction and be answerable to the courts.

Missouri v. Jenkins (p. 40)

In order to integrate the public schools in the district, a federal judge ruled that the school district must make a number of improvements. He further ordered these be paid for by an income tax surcharge and a property tax increase. The state argued that the judge had exceeded his authority in imposing these taxes.

The Supreme Court held that the district court had overreached its authority. The court did not have this right to displace local governance unless there were no allowable alternatives. In this case there were alternatives such as requiring the school district to raise taxes. That remedy would have protected the function of the school district as well as requiring it to correct the situation it created.

Aetna Life Insurance Co. v. Lavoie et al. (p. 47)

This case illustrates the law's self-scrutiny and the enforcement of proper judicial conduct. The United States Supreme Court reviewed an appellate decision participated in and written by an Alabama justice who ruled against an insurance company for bad-faith failure to pay a claim. The insurance company argued that this justice should not have participated in the case because he personally had a case against this particular insurance company. The Supreme Court agreed with the insurance company but made it clear that it was not judging whether the justice had been biased, only that because of his interest, he should not have been involved. The case was sent back to the Alabama appellate court to be redecided by other justices.

Nix v. Whiteside (p. 50)

The issue in this case is whether the Sixth Amendment right of a criminal defendant to assistance of counsel is violated when the attorney refuses to allow the defendant to perjure himself in court. The Supreme Court relied on *Strickland v. Washington* as precedent. This case held that the defendant must show serious attorney error and prejudice.

Applying these rules to the *Nix* case, neither error nor prejudice was shown. The attorney was within his rights and duties as an officer of the court in not allowing the defendant to perjure himself on the stand. As for prejudice, the defendant had to show that there was a reasonable probability that the result of the trial would have been different. The court held that even if the perjury had been believed by the jury, the result might well have been the same.

SELF-TEST QUESTIONS

True/False

_____ 1. Judicial lawmaking includes both the creation of law and the interpretation of statutes and the Constitution. (p. 23)

_____ 2. In order to hear a case, a court must have jurisdiction over both the subject matter and the parties. (p. 24)

_____ 3. Federal courts can hear only cases involving a question of federal law. (pp. 31-32)

_____ 4. The organization of courts within a state is very different from the organization of the federal court system. (p. 35)

_____ 5. An appellate court corrects errors of law made by the trial judge, but does not make determinations about the facts in the case. (p. 38)

_____ 6. If an appellate justice disagrees with the majority decision, he or she may write a dissenting opinion. (p. 38)

_____ 7. A court's lawmaking activity is confined to the particular disputes that appear before the court. (p. 40)

_____ 8. One effect of judicial activism is to shift some political decisions from the legislature to the judiciary. (p. 42)

_____ 9. Federal judges are initially appointed by the president with the advice and consent of the Senate but must be periodically approved by the voters in a general election. (p. 43)

_____ 10. Independence of the judiciary is necessary to insure that judges make decisions based upon the law and the facts in dispute rather than political considerations. (pp. 44-45)

_____ 11. As a general rule, judges are immune from suits brought by unhappy litigants. (p. 46)

_____ 12. Most lawyers primarily practice preventative law by attempting to keep their clients from having to go to court. (p. 48)

_____ 13. The attorney-client privilege most often keeps the truth from being discovered during a trial. (pp. 51-52)

_____ 14. In our legal system, the question of guilt depends simply upon whether the accused did or did not commit the act in question. (pp. 52-53)

_____ 15. Our adversary system is based on the theory that justice can best be served through vigorous argument and testing in a courtroom. (p. 53)

Multiple Choice

1. In the *International Shoe* case which dealt with a state obtaining in personam jurisdiction over a shoe company, the Supreme Court held there was:
   a. in personam jurisdiction because the activities were systematic and continuous.
   b. in personam jurisdiction because there were 11 salespersons employed and 10 or more connotes enough of a presence.
   c. no in personam jurisdiction because there was no office in Washington.
   d. no in personam jurisdiction because the activities were irregular and casual.

   (pp. 27-28)

2. Venue concerns:
   a. in which state an action may be brought.
   b. the geographic area in a state in which an action may be brought.
   c. whether an action may be brought in a federal or state court.
   d. whether the plaintiff has the proper jurisdiction. (p. 29)

3. John, a resident of Colorado, was arrested for carrying a picket which read "Only Animals Wear Fur Coats" at a demonstration. John claims he was entitled to his opinion under the First Amendment of the Constitution which guarantees freedom of speech. In regard to John's lawsuit:
   a. John may choose to have his case heard in a state or federal court.
   b. John may choose a federal court in any geographic circuit.
   c. If there is no precedent for John's case where the trial is held, the court must follow the precedent set by another geographic area.
   d. Since this a constitutional issue, the result will be automatically appealed.

   (pp. 30-35)

4. While visiting a tourist attraction in Florida, Osgood, a Michigan resident, was involved in an automobile accident that resulted in $75,000 in damages to Quimby, a Florida resident. If Quimby wishes to sue Osgood for the injuries that he sustained, he may do so:
   a. only in Michigan, where he can get personal service on Osgood.
   b. in Florida, through the use of the Florida long arm statute.
   c. in federal district court, because the parties are residents of different states.
   d. both b and c. (pp. 31-32)

5. Which of the following is true concerning the United States Supreme Court?
   a. It can only hear cases appealed from the United States Courts of Appeals.
   b. It can hear cases from state supreme courts only if a constitutional question is involved.
   c. It must take all cases appealed to it for it is the highest court in the nation.
   d. It never hears cases of original jurisdiction, only cases on appeal. (pp. 34-35)

6. An appellate court:
   a. conducts a new trial.
   b. does not conduct a new trial but may recall witnesses if clarifications are needed.
   c. relies on juries known as "special juries."
   d. produces a written opinion which is usually published. (p. 38)

14

7. Which of the following would *not* be proper grounds for an appellate court to use in reversing the decision of a trial court?
   a. An error in instructions to the jury.
   b. An error in rulings on the admissibility of evidence.
   c. An error in the factual determinations.
   d. An error in the interpretation of applicable law. (p. 38)

8. Which of the following decisions would best be described as judicial activism?
   a. The court voids a criminal statute because it is vague and imprecise.
   b. The court overturns a murder conviction because the arresting officer used improper interrogation techniques.
   c. The court orders a school system to institute a series of special programs for handicapped students.
   d. The court rules that a state may withhold welfare payments from able-bodied adults who refuse employment. (pp. 40-43)

9. In the *Jenkins* case which involved a court order of a property tax increase, the court:
   a. upheld the court order through the remedial powers of an equity court.
   b. upheld the court order because there was no real alternative.
   c. did not uphold the court order because the court circumvented local authority.
   d. did not uphold the court order because courts are never allowed to order tax increases. (pp. 40-41)

10. Judges are kept accountable to the population by:
   a. peer pressure.
   b. the Missouri plan.
   c. threat of removal for incorrect discussions.
   d. judicial temperament. (pp. 44-45)

11. The factor that exerts the *least* amount of control on the judiciary is:
   a. the possibility of removal from the bench for misconduct.
   b. the threat of civil suits by unhappy litigants.
   c. reversals by a higher court.
   d. criticism by attorneys and legal scholars. (pp. 45-47)

12. Which of the following statements concerning lawyers is *not* true?
   a. Most lawyers never appear in court.
   b. Lawyers can never refuse to represent a client.
   c. A lawyer's first duty is to represent his or her client vigorously.
   d. A lawyer has a duty to the courts and the legal system. (pp. 48-49)

13. John is arrested for vandalism and admits to his attorney that he did commit the act. John's attorney:
   a. may not divulge this information without John's consent.
   b. must insist that John testify so that this evidence will be available to the trial court.
   c. as an officer of the court, should report the confession to the trial judge.
   d. should withdraw from the case rather than represent a guilty client. (pp. 49-53)

14. In the *Nix* case, where the attorney would not allow his criminal client to testify because he believed the client would commit perjury, the Supreme Court held:
    a. the attorney acted within accepted limits of professional conduct.
    b. the attorney acted against accepted limits because a defendant has the right to testify in court.
    c. the attorney acted against accepted limits because his client was found guilty.
    d. the attorney acted against accepted limits because he had the duty to do everything in his power to help his client. (pp. 50-51)

15. A lawyer's duty to his or her client involves:
    a. deciding if the client is telling the truth.
    b. keeping privileged statements confidential.
    c. never knowingly representing a guilty client.
    d. giving his or her personal opinion of a case during the summation. (pp. 51-53)

Essay Questions

1. What are the major differences in jurisdiction between the federal and state courts?

2. Discuss the rationale for an attorney defending a guilty party.

Chapter 3

Civil Litigation and Alternative Dispute Resolution

In order to understand the legal environment of business, one must understand the process or procedure of the court system. The first part of the chapter examines civil procedure, or the formal steps in a noncriminal proceeding.

It is important to note that there are pretrial, trial, and post-trial procedures. There are many opportunities, through the use of motions, for one party to attempt to have the court find in his or her favor without continuing the trial. The second part of the chapter describes alternative dispute resolutions which are different procedures that substitute for a court trial. Since trials are both expensive and time-consuming, the parties are encouraged to utilize one of these methods if possible. The parties are encouraged to eliminate all or a portion of the trial if it can be shown that one party has a weak case, which should not be heard or continue to be heard by the court.

CHAPTER OBJECTIVES

After reading Chapter 3 of the text and studying the related materials in this chapter of the *Study Guide*, you will be able to fulfill the following objectives:

1. Define the various pretrial motions and procedures.

2. Define the various motions and procedures used during the trial.

3. Appreciate the importance of a jury to trial.

4. Describe the alternatives to civil litigation.

MAJOR POINTS TO REMEMBER

Civil Litigation

1. A trial is an adversarial process. Each side attempts to convince the judge and jury, if one is present, that its arguments and causes are correct. In addition, each side attempts to discredit the opposing side.

2. When a plaintiff has selected the correct jurisdiction in which to bring his or her legal dispute (cause of action), he or she files a petition or complaint, detailing his or her version of the facts and asking for relief. The defendant is served a summons advising him or her of the petition and giving a stated period of time in which to file an answer or the defendant's version of the facts. The defendant may, in the answer, assert a counterclaim or a grievance against the plaintiff. The petition and the answer are called the *pleadings*.

3. If the defendant does not believe the plaintiff has a cause of action or a justiciable dispute that should be decided by the court, he or she may file a motion to dismiss. If the judge grants this motion, the lawsuit is dismissed. If the judge does not grant the motion to dismiss, the defendant must file an answer or be in default.

4. After the pleadings are filed, either party may ask the judge to make a judgment on the pleadings. This request is the same as a motion to dismiss except that it is filed after the answer. After the pleadings are filed, either party may make a motion for summary judgment. The party who makes this request feels that there are no disputes about the facts and that the judge should make a decision about who is legally correct. If the judge grants this motion, there is no further court action. These filings must be brought by the legal time limit or the statute of limitations is said to have run out and it is too late for a trial. These time limits vary with the type of lawsuit.

5. If the case is going to be heard in court, there is a discovery period in which each side is required to inform the opposing side of its witnesses. Either side may question the opposing witnesses by oral questioning called *depositions*, or written questions, called *interrogatories*. Occasionally, there are discovery abuses such as evasive answers or an overly long list of questions. Some legal critics view such dilatory tactics as unethical.

Trial Procedure

6. Once the discovery process is completed, the attorneys meet with the judge for a pretrial conference where the issues to be tried are simplified.

7. If either party is entitled to a jury trial, either under the Constitution or under state statutes, he or she may request one. There are two types of juries:
   a. Grand juries -- These are used only in criminal cases to determine if there is enough evidence to accuse the defendant. If so, this finding is an indictment and the defendant must stand trial.
   b. Petit juries -- These are used in both criminal and civil cases. This jury's job is to determine the facts of the situation. The judge determines the law. If no jury is present, the judge determines both the facts and the law.

8. If a jury is to be present, the judge and both attorneys participate in jury selection. The judge may exempt or excuse people from service who have valid reasons for not serving. The other people are then questioned under the *voir dire* proceeding. Each attorney may challenge a prospective juror's ability to serve. There are two types of challenges:
   a. Challenge for cause -- These are unlimited in number and are used if a juror is believed to be biased.
   b. Peremptory challenge -- These are limited in number and may be used to keep the person from serving. No explanation need be given to the court.

9. Obtaining the right jury is very important as shown in the MCI example. Once the jury has been selected, the trial begins with the plaintiff's attorney making an opening statement. This is an overview of the plaintiff's position in the case. The defendant's opening statement either follows directly or is given at the end of the plaintiff's entire case, depending on the court procedure.

10. In a civil case, the plaintiff has the burden of proof. If he or she does not prove the case by a preponderance of the evidence, the defendant may make a motion for a directed verdict. If the judge agrees with the defendant, the case is dismissed. Otherwise the defendant presents his or her side.

11. A defeated party may ask that the judge rule in his or her favor even though the jury verdict finds for the other party. This is a motion for a judgment notwithstanding the verdict.

12. During the trial, rules of evidence of that particular jurisdiction must be followed. For example, the hearsay rule excludes testimony which is not the firsthand knowledge of the witness. If an attorney objects to a piece of evidence, the judge must apply the law by allowing or disallowing the objection. A party's challenge that the judge has made an error of law is one of the grounds for an appeal.

13. When a witness is questioned by the attorney of the party who called him or her, this is called *direct examination*. When the opposing attorney then questions the party, this is called *cross examination*. Remember, the purpose of cross examination is to shake the jury's belief in the witness's credibility.

14. At the end of the trial, each attorney presents a closing argument, which summarizes the case, and which the attorney hopes will persuade the judge or jury to find for that party. If there is a jury, the judge gives instructions and the jury must arrive at a verdict. Note that the rules in the jurisdiction may or may not require a unanimous jury vote for a verdict.

15. There are two types of proper verdicts that a jury may give:
    a. General verdict -- A jury simply finds in favor of the plaintiff or the defendant.
    b. Special verdict -- A jury decides the answer to a number of questions concerning specific issues in the case. The judge then applies the law to the facts that the jury has found.

16. Post-trial motions include motions for judgment notwithstanding the verdict and motions for a new trial. The first motion is granted if the judge believes that the verdict is inconsistent with the evidence. The second motion is granted if the judge believes that there were reversible errors during the trial.

The Appeal

17. If all his or her motions are defeated and a party is still dissatisfied with the results of the trial, he or she may file an appeal to the proper appellate court. The person appealing the decision is referred to as the *appellant*, and the other party is referred to as the *appellee* or *respondent*. The appellate court may agree with the trial court (affirm the decision), disagree with the trial court (reverse the decision), or reverse and remand (send it back to the trial court for a new decision).

Alternate Dispute Resolution Procedures

18. Most legal disputes are resolved out of court in order to save both the time and the expense of a court hearing. In addition, these alternative methods are generally more informal and private. This section of the chapter discusses the various alternatives which are available to parties.

19. *Settlements* are agreements made by the parties themselves. In addition to eliminating the time and expense factors of a court hearing, this method eliminates any risk of an adverse judgment. Note the Apple Computer example.

20. *Arbitration* is when an impartial third party or parties are selected to hear and decide the dispute. It is dependent upon the parties' agreement to be bound by the arbitration decision. If there is a clause in a contract to arbitrate, courts will enforce it. If the clause is ambiguous, the courts will order arbitration unless it is clearly against the interest of the parties. *Kansas City Royals Baseball Corp. v. Major League Baseball Players Assn.* is a case in point.

21. Originally courts were reluctant to enforce arbitration clauses. The Federal Arbitration Act required that arbitration agreements be upheld by the courts. In *Shearson/American Express, Inc. v. McMahon* the Supreme Court held that even statutory claims could be arbitrated. In addition, the adoption of the Uniform Arbitration Act by the majority of states encourages arbitration. Even if there has been an error of law or a grave injustice, an arbitration award is final as *Moncharsh v. Heily & Blase* illustrates.

22. Occasionally when parties do not have an agreement to arbitrate or do not voluntarily seek to arbitrate, courts order a *court annexed arbitration*. The purpose of this is to induce the parties to settle certain issues in order to avoid a long jury trial.

23. The alternative of *mediation* is quite similar to arbitration except that it is not binding on the parties. The mediator attempts to assist the parties in coming to an agreement, but does not have the power of an arbitrator to decide the case.

24. Another method of resolving a dispute is a *minitrial*. Here three panelists each give his or her point of view on how the case is likely to be determined in court. Hopefully, the parties will see the strengths and weaknesses of their case and settle. If this does not happen, the parties may still take their case to court for a judgment. A trial with persons acting as a jury is called a *summary jury trial*.

25. As seen earlier in this chapter, often the *settlement conferences* presided over by the judge before the trial leads to an agreement between the parties and no need for a trial.

26. Another alternative is *expert fact-finding*. In these instances a neutral party makes a determination on the facts. This may include all the relevant facts or merely a limited number of facts. Since this alternative is similar to agreements to arbitrate by the parties, most courts would enforce the finding.

27. Parties may hire a referee to act as a judge in an alternative known as *private judging*. Business may set up methods like *private panels* to deal with consumer complaints. If this fails, the consumers may request arbitration.

28. The last alternative resolution procedure is the utilization of *small claims courts*. Depending on the state, persons with claims of $1,000-$5,000 may have their cases heard. Small claims courts are more informal as parties represent themselves. However, a judge does preside.

29. The advantage to using alternative dispute resolution procedures include:
    a. Non-westerners prefer it.
    b. It is designed to facilitate a decision rather than impose one.
    c. Parties in a nonbinding procedure can still go to the trial court if the resolution is unsatisfactory.
    d. The procedures are usually confidential and attract no publicity.

30. A disadvantage to using alternative dispute resolution procedures is that if one of the parties is opposed to the idea, he or she may not agree to any suggestions or results.

31. Even though a contract may require alternative disputes resolution, occasionally one party will refuse to go along with the procedure or the results. Whether a party can be forced to cooperate is the issue in *AMF Inc. v. Brunswick Corp.*

32. Occasionally an unwilling party shows up voluntarily or through contractual obligation attends, but does not participate in the alternative dispute resolution. The other party may assert that the uncooperative appearance is a bad faith breach of contract. *Gilling v. Eastern Airlines, Inc.* is an example of a case of this type. In their contracts, parties often include good faith clauses, clauses forbidding parties from filing suit for a certain period of time, and liquidated damages clauses which stipulate the monetary amount a party will receive if the other party breaches the agreement.

MAJOR POINTS OF CASES

Kansas City Royals Baseball Corp. v.
Major League Baseball Players Assn. (p. 78)

The issue in this case is whether the arbitrators had the jurisdiction to hear the Messersmith-McNally grievances. The lower court held that they did.

The club owners' argument was that although Article X of the agreement between the players and the teams gave provisions for grievances, Article XV excluded any dispute concerning the "core" or "heart" of the reserve system.

The court conceded that a party need only arbitrate what it has agreed to but that the clauses and language must be clear. Because Article XV was not clear, the appellate court held that the Messersmith-McNally grievances should have been decided by the arbitrators.

Shearson/American Express, Inc. v. McMahon (p. 80)

Shearson and McMahon had an arbitration agreement. The issue in this case is whether such an agreement applies when the dispute involves statutes (laws made by legislators) like the Exchange Act and RICO. The Supreme Court held that the arbitration agreement applies.

The court described the Federal Arbitration Act and stated that nowhere in this act is there any suggestion that arbitration not apply to disputes over statutory law. Since the purpose of the Act was to encourage arbitration, the court held that unless one of the parties had shown evidence that Congress wished to make an exception for statutes, the arbitration agreement would be enforced.

Moncharsh v. Heily & Blase (p. 81)

    As a condition of employment, Moncharsh signed an employment agreement with Heily & Blase. He agreed, in the event he left the firm, to pay Heily & Blase eighty percent of any fees collected from clients who went with him. He also agreed that any contractual dispute would be resolved by a final and binding arbitration, After leaving the firm, Moncharsh did not pay the agreed upon eighty percent to Heily & Blase who took the matter to arbitration. The arbitrator found for Heily & Blase. Moncharsh requested the court to amend the decision, claiming that the arbitrator had incorrectly applied the law.

    The issue the court had to decide was whether and when a trial court can review an arbitrator's decision. The court held that statutes favor arbitration. When parties choose this means of solving a dispute, they benefit from the fact that it is quick and inexpensive. Those benefits offset errors which may occur. The court will only become involved if there is grave misconduct such as fraud or a minor correction of an arbitrator's award such as a miscalculation of figures.

    The court stated the general rule of arbitration is that it is final and binding. This would be true even if this fact had not been stated in the contract between Moncharsh and Heily & Blase.

AMF Inc. v. Brunswick Corp. (p. 90)

    AMF and Brunswick agreed to submit to an arbitrator any disputes concerning advertising of either party which was based on data alleging that one product was superior to the other. Two years after the agreement, Brunswick advertised in such a fashion. When Brunswick refused to show the data to AMF, or to an arbitrator, AMF brought suit for the courts to enforce the agreement.

    The issue in this case is whether arbitration can be forced if the action requires "specific performance" like turning over data to a third party. The court held that the agreement was enforceable because public policy favors substitution to court hearings especially when it is agreed upon as in this case.

Gilling v. Eastern Airlines, Inc. (p. 92)

    The passengers aboard an Eastern Airline flight claim they were wrongfully evicted due to Eastern's negligence and breach of contract. The court ordered compulsory arbitration to settle the matter. Eastern executives did not appear but sent their attorneys who participated minimally. When the arbitrator found for the passengers, Eastern requested a trial de novo (new trial) claiming that it was denied its constitutional right to a jury trial. The passengers and arbitrator argued that Eastern did not "participate in a meaningful manner" and so a new trial should be denied.

    The court held that Eastern was entitled to a trial de novo. Although Eastern did not "participate in a meaningful manner" the court felt that denying a new trial was too harsh a penalty since there are other remedies which can be used to penalize Eastern such as paying for both the arbitrator and hearing opposing the trial de novo. Since these other remedies are being used, the court did not have to reach the constitutional question.

SELF-TEST QUESTIONS

True/False

_F_ 1. A trial is a perfect mechanism for obtaining the truth. (p. 56)

_F_ 2. The pleadings consist of the petition, the summons, and the answer. (pp. 57-58)

_T_ 3. A party making a motion for summary judgment is saying that there is no genuine issue of material fact to be decided. (p. 61)

_F_ 4. The statute of limitations puts a restriction on the amount of money damages a party can request in a civil case. (p. 61)

_T_ 5. A major purpose of the discovery procedures is to encourage settlement out of court. (p. 62)

_F_ 6. Since the discovery procedures are designed to operate without court order, courts have very little authority to limit discovery. (pp. 62-63)

_T_ 7. The major function of the pretrial conference is to narrow and simplify the factual issues involved in a case. (p. 64)

_F_ 8. The court will allow the removal of a prospective juror by peremptory challenge only if the attorney requesting the removal can show a good reason for the challenge. (pp. 65-66)

_T_ 9. In a civil case the plaintiff has the burden of proof which, if not established, may cause the case to be dismissed even if the defendant has presented no evidence at court. (p. 71)

_T_ 10. The hearsay rule applies to both oral and written statements. (pp. 71-72)

_T_ 11. If the jurors in a particular case are unable to arrive at a verdict, the judge declares the jury a hung jury and dismisses the case. (p. 74)

_F_ 12. A special verdict requires the jurors to merely make a decision in favor of one of the parties. (p. 75)

_F_ 13. Court annexed arbitration occurs when the arbitrator is a judge or a lawyer. (pp. 83-84)

_F_ 14. Small claims courts are exactly like regular courts except that the proceedings are more informal. (p. 88)

_T_ 15. A major disadvantage to alternative dispute resolution proceedings is that some parties refuse to abide by the decision. (p. 90)

Multiple Choice

1. Civil litigation involves all of the following except:
   a. contract law.
   b. property law.
   c. criminal law.
   d. labor law. (p. 56)

2. A trial:
   a. is an adversarial process.
   b. is the decision maker's function to select the truth teller.
   c. must eliminate all personality factors of the decision maker.
   d. is usually preferable to settling out of court because a lawyer is a good predictor of the outcome. (pp. 56-57)

3. Walter sends Henry a petition and summons. After reading Walter's petition, Henry's attorney is convinced that even if all of Walter's allegations are true, Walter is not entitled to a remedy. Before the close of pleadings, Henry's attorney should ask the court for a:
   a. motion to dismiss.
   b. motion for summary judgment.
   c. motion for a counterclaim.
   d. motion for judgment on the pleadings. (pp. 58-61)

4. When an attorney is using discovery techniques he or she may:
   a. refuse to answer questions the opposing attorney asks if they are unfair to the client.
   b. provide evasive answers to questions which are unfair to the client.
   c. ask the opposing party so many questions that it will encourage a settlement.
   d. request the court to order the opposing side to pay attorney's fees if it refuses to answer questions. (pp. 62-63)

5. The difference between a grand jury and a petit jury is that:
   a. a grand jury is used only in criminal cases; a petit jury is used only in civil cases.
   b. a grand jury is used only in federal cases; a petit jury is used only in state cases.
   c. a grand jury tries issues of law; a petit jury tries issues of fact.
   d. a grand jury determines whether a criminal trial should be held; a petit jury determines guilt or innocence of the defendant. (pp. 64-65)

6. Mitzi, a busy college student, is called for jury duty. Since she has three exams, a term paper, and a sorority party scheduled, she would like to avoid her civic responsibility. Mitzi can do this legally:
   a. only by finding a statutory exemption that applies to her.
   b. simply by not showing up on the appointed day.
   c. by convincing the judge to excuse her.
   d. by informing the court in writing that she is too busy to serve. (p. 65)

7. Voir dire:
   a. is limited in length at the judge's discretion.
   b. is always conducted by the judge on the basis of written questions from the attorneys.
   c. applies to exemptions granted to categories of persons who will better serve society by continuing at their job.
   d. applies to exemptions of state workers in criminal cases because it is expected they would support their employer. (p. 65)

8. Peremptory challenges:
   a. are limited in number.
   b. allow for removal of the biased juror.
   c. must be approved by the judge.
   d. all of the above. (p. 66)

9. In preparing for *voir dire*, attorneys:
   a. are hoping to find unbiased jurors.
   b. tend to stereotype people.
   c. must be provided with background information on each juror by the court.
   d. believe a person's personal appearance can be discounted. (pp. 66-70)

10. The opening statement made by an attorney:
    a. cannot refer to the burden of proof as this is part of the judge's instruction to the jury.
    b. is a part of the presented evidence.
    c. is made first by the plaintiff's attorney in both a civil and a criminal case.
    d. is of little importance because of the limited attention span of most jurors. (p. 70)

11. The only type of alternative dispute resolution procedure listed below which is binding is:
    a. arbitration.
    b. mediation.
    c. minitrial.
    d. expert fact-finding. (pp. 76-77)

12. In the *Kansas City Royals* case where the issue was whether the owners had to arbitrate, the court held:
    a. the agreement excluded disputes by arbitration concerning the reserve system.
    b. the owners only have to arbitrate if it was clearly written in the agreement.
    c. the contract contained contradictory language and the conflict was resolved against those who wrote the contract - the owners.
    d. the contract contained contradictory language and the conflict was resolved against those who signed the contract - the players. (pp. 78-79)

13. In the *Shearson/American Express* case where the court had to determine whether arbitration applied to statutes, the court held that arbitration:
    a. did apply because the Federal Arbitration Act expressly includes statutes.
    b. did apply because the Federal Arbitration Act establishes a federal policy favoring arbitration.
    c. did not apply because the defendants proved that inclusion of statutes was not the Congressional intent in the passage of the Federal Arbitration Act.
    d. did not apply because the defendants did not willingly sign the agreement to arbitrate. (pp. 80-81)

14. Which is *not* an advantage to using nonbinding alternative dispute resolution procedures?
    a. It is mandatory for parties to come to a decision.
    b. If party disagrees with the outcome he or she has no recourse but to obey.
    c. Non-westerners feel ill at ease in this type of proceeding.
    d. There is generally little publicity. (pp. 88-89)

15. In the *Gilling* case where Eastern was dissatisfied with the arbitration outcome and requested a trial *de novo*, the court held:
    a. *Eastern* was deprived of its constitutional right to a jury trial.
    b. the finding of the arbitrator that Eastern had not fully participated in the arbitration should be overruled.
    c. *Eastern* had to pay for the plaintiff's costs of the arbitration and in defending the action for a trial *de novo*.
    d. under statute, it must grant *Eastern* a trial de novo. (p. 92)

Essay Questions

1. What are the major differences between a hearing in a trial court and an appeal to the appellate court?

2. What are the advantages of using alternative dispute resolution procedures?

Chapter 4

Judicial Reasoning and Decision Making

This chapter focuses on the judicial decision-making process. A judge in a trial court or a justice in an appellate court is a product of his or her upbringing and times. They form his or her personality, the ability to decide what is right or wrong, what is just or unjust. They influence the decision in any case.

There are standard factors in reaching a legal decision. A certain judge may view some of these factors as generally more important than others in all cases, or he or she may view some factors as more important in one case than in another.

CHAPTER OBJECTIVES

After reading Chapter 4 of the text and studying the related materials in this chapter of the *Study Guide*, you will be able to fulfill the following objectives:

1. Understand the importance of a judge's particular set of values to his or her role as a judicial decision maker.

2. Identify and analyze the six factors that can be used to justify a judicial decision:
   a. History and custom.
   b. Balance of interest.
   c. Doing "what is right."
   d. Deferring to the other branches of government.
   e. Use of social science data.
   f. Precedent: The doctrine of stare decisis.

3. Recognize these factors in legal decisions and be able to apply various factors that might result in a different decision.

MAJOR POINTS TO REMEMBER

The Judge as a Person: The Personality Factor

1. All judges are products of their environments. Laws are applied by different judges, who may come to varying conclusions. Some cases in the text include a dissenting opinion by a judge who believes that the majority opinion is incorrect.

2. When the President appoints a justice to the United States Supreme Court, he considers both the background and the personality of the justice.

3. Lawyers realize that the personality factor of the judge may affect the outcome of a case, and lawyers therefore may have preferences about which judge they would prefer to have preside at a particular trial. For this reason many lawyers "judge-shop."

4. A judge may decline to hear a certain case because of a conflict of interest. This procedure is called *recusal*.

5. Most judges attempt to remain impartial and to keep their personal feelings from affecting a legal decision. A lawyer or any other party who feels that the judge has not been able to achieve this ideal may attempt to have the judge removed from the case. *State of Israel v. Adolph Eichmann* is an example of this type of proceeding.

Factors in Judicial Decision Making

6. The six factors in legal reasoning discussed in the text are not weighted equally by every judge. Some judges use different factors depending on the content of the lawsuit before them. This is another example of the effect of a judge's beliefs and values on the judicial decision.

7. History and custom make up the first factor that can be applied in judicial reasoning. As Chapter 1 indicated, a past history and present custom reflect the values of the citizens, which are generally reflected in the law. *Ghen v. Rich* embodies a court's use of custom to explain its legal decision.

8. The factor of balance of interests involves a judge's projection of how the outcome of this particular case might involve other people with the same interest. Sometimes an amicus curiae brief is filed on the behalf of the people who will be affected by the result. Note that this brief is a legal argument filed by "friends of the court" to persuade the judge to rule for one of the parties involved in the lawsuit.

9. A third factor considered by judges in their legal reasoning is the attempt to do "what is right," or to reach, in the judge's view, the most fair result to each of the parties. This type of reasoning often reflects the ethics or lack of ethics of the parties.

10. There are many legal doctrines that reflect "what is right" reasoning. These doctrines are:
    a. Equity - Doing what is fair or equitable.
    b. The due process clause in the United State Constitution, which represents the concept of "fundamental fairness."
    c. The unconscionable (against the conscience) clause in contracts.
    d. Public policy - Beliefs in fairness held by the public. Many of these beliefs are reflected in the case of *Riggs v. Palmer*.

11. The fourth factor often used by judges is deferring the decision to other branches of the government. A judge may believe that a dispute is better suited to resolution by the legislature (elected by the people) or administrative agency (which has expertise in the area). *TVA v. Hill* is an example of a court's belief that the legislature is sometimes the better government unit to solve the problem.

12. Another factor that judges use in legal reasoning is data from social-science studies. Note that these studies were not performed with a particular lawsuit in mind, but the studies' results are a factor that should be considered. Arguments that contain social science data are called *Brandeis briefs*. Use of these data has been criticized by some who argue that as the data change, the laws are not modified.

13. The last factor in legal reasoning is following precedent or the doctrine of stare decisis. This doctrine means that a court applies past decisions to present cases that are similar. An appellate court decision is binding on the lower courts in that jurisdiction. Neighboring jurisdictions may adopt the precedent if they choose, but it is not mandatory. This is why there can be differing laws in various states. Note that if a federal appellate court sets precedent, this applies to all the federal courts in that district, not just to one state. If the Supreme Court makes a ruling, this is precedent for all jurisdictions.

14. Precedent is justified by the element of predictability, which is important for citizens to rely upon in their daily actions. For this reason, judges are very careful to follow precedent. *Flood v. Kuhn* is a case that emphasizes the importance of the certainty in the law.

15. Flexibility in the law is also important. If there is an outdated or unjust law, it should be changed. For this reason precedent is not always followed. Sometimes a lawyer will argue that precedent does not apply because the current case does not contain enough similarities to past cases. Since no two cases are exactly the same, this argument can often be used.

16. Another way to break precedent is to argue dicta from previous cases. Dicta is discussion in a previous opinion that did not apply directly to that particular case or was not used as the ruling. Dicta can be an indication that the groundwork for a change in precedent is being laid.

17. The last way that a court may choose to break precedent comes about when the judge strongly believes that a change in the law is needed. It is unusual for a judge to take on that responsibility, for judges must weigh the importance of predictability with the need for change. *Flagiello v. Pennsylvania Hospital* is a case in point.

MAJOR POINTS OF CASES

State of Israel v. Adolph Eichmann (p. 100)

The defendant's lawyer raised the question of whether all three of the Jewish judges would be able to remain impartial in their judgments against a person who was responsible for the extermination of many Jews in Nazi Germany. The decision reached by the judges was that they were trained to be impartial and work under public scrutiny and would therefore be able to separate personal bias from their work as judges.

Ghen v. Rich (p. 102)

The issue in this case is the ownership of a whale. Because whales sink after being shot, the killer cannot take possession until the whale resurfaces. The custom on Cape Cod was for any finder of a whale to notify the killer whose marks were on the whale. The killer would then pay a finder's fee.

In this case, the finder of the whale sold it. The court held that custom should be followed because to find otherwise would be detrimental to those in the whaling industry.

Riggs v. Palmer (p. 105)

The discussion in this case centers around whether an individual who murdered to receive property left him in the victim's will should receive it. The appellate court held that the lower court had the right to apply fundamental maxims or principles of the common law to modify this particular law concerning wills. The maxim is that no one should be allowed to take advantage of his or her own wrong. The court felt that the nephew, who had murdered his uncle in order to receive his share of the bequest, should not be able to benefit from his wrongful actions.

TVA v. Hill (p. 107)

This issue here is whether the Tennessee Valley Authority should be allowed to continue construction of a dam that would endanger a legally protected species of snail darter.

The Court held that it must uphold rulings of other government units. Each branch of government has its function. Deciding whether the legislation under dispute is wise or unwise or whether Congress would have amended the legislation had it anticipated such a result is not the function of the court.

Flood v. Kuhn (p. 110)

Curt Flood was traded to the Philadelphia Phillies without notice. His request that he be made a free agent was denied. He sued claiming violation of the antitrust laws. The trial and appellate courts held that the precedent that baseball was not covered by antitrust law was controlling. The Supreme Court agreed to hear the case.

The Supreme Court stated that this was the third time that it had dealt with the issue of whether baseball is exempt from antitrust law. The court held, as it had in the two earlier cases, that if there is any inconsistency in the law, it should be remedied by the Congress.

The Court pointed out that the original intent of Congress was to exempt baseball from the antitrust laws. If the intent had changed, Congress - not the courts - should amend the law.

Flagiello v. Pennsylvania Hospital (p. 113)

The charitable immunity doctrine is challenged in this case. If the court had followed the precedent in the state, it would have held that a hospital could not be sued, because it was a charitable institution.

The court felt that precedent should be broken for several reasons. The first was that hospitals today are more of a business institution than a charitable institution and therefore should be accountable for any negligent acts.

The second reason was that twenty-four other states have discarded this concept entirely and fourteen states have modified it. Note that while Pennsylvania is under no obligation to follow precedent in other states, it may if it is felt to be desirable and just.

The third reason for breaking precedent was that the court felt that it was irrational for precedent to be followed because it exists. When a law or doctrine is outdated and unjust, it should be abolished.

SELF-TEST QUESTIONS

True/False

_T_ 1. Judges use factors such as balancing the interests involved in a case to justify their decisions. (p. 96)

_T_ 2. Because of personality factors, judges may respond to certain legal arguments in different ways and, as a result, two similar cases, applying the same legal rules, may have different outcomes. (p. 97)

_F_ 3. Studying personality factors of judges indicates that they cannot separate their personal feelings from their professional efforts. (p. 97)

_F_ 4. When attorneys judge-shop, this evidences their belief that a particular judge is biased. (p. 100)

_T_ 5. Competent judges realize that personality factors play a role in their perception of legal issues and attempt to separate their personal feelings from the final decision. (p. 100)

_T_ 6. In cases involving commercial transactions, the outcome is often determined by what is customary within a particular industry. (p. 102)

_F_ 7. Courts may not refuse to enforce certain contracts simply because it would be against public policy to do so. (pp. 104-105)

_T_ 8. Judges can only make law in the context of the issues brought before them and the facts and information involved in a particular case. (p. 106)

_T_ 9. Courts often decide to uphold an administrative agency rule merely because the agency possesses superior knowledge in the area. (p. 106)

_F_ 10. A judge may not refuse to change a legal rule merely because he or she believes that the proposed change should be considered by the legislature. (p. 106)

_F_ 11. Social science data is gathered by sociologists and psychologists at the request of the judge, not the parties. (p. 108)

_T_ 12. Keeping the law stable but flexible is a major function of the doctrine of stare decisis. (p. 109)

_____ 13. Judges usually maintain tradition by following precedent in deciding cases. (p. 110)

_____ 14. When precedent is not followed in a case, it is usually because one of the attorneys has made misrepresentations to the court. (p. 112)

_____ 15. The struggle in the law to balance stability and flexibility is most clearly seen in areas involving stare decisis or precedent. (p. 113)

Multiple Choice

1. Which of the following does *not* affect judicial decision making?
   a. Deferring to other branches of government.
   b. Dicta.
   c. Following precedent.
   d. The judge's personality. (p. 96)

2. A judge's personality includes:
   a. likes and dislikes.
   b. his or her knowledge of the law.
   c. a computer-like mind programmed to decide cases.
   d. a deliberate bias. (pp. 97-98)

3. The personality factor of a judge is balanced by:
   a. removal of all aspects of a judge's personality during a case.
   b. the ability of attorneys to judge-shop.
   c. the ability of a judge to decline to hear a case.
   d. the removal of a judge for incorrect decisions. (p. 100)

4. Judges may avail themselves of the action of recusal when:
   a. they intensely dislike one of the parties.
   b. they strongly believe one of the parties is guilty.
   c. they have formerly represented one of the parties.
   d. they have had to make too many decision in cases of this type. (p. 100)

5. Which of the following is true about judicial decision making?
   a. A judicial decision must contain at least two of the six factors discussed in this chapter.
   b. The judge uses the factors before making a decision based on the law.
   c. The judge uses the applicable factors to justify a legal decision.
   d. If the law is not justified by the factors used, the judge will change the factors. (pp. 101-102)

6. In the *Ghen* case where the issue was if the finder of the whale was the owner, the court justified its decision by:
   a. history and custom.
   b. a balancing of the conflicting interests.
   c. a concept of natural rights.
   d. the doctrine of stare decisis. (pp. 102-103)

7. Since balance of interest cases affect many interested parties, oftentimes these parties will file their own writings known as a(n):
   a. Brandeis brief
   b. amicus curiae brief
   c. unconscionability brief
   d. certiorari brief (p. 104)

8. Judicial decisions which involve doing what is right have been applied specifically to areas of law such as:
   a. the law of equity.
   b. the due process clause.
   c. natural law.
   d. all of the above. (pp. 104-105)

9. In the *Riggs* case where the grandson killed his grandfather to inherit his estate, the court used the following reasoning:
   a. balancing-of-interests factor.
   b. deferring-to-other-branches factor.
   c. following-precedent factor.
   d. doing-what-is-right factor. (pp. 105-106)

10. Courts may refuse to change the law in a particular case and defer the possibility of change to the legislation because:
    a. lawmaking is not a proper function for a court.
    b. courts can only follow precedent in deciding a case.
    c. judges are more subject to political pressure than legislators.
    d. legislatures are able to gather more information and are more accountable to the people. (p. 106)

11. The use of social-science data by the courts in making decisions has been criticized because:
    a. judges are not social scientists.
    b. studies are not always accurate.
    c. as data from the studies change, the law does not always change.
    d. unless both sides have studies, it's unfair under our adversarial system. (pp. 108-109)

12. Which of the following statements concerning precedent is correct?
    a. The major value of precedent is the flexibility that it brings to the law.
    b. Precedent is useful when a case comes to trial but is of little use to an attorney in advising clients.
    c. Judges generally follow precedent in deciding cases.
    d. A judge who routinely ignores precedent is generally considered by attorneys to be clever and innovative. (pp. 109-113)

13. Which of the following is *not* a sufficient reason for a court's failure to follow precedent?
    a. The existing rule is outdated.
    b. The judge personally dislikes the rule.
    c. Injustice will result if the existing rule is used.
    d. The purposes and reasons for the rule no longer exist. (pp. 109-113)

14. Dicta is the portion of the judge's decision which:
    a. explains the rationale of the decision.
    b. is the ruling of the case.
    c. is a remark about the case but does not involve the issue.
    d. can never be used as precedent. (pp. 112-113)

15. In the *Flagiello* case which dealt with the issue of charitable immunity for hospitals, the court disregarded longstanding precedent because:
    a. there is no longer justification for the charitable immunity doctrine.
    b. most of the other states have discarded the charitable immunity doctrine.
    c. the number of accidents in hospitals would not necessarily rise if the doctrine were changed.
    d. all of the above. (pp. 113-114)

Essay Questions

1. There are six factors which can be used to justify a judicial decision. In which is the personality of the judge most apparent? In which is it least apparent?

2. What are the arguments used to break precedent?

Chapter 5

The Legislature, Legislation, and the Executive Branch

Although the judicial branch of the government is the primary focus of this text, some familiarity with the other branches is necessary for understanding the function of law in our society. Business managers need to learn how to work with and influence the legislature and executive branches in order to protect business interests.

The first section of this chapter focuses upon the legislative branch and legislation. Occasionally, the courts are prevailed upon to determine the meaning of legislative statutes. Some of the techniques used by the courts are discussed.

The remainder of this chapter concentrates on the lawmaking function of the executive branch. In addition, the judicial relationship with the executive branch is examined.

CHAPTER OBJECTIVES

After reading Chapter 5 of the text and studying the related materials in this chapter of the *Study Guide*, you will be able to fulfill the following objectives:

1. Identify the functions of legislators.

2. Discuss the reasons for judicial interpretations of statutes.

3. List and understand the techniques used to interpret statutes.

4. Discuss the executive's lawmaking powers and limitations.

MAJOR POINTS TO REMEMBER

A Comparison of Lawmaking by the Courts and the Legislature

1. The judicial approach to lawmaking is to decide each case on its particular facts as it is brought before the court.

2. Courts have no power to decide hypothetical cases or to perform informational surveys. A court can judge only what is presented before it.

3. The legislative approach to lawmaking is much broader. Statutes are not written to settle private disputes, but rather because the legislature has determined certain laws are needed. Unless the Constitution limits an area, the legislature has the power to research issues and recommend certain statutes.

4. The judicial approach to lawmaking is also concerned with the doctrine of stare decisis. If a court is reluctant to change the existing law, it often yields to the legislature.

5. The legislative approach to law, although not bound to stare decisis, is also concerned with stability and certainty in the law. It tends to enact laws similar to those that already exist or that have proved themselves in other states.

The Legislature and Lawmakers

6. Legislation as a means of regulating conduct is relatively new in the United States. Prior to this, most of the law was common law. But common law could only deal with issues brought before the courts. The legislature was able to eliminate confusion caused by conflicting precedents and provide uniformity by passing one act governing a given area.

7. There are three major roles of legislators:
   a. Lawmaking function -- Enact statutes.
   b. Overseer function -- Investigate.
   c. Ombudsman -- Serve constituents.

8. A statute is a law passed by the legislature. The other branches of government are often involved as well. The executive branch may influence the debate and passage of a statute, and the judicial branch may have to interpret the statute.

9. A statute can pertain to the legal environment of business. For this reason, business may try to influence the debate and passage of a statute. It can do so by lobbyists or by contributions to certain legislators' campaigns for election or reelection.

Statutory Construction

10. Some statutes are ambiguous or vague. At times, they are written in this way deliberately so that a statute will cover may types of situations without requiring all of them to be listed.

11. Courts are often requested to interpret statutes that are technical or vague because of the nature of the language.

12. Judges generally use three methods to interpret these statutes:
   a. Legislative history -- The reports and materials generated during the passage of the statute may be helpful in determining what the legislature intended. *United Steelworkers of America v. Weber* is an example of this approach.
   b. Construing the meaning of the words themselves -- There are three ways of doing this:
      1. Plain meaning or ordinary usage doctrine, in which a standard dictionary definition is used. *Diamond v. Chakrabarty* focuses upon this doctrine.
      2. Ejusdem generis doctrine, in which a general word following a list of specific words is interpreted as including all similar specific words.
      3. Referring to other parts of the statute in which the surrounding material is an aid to the meaning.

c. The spirit or purpose of the statute -- Instead of taking the plain meaning of a statute, a court may interpret the general intention of the statute. For an example of this doctrine, see *Lennon v. Immigration and Naturalization Service*.

The Executive Branch

13. The executive branch of the government is composed of those making and enforcing the laws. One may consider the executive's primary role as the enforcer of law by *carrying out* legislative statutes and court orders. However, the executive also makes law through executive orders, by carrying out executive duties, and by initiating policy. The text focuses on the president as an example. Note that the Constitution, the legislature, and the courts limit the executive's power.

14. The executive has the power to enact executive orders such as President Reagan's Drug-Free Federal Workplace. Sometimes the judicial branch of the government will limit executive orders, as when the court held that President Truman did not have the authority to seize the steel mills. The executive also has the power to veto laws, appoint judges, commute (reduce) a sentence given by a judge, or pardon a person. An executive can use policy to set priorities for the legislature's consideration of certain laws.

15. Courts are empowered to set limits on executive activities but are generally hesitant to do so because the executive must voluntarily accept the limits. Some difficulties have arisen in the areas of political questions due to the often held belief that certain questions are best answered by the voters. *Orlando and Berk v. Laird* is a case of this type.

MAJOR POINTS OF CASES

United Steelworkers of America v. Weber (p. 129)

This is a dissenting opinion, which argues against the finding of the majority of the Court holding that voluntary affirmative action plans do not violate the Civil Rights Act of 1964.

Justice Rehnquist felt that the legislative history of the act showed that just the opposite should be true. The purpose of the act was to prohibit any type of racial discrimination, and to favor neither whites or blacks. When passage of the act was being debated, those in favor stated that it would not permit racial quotas, or have any effect on seniority rights or be used to give preference to black workers.

Diamond v. Chakrabarty (p. 130)

The issue in this case is whether an invention of bacterium to break down crude oil should be patentable. The statute that applies to the granting of patents includes such categories as "manufacture" and "composition of matter."

The Supreme Court applied the plain meaning doctrine to the statute and determined that the categories listed were quite broad. The nonnatural bacteria were in a sense a "manufactured composition of matter" invented by Chakrabarty and a patent should be granted.

Lennon v. Immigration and Naturalization Service (p. 133)

The Immigration and Nationality Act exempts thirty-one classes of people from permanent residency in the United State. Because John Lennon was convicted of possession of marihuana under an English statute, he was denied permanent residency in the United States under this act. He appealed this decision.

The appellate court first looked at the plain language of the British statute and stated that this statute made guilty knowledge irrelevant and that the deportation of everyone found guilty under this act was grossly unfair. The court then looked to the general purpose of the act, which was to keep undesirables such as drug traffickers and addicts from establishing permanent residency. Thus, the court held that to deny Lennon permanent residency in the United States was unfair.

The dissent argued that the act was clear and that it included possessors of drugs as well as sellers and addicts. The dissent also argued that the British statute was fair, as it would be very unusual for a person to unknowingly possess drugs.

Orlando and Berk v. Laird (p. 142)

In this case, the executive branch is challenged on its authority to wage war in Vietnam, because war had not been declared by Congress.

The court held that there were resolutions and consent for the war by the legislature. It was felt that whether there had to be a formal declaration of war was a question that constitutionally the court did not have the competence to decide.

SELF-TEST QUESTIONS

True/False

___F___ 1. The legislature, like the courts, makes law on a case-by-case basis. (p. 119)

___T___ 2. Abuses of the investigative process may pose a danger to individual freedom; therefore, the courts have the power to review the scope of legislative investigations. (p. 119)

___T___ 3. Codification of laws began as an attempt by legislators to limit judicial power. (p. 121)

___F___ 4. Like the executive and the judicial branches, power in the legislative branch is centralized. (p. 122)

___F___ 5. Eventually, all statutes become subject to judicial scrutiny. (p. 124)

___F___ 6. One reason that statutes are vague is because language itself is vague. (p. 125)

___T___ 7. The legislature may draft a deliberately ambiguous statute in order to give the courts greater leeway in closing potential loopholes. (pp. 126-127)

_____ 8. Legislative history may often be used to justify two entirely different interpretations of the same statute. (p. 128)

_____ 9. In interpreting a word or phrase in a statute, the courts often interpret that word or phrase within the statutory context in which it is used. (p. 132)

_____ 10. The executive can affect the legal environment by the vigor or lack of vigor in his or her enforcement of policies. (p. 137)

_____ 11. The only check that the legislative branch has on the power of the executive is the power to impeach and remove the president from office. (p. 137)

_____ 12. The president makes laws through the drafting of executive orders, by policy initiation, and through the execution of his general executive duties. (pp. 138-139)

_____ 13. The executive's lawmaking powers are no more limited than the power of the other branches of government. (p. 139)

_____ 14. A president may be able to influence the legal environment by his appointment of federal and state judges. (p. 139)

_____ 15. Courts may not refuse to hear a challenge to an action taken by the president merely because it presents a political question. (p. 142)

Multiple Choice

1. The Tennessee legislature is convinced that a principle of common law is unfair and should be radically changed. Which of the following factors will be the *least* useful to the legislature in drafting the new statute?
   a. Prior cases decided by the Tennessee Supreme Court.
   b. An older but similar Tennessee statute.
   c. A current Georgia statute dealing with the same subject matter.
   d. The results of an investigation by a legislative subcommittee.

   (pp. 119-121)

2. Which of the following is *not* a reason for courts to defer to the legislature to make laws?
   a. Legislatures are not bound by stare decisis.
   b. Legislatures' statutes cannot be interpreted by the courts.
   c. Legislatures have broader investigative powers than the courts.
   d. Legislatures can look to model statutes in other states.

   (pp. 119-121)

3. Which of the following is the best reason for the courts to defer to the legislature to make laws?
   a. The courts are overworked.
   b. The legislature has the power to thoroughly study the probable effect of a statute before enacting it.
   c. The legislature must look to other state legislatures for guidance as this reveals the effects of the statute.
   d. The legislature is bound by stare decisis. (p. 120)

4. Which of the following is *not* true?
   a. The first legal area to receive serious legislative attention was criminal law.
   b. Originally legislation was merely a means to fill in the gaps in common law.
   c. Much of commercial law has been codified.
   d. Statutes are a newer means to regulate conduct than the common law. (p. 121)

5. When creating statutes, the legislature is often under the influence and guidance of:
   a. the executive branch.
   b. lobbyists.
   c. contributors to legislative campaigns.
   d. all of the above. (p. 122)

6. The major function of the courts in statutory interpretation is:
   a. to insure that the statute is interpreted in accordance with existing case law.
   b. to correct errors made by the legislature in drafting the statute.
   c. to give meaning to a statute as it applies to specific facts.
   d. to rewrite the statute in accordance with basic concepts of justice. (p. 127)

7. A local ordinance prohibits "chickens, ducks, geese, and other barnyard fowl" from "wandering loose in the city" and provides for a fine of $50 to be paid by "the owner of such fowl." Roger allows his pet pig to wander unrestrained throughout his neighborhood. If Roger is arrested for violating the statute, he is most likely to be found guilty if the court:
   a. examines the legislative history of the statute.
   b. applies the doctrine of ejusdem generis.
   c. refers to the statutory context.
   d. examines the purpose of the ordinance. (pp. 127-132)

8. A technique *not* used by the courts in interpreting vague statutes is:
   a. the ombudsman doctrine.
   b. legislative history.
   c. the plain meaning doctrine.
   d. ejusdem generis. (pp. 127-132)

9. In the *United Steelworkers of America* case, where the majority of the justices held that voluntary affirmative action plans did not violate the Civil Right Act of 1964, the dissent felt:
    a. the affirmative-action plan was too vague.
    b. the affirmative-action plan was too technical.
    c. the affirmative-action plan violated legislative history.
    d. the affirmative-action plan would upset the majority of workers in the country.
    (pp. 129-130)

10. The technique of statutory interpretation, which is best illustrated by *Diamond v. Chakrabarty*, which dealt with patent claims, is:
    a. the statute's legislative history.
    b. the plain meaning doctrine.
    c. the doctrine of ejusdem generis.
    d. the reference to other parts of the statute.
    (pp. 130-131)

11. The executive branch of government:
    a. is limited to the top hierarchy of executives such as the president, the governor, and the mayor.
    b. can affect the legal environment by enforcing some laws more strongly than others.
    c. merely enforces the law, but does not make it.
    d. has the most power of the three branches of government.
    (pp. 135-137)

12. The authority of the president to issue executive orders:
    a. is limited to rules involving the day-to-day operation of the government.
    b. is limited by the Congress and the Constitution.
    c. is limited only by the Constitution.
    d. is unlimited.
    (pp. 137-139)

13. With regard to the judicial branch of government, the president has a right to:
    a. appoint justices to the Supreme Court only.
    b. appoint all federal judges.
    c. appoint some federal and state judges.
    d. encourage judicial review.
    (pp. 139-141)

14. Limits on executive lawmaking power:
    a. are explicitly stated in the Constitution.
    b. are usually adjudicated by the courts.
    c. are enforced by the executive branch itself through unwritten rules.
    d. are limited by past practice in some areas.
    (p. 141)

15. In the *Orlando* case, the court declined to decide if the Vietnam War was constitutional because of:
    a. the legislative history.
    b. the doctrine of ejusdem generis.
    c. the belief that political questions are best answered by voters.
    d. the belief that the executive is an expert in foreign policy.
    (pp. 142-143)

Essay Questions

1.   Discuss the differences between statutes and the common law.

2.   What are the limitations on executive power by the legislative and judicial branches of government?

Chapter 6

Constitutional Law and Business

The two major functions of the United States Constitution are to create the general structure of government and to protect the individual's rights against the government.

This chapter focuses upon the working of these functions. The Constitution grants certain powers to both the federal and state government to regulate business. This chapter concludes with an analysis of some individual rights granted by the Constitution through limitations on governmental power.

CHAPTER OBJECTIVES

After reading Chapter 6 of the text and studying the related materials in this chapter of the *Study Guide*, you will be able to fulfill the following objectives:

1. Describe the two major functions of the Constitution. These are:
    a. Creating the general structure of government.
    b. Protecting individual rights.

2. Identify certain federal and state powers granted by the Constitution to regulate business. These are:
    a. The commerce clause.
    b. The supremacy clause.
    c. The police power of the states.

3. Identify certain individual rights guaranteed by the Constitution, including those given by:
    a. The due process clause.
    b. The equal protection clause.
    c. The First Amendment right to freedom of speech.

MAJOR POINTS TO REMEMBER

The United States Constitution

1. One of the major functions of the Constitution is to create the organizational structure of the federal government and to create the structural relationship between the federal and state governments. Note when reading the Constitution that the structure of the federal government gives certain powers to each of the three branches of government. This arrangement provides a system of checks and balances, which protects against any one branch acquiring too much power.

2. The second major function of the Constitution is to protect individual rights against the government. Most of these individual rights are found in Constitutional amendments. For example, the Fourteenth Amendment provides that certain individual rights are protected from state interference as well as federal interference.

Federal Power to Regulate Business

3. The commerce clause of the Constitution grants Congress the right to regulate commerce among Indian tribes, among foreign nations, and among the states. Only the latter two areas are emphasized in the text. Note that since the federal government has the right to regulate commerce, this is a limitation on the states.

4. Although there was never any challenge to federal control of foreign commerce, the Supreme Court was called upon to interpret the commerce clause as applied to the states. The Court's interpretation underwent several changes from the time the statute was first challenged to the present day. Currently, Congress has the power to regulate commerce that is intrastate (in state), interstate (between states), and noncommerce areas that could have a substantial effect on commerce. *Katzenbach v. McClung* is a case that demonstrates the effect on commerce of a restaurant that refused to serve blacks.

State Power to Regulate Business

5. The state power to regulate business is known as *police power*. As previously noted, this power is limited. It does not include:
   a. Powers granted to the federal government under the commerce clause.
   b. Powers granted by the state to local governments, such as municipalities.
   c. Areas where national uniformity is necessary. *Cipollone v. Liggett Group, Inc.* is a case which discusses a preemptive statute in the area of cigarette labeling.
   d. Areas where Congress has preempted or taken possession of that particular domain. *Silkwood v. Kerr-McGee* is a case that deals with the right of a state court to order punitive damages to be paid by a company that manufactured nuclear fuel.
   e. Any state law in conflict with a federal law. The supremacy clause of the Constitution declares that federal law is controlling over state law.
   f. Any state law that discriminates in favor of in-state businesses over out-of-state businesses. *Maine v. Taylor* is a case in which a state was accused of discriminating against interstate commerce.

Limitations on Governmental Power

6. The Constitution provides protection of individual rights from the state action of the government. The term *state action* applies to both the state and federal government, but not to the actions of private parties. For example, NCAA actions are private, not state actions.

7. Most individual rights are found in amendments to the Constitution. For example, the Fourteenth Amendment contains the due process clause, which specifies that no state may "deprive persons of life, liberty or property without due process of law." Due process comprises two general types of rights:
   a. Substantial due process, which requires that the law be fair and reasonable.

b. Procedural due process, which requires that the procedures used by the courts to enforce the laws be fair and reasonable. Some of these procedures include notice of an action, a fair hearing, and the right to present and rebut evidence. *Connecticut v. Doehr* is a case in which the defendant claimed that he was denied due process of law.

8. Another individual right granted by the Fourteenth Amendment is the equal protection clause, which holds that no state shall "deny to any person within its jurisdiction the equal protection of the laws." Note that this clause does not entirely prohibit discrimination by the state. It rather means that if the state discriminates, it must show a legitimate reason for doing so. Different classifications of discrimination require differing rationales for the state's action.
    a. The strict scrutiny test is the most rigid test and is applied to classifications of race. To deny equal protection because of race, the government must show a compelling purpose that cannot be achieved by any other method.
    b. The rational basis test is the least exacting test and is generally the test applied to the regulation of business. The government need only show a reasonable purpose for a valid objective. Courts generally defer to the legislature in these instances, as shown in *State by Humphrey v. Ri-Mel, Inc.*

9. There are different levels of tests between the strict-scrutiny and rational-basis tests. *Craig v. Boren* is a case demonstrating the test applied by the courts in a sex-discrimination case.

The First Amendment and Business

10. One of the guarantees to an individual under the First Amendment is freedom of speech. Much debate exists whether this should be total or restricted freedom of speech. The laws limiting speech to reasonable times, places, or manner show that the majority of courts have concluded that this is a restricted guarantee. Note the examples of Penn State's "open canvassing" procedures and New York's prohibition on begging. Sometimes there is a conflict of cultures between countries as in the Salman Rushdie situation.

11. Another debated question in this area has been whether freedom of speech applies to commercial speech, or speech by business. *First National Bank of Boston v. Bellotti* deals with the issue of freedom of speech for a corporation. Although the content of commercial speech has received First Amendment protection, it can be restricted if there is a "reasonable fit" between the restriction and the interest the government is attempting to protect. *Cincinnati v. Discovery Network, Inc.* reflects some of the court's concerns in this area.

12. A third debated question has been whether professionals such as doctors and lawyers have the right to advertise. The Supreme Court held that the First Amendment gives them this right. As with other types of speech, advertising is limited by restrictions on false or deceptive advertising. Advertising is also subject to reasonable time, place, and manner restrictions.

MAJOR POINTS OF CASES

Katzenbach v. McClung (p. 149)

This case involves the Civil Rights Act of 1964, which prohibits racial discrimination. A restaurant that purchased food from other states refused to serve black interstate travelers. The plaintiff argued that this practice was illegal under the commerce clause. Note that the federal government, by the commerce clause, has the power to regulate commerce.

The Court held that this antidiscriminatory result of the Civil Rights Act of 1964 was constitutional. Although it was argued that the discrimination did not substantially affect interstate commerce, the Court felt it did. The rationale is that blacks do not travel or relocate frequently in areas that allow discrimination. This affects the economy of those areas and has a serious effect upon interstate commerce.

Cipollone v. Liggett Group, Inc. (p. 152)

This case deals with whether a federal statute requiring warning labels on cigarette packages and in cigarette advertising preempts state law damage actions in general and the plaintiff's claims in particular.

The Supreme Court held that when Congress defines what is preempted in a field, areas beyond that definition are not preempted. In this particular case, the statute limited itself to health warnings on cigarette packages and in advertising. The Court went on to discuss the philosophy behind its holding. The first reason is to protect state police power. The second is that the statute itself says nothing about restricting other state remedies. The third reason is that there is no conflict between the federal preemption and state common law damages.

Silkwood v. Kerr-McGee Corporation (p. 155)

Karen Silkwood was contaminated by plutonium at her job at the defendant corporation, which manufactured fuel for nuclear power plants. Her father sued the corporation under state tort law and was awarded both actual and punitive damages.

The corporation appealed, arguing that the nuclear energy field was preempted by federal law from having to pay punitive damages.

The court looked at the legislative intent behind the federal laws in the nuclear energy and safety areas and held that Congress intended both state and federal law to coexist as much as possible. Therefore the court ruled that punitive damages were not preempted in this case by federal law.

Maine v. Taylor (p. 156)

The issue in this case is whether a Maine statute that prohibited the importing of fish was unconstitutional because it burdened interstate commerce.

The Supreme Court stated that the commerce clause is controlling but not absolute. States may regulate if the statute serves a legitimate local purpose that cannot be served as well by nondiscriminatory means. The court held that Maine had a legal interest in guarding the environment.

46

Connecticut v. Doehr (p. 160)

Under Connecticut law, a creditor could attach a debtor's real estate after a finding that there was probable cause to believe the creditor's claim. This attachment could occur without giving the debtor notice and before a hearing on the issue between the debtor and the creditor. When Doehr's house was attached in this manner, he sued the state of Connecticut claiming that this statute was unconstitutional under the due process clause.

The Supreme Court had to decide two issues in the case. The first was whether the due process clause applied in this case. The Court held that although debtor-creditor hearings usually involve private individuals, the fact that the creditor made use of state procedures with state officials involved sufficient state action to invoke the due process clause.

The second issue to be determined was whether the Connecticut statute procedures were fair. The court held that they were not because the debtor has a significant interest in his or her property and because there is a risk of an erroneous taking of property without a hearing involving both parties. The court held that a hearing should be held after attachment only in urgent circumstances such as a creditor's belief that the debtor was going to dispose of the property before attachment.

State by Humphrey v. Ri-Mel, Inc. (p. 163)

This case examines the equal protection clause and the various tests which courts must use to test whether discriminatory treatment is permissible. Minnesota distinguished between for profit and nonprofit health clubs by requiring the for profit clubs to post a bond to protect consumers in the event that the club went out of business.

Ri-Mel, Inc., a for profit health club, challenged this law. Ri-Mel argued that freedom of contract was a fundamental right and so a higher standard than the rational basis test should be used to determine whether the law was permissible under the equal protection clause.

The court held that freedom of contract was not a fundamental right and that the rational basis test should be applied. Under this test the discriminatory practice is allowable if the state can show a rational (or reasonable) governmental purpose for the rule. The purpose in this particular case was to protect the consumer. In the past, members of for profit health clubs had lost their prepayments when the club went out of business. Since non-profit health clubs did not require prepayments, it was not necessary for them to post bonds.

Craig v. Boren (p. 164)

The issue in this case is whether a statute legalizing 3.2 percent beer for females at age eighteen and for males at age twenty-one is sex discrimination.

The general rule is that the government may discriminate on the basis of sex only if the government can show that important objectives are met by this discrimination.

The court held that although the government objective of public health and safety was clearly important, the government failed to show an effective rationale for the discrimination. Since the state government did not meet the required burden of proof, the law was held unconstitutional on the basis of sex discrimination.

First National Bank of Boston v. Bellotti (p. 168)

This case is a challenge to a state statute prohibiting corporations from publicizing their views to the voters.

The Court held that the statute is unconstitutional. The rationale given is that the First Amendment guaranteed freedom of speech. The statute itself recognized the right of the corporations to speak on certain issues, and the Court felt that this was supportive of its position. A state may not dictate the content of speech. Thus corporations are guaranteed the right of free speech.

Cincinnati v. Discovery Network, Inc. (p. 170)

The city of Cincinnati allowed free standing newsracks on public property. 1500 to 2000 of these newsracks contained local newspapers and 38 of these newsracks contained promotional material for the Discovery Network's adult education programs. Cincinnati withdrew Discovery's permit on the grounds that it was protecting the safety and esthetics of the city and that commercial speech had a low value. Discovery sued alleging its First Amendment rights had been violated.

The Supreme Court agreed with the lower courts that the city had failed to meet its burden of showing a "reasonable fit" between the interests of safety and esthetics and its discussion to revoke Discovery's permit. The Court pointed out that removal of such a small number of newsracks would have little effect on safety and esthetics.

As for the argument that commercial speech has a low value, the Court held that the distinctions between commercial and noncommercial speech bears no relationship to the goals the city is protecting. The court went on to say that its holding does not reach the question of whether a community with different circumstances might be able to justify different treatment between the two types of speech. The Court only held that Cincinnati had failed to justify different treatment in this instance.

SELF-TEST QUESTIONS

True/False

F 1. The two major functions of the Constitution are to protect individuals from the government and from corporations. (pp. 146-147)

F 2. Under the commerce clause, the federal government can regulate only activities that are clearly interstate in character. (p. 149)

T 3. The power of the state to regulate is called police power. (p. 151)

T 4. Congress may preempt a field by implication when congressional legislation is extensive in a particular area. (p. 154)

T 5. Under the supremacy clause of the United States Constitution, a state law that conflicts with federal law generally must give way to federal law. (p. 156)

T 6. Purely private activity is not covered by the Bill of Rights. (p. 158)

48

_____ 7. The Fourteenth Amendment extends the concept of due process found in the Fifth Amendment to the states. (p. 159)

_T_ 8. Substantive due process requires notification and a fair hearing. (p. 159)

_F_ 9. The equal protection clause prohibits the law from treating different groups of people differently. (p. 162)

_F_ 10. In equal protection cases the classification most often applied to business is the strict security test. (p. 162)

_T_ 11. The Constitution was purposely drafted in general language to allow reinterpretation as times change. (p. 166)

_F_ 12. When interpreting the First Amendment, the Supreme Court has only allowed federal, not state, restrictions on speech. (p. 167)

_F_ 13. Constitutional protection of free speech does not apply to speech other than that with some political content. (p. 167)

_____ 14. For commercial speech to be protected by the First Amendment, it must do more than propose a commercial transaction. (p. 169)

_F_ 15. Under the First Amendment, advertising by professionals may no longer be regulated by time, place, and manner restrictions. (p. 174)

Multiple Choice

1. The United States Constitution:
   a. has one major purpose which is to set forth the basic structure of government.
   b. includes some amendments pertaining to governmental organization.
   c. contains limitations on the power of the federal government, but not the state government.
   d. only provides for individual rights in the Bill of Rights and later amendments.
   (pp. 146-147)

2. Under modern interpretations of the commerce clause, the federal government may regulate:
   a. commercial activities that actually involve or affect more than one state.
   b. commercial activities that are intrastate in character but have a substantial effect on interstate commerce.
   c. noncommercial activities that have a substantial effect on interstate commerce.
   d. all of the above.
   (pp. 147-149)

3. In the *Katzenbach* case which deals with the refusal of the owner of Ollie's Barbeque to serve blacks, the court held:
   a. the owner can't discriminate because of the effect on interstate commerce.
   b. the owner can't discriminate because of the due process clause.
   c. the owner can discriminate because the barbeque is a small business.
   d. the owner can discriminate in this case, but the same finding would probably not be true today. (pp. 149-151)

4. Police power is:
   a. the power of *both* state and local government to regulate business.
   b. unlimited unless it affects interstate commerce.
   c. unlimited unless the federal government has completely occupied the field.
   d. all of the above. (pp. 151-152)

5. Under Congress's right of preemption:
   a. the preemption must be expressly stated by an act of Congress.
   b. most regulations relating to the banking industry have now been preempted by the federal government.
   c. states still have a great deal of regulatory power.
   d. only local, not state, regulations are affected. (pp. 152-154)

6. In the *Silkwood* case, where the issue was whether punitive damages could be granted, the court held:
   a. since Silkwood was dead, no punitive damages would be given.
   b. since the state statute dealt with punitive damages only, it was not preempted by federal nuclear power law.
   c. since the case dealt with the effects of nuclear power, federal law applied and punitive damages could not be given.
   d. there is never any instance where federal law can preempt state damages law. (pp. 155-157)

7. Mary refused to sell her stereo to Jim because he only listened to rock music. Jim claims this refusal to sell is unconstitutional. Mary disagrees.
   a. Mary is right because this would be a private sale and no state action is involved.
   b. Mary is right because the Commerce Clause of the Constitution gives her the right to refuse.
   c. Jim is right because Mary's action is preempted by federal law.
   d. Jim is right because Mary is discriminating against him and discrimination is illegal. (pp. 157-158)

8. Most of the individual rights guaranteed by the Bill of Rights are applicable to the states as well because:
   a. the state governments are specifically mentioned in the Bill of Rights.
   b. basic concepts of fairness and justice require such a result.
   c. the courts have interpreted the Fourteenth Amendment's due process clause to require such a result.
   d. no states include bills of rights in their constitutions. (pp. 159-160)

50

9. All of the following are true about the due process clause except:
   a. There is no universal agreement as to what precisely due process is.
   b. Originally the due process clause applied only to federal, not state, actions.
   c. One agreed-upon principle is that individuals must have notice of governmental actions being taken against them.
   d. Due process generally refers to what the government can do to individuals, not the process being used. (pp. 159-160)

10. The legislature of State X has passed a statute that requires Mexican-Americans to show proof of citizenship when applying for employment. If this law is challenged on the grounds that it violates the equal protection clause, it probably will be declared:
    a. unconstitutional, because the equal protection clause prohibits all classification.
    b. unconstitutional, unless the state can show that it had a compelling interest in making the classification that could not be served in any other way.
    c. constitutional, if the state can show a reasonable basis for the classification.
    d. constitutional, because classification is generally presumed to be reasonable under the equal protection clause. (p. 162)

11. In the *Craig* case, involving a statute which prohibited the sale of beer to males under 21 and females under 18, the court held that the statute:
    a. was constitutional because the protection of public health and safety represents an important function of state government.
    b. was constitutional because the statistics presented were in support of the statute.
    c. was unconstitutional because the statute unreasonably discriminated.
    d. was unconstitutional because the statute invidiously discriminated. (pp. 164-165)

12. The First Amendment to the Constitution:
    a. gives unlimited freedom of speech.
    b. requires a literal reading of the Constitution.
    c. is an area where judges use considerable discretion in interpretation.
    d. applies to business only in the area of advertising. (pp. 165-166)

13. Commercial speech:
    a. is governed by the commercial speech doctrine which states the public has a need to receive commercial information.
    b. can only be limited by the government in the least restrictive manner possible.
    c. cannot be restricted unless the government can show a substantial interest in doing so.
    d. all of the above. (pp. 169-170)

14. In the *Cincinnati* case, where the city attempted to ban commercial speech from newsracks, the court held:
    a. commercial speech has less value than noncommercial speech.
    b. the city showed a reasonable fit between its actions and the protection of safety and esthetics.
    c. under no circumstances would the court allow different treatment of commercial speech.
    d. there was insufficient justification by the city for its discrimination against commercial speech. (pp. 170-171)

15. State Y wishes to regulate advertising by physicians, dentists, and other health-care professionals in order to protect the public from unethical practitioners. The state may do this by:
    a.   prohibiting all advertising by health-care practitioners.
    b.   prohibiting the advertising of prices for health-related services.
    c.   prohibiting deceptive or misleading advertising.
    d.   both b and c.   (pp. 171-174)

Essay Questions

1. Why did the framers of the Constitution limit the due process and equal protection clauses to instances where governmental action was present? How has the expansion of the commerce clause affected the equal protection clause?

2. What was the major reason for extending First Amendment protection to business and professionals? How are these rights similar to freedom of speech enjoyed by individuals?

Chapter 7

The Administrative Agency

This chapter presents an overview of administrative agencies. These government bodies are unique in that each administrative agency has attributes of the three other branches of government. The agency can make or amend regulations, like the legislative branch; investigate to ascertain if these rules are complied with, like the executive branch; and hold hearings to decide cases, like the judicial branch.

In this chapter, general characteristics of agencies are discussed, with particular attention given to their three major functions. In addition, the limits of these agencies are described.

CHAPTER OBJECTIVES

After reading Chapter 7 of the text and studying the related materials in this chapter of the *Study Guide*, you will be able to fulfill the following objectives:

1. Describe the importance and power of administrative agencies.

2. Debate both sides of popular criticism of agency functions, powers, and operations.

3. Describe the three functions of the agencies. These functions are:
   a. Executive -- Investigating the need for and enforcing regulations.
   b. Judicial -- Conducting hearings.
   c. Legislative -- Distributing regulations.

MAJOR POINTS TO REMEMBER

Administrative Agencies and Administrative Law

1. Administrative agencies are created by Congress through enabling acts to create, enforce, and adjudicate laws in specialized areas such as labor-management relations, product safety, and the environment. These rules affect nearly every aspect of business decision making today.

2. Because each agency focuses on a particular legal area, it is argued that the agency has the expertise to perform all three governmental functions. The agency makes rules, investigates to make sure that these rules are followed, and decides cases in its particular area.

3. Administrative agencies have been criticized because they encompass all three branches of government. Many people feel that this is too much power and argue that the bureaucrats in these agencies should be accountable to the voters.

4. However, there are controls over administrative agencies. The courts review agency decisions if they are appealed. The legislature can do several things:
   a. Change or terminate the agency.
   b. Control the funding of the agency.
   c. Enact statutes, such as the Administrative Procedure Act.

5. Critics maintain that although the legislature does supervise agency policies, since there are so many agencies and legislators occupied with many other issues, they do not supervise agencies closely enough.

6. Other common criticisms of administrative agencies are that they can become complacent and that the cost of implementing their regulations outweigh the benefits to the public, which indirectly pays the cost.

7. Supporters argue that agencies provide a valuable service in dealing with complex issues that other branches of government are not capable of handling.

Functions of Administrative Agencies

8. One executive function of the agency is to gather and interpret information. Some of the information is given voluntarily, and other information may be gathered by a subpoena ordering that such information be forthcoming. The agencies also have the power to inspect a business's books, its records, and its building. Whether an agency needs a warrant, or permission by the court to do this, is the issue in *Marshall v. Barlow's Inc.*

9. Another function of an agency's executive power is giving advice on how a business can comply with its regulations. Note that the agency is not legally bound by the advice given by one of its employees. Although this perhaps is unfair to the business that asked for advice, the rationale is that this is really a means of control, so that an agency does not take on more power than the legislature granted. *Federal Crop Insurance Corp. v. Merrill* is an example of this type of problem.

10. The administrative agency also has the function of the judicial branch of government. The agency hears complaints, weighs evidence, and reaches a decision in favor of one party over another.

11. Courts review agency decisions in an appellate capacity, rather than treating them as a trial de novo, or new trial. The courts do not retry the case; they look to see if the agency acted fairly and impartially in its ruling. Two examples of judicial review of agency rulings are *Federal Trade Commission v. Colgate-Palmolive Co.* and *Citizens to Preserve Overton Park v. Volpe.*

12. The legislative function of an administrative agency is to make regulations. The Administrative Procedure Act requires that three steps be followed by agencies. They must:
   a. Give notice in the Federal Register of an impending rule.
   b. Give interested parties the chance to give their opinions of the proposed regulation.
   c. Publish the final version of the rule in the Federal Register.

13. When courts review administrative regulations, one of the questions to be answered is whether the agency had the authority to make this rule. *Forging Industry Association v. Secretary of Labor* is a case that deals with the issue.

14. Another question that the courts address is whether the procedures used by the agency to make the regulation were fair.

15. A third question that the courts are sometimes called upon to answer is whether the rule is reasonable. *Federal Security Administration v. Quaker Oats Co.* and *Home Box Office, Inc. v. Federal Communications Commission* are cases in which the courts were asked to decide this question. Note that in the second case the decision was given per curiam, or by the court as a whole.

16. The courts use the same standards when an agency wants to rescind or revoke a certain regulation. *State Farm Mutual Automobile Insurance Company v. Department of Transportation* is an example of an agency attempting to rescind a certain regulation.

MAJOR POINTS OF CASES

Marshall v. Barlow's, Inc. (p. 182)

The question raised in this case is whether a business's facility may be checked for safety by OSHA without a warrant.

The Court held that a warrant was required. The rationale for this decision is that the Fourth Amendment and the Constitution protects business facilities as well as private dwellings.

The Court went on to say that it did not feel that requiring a warrant would place a serious burden on OSHA. First, many businesses voluntarily submit to an inspection. Second, the standards for obtaining a warrant for inspection purposes are not as strict as those for obtaining a warrant in a criminal case.

The benefits of requiring a warrant are that it would assure reasonable inspection and define the area and objects of this search.

Federal Crop Insurance Corp. v. Merrill (p. 183)

The issue in this case is whether a government-owned insurance company that accepted an application for insurance must pay for a loss. The lower court held that it should and compared the situation to that of a private insurance company that, even though making a mistake by accepting the application, still would be responsible.

The Supreme Court reversed this holding by stating that anyone who deals with the government is required to be familiar with the regulations. If an application is wrongfully submitted, the applicant is responsible for the consequences.

Federal Trade Commission v.
Colgate-Palmolive Co. (p. 186)

This case is an example of judicial review of an administrative judgment. The Federal Trade Commission had interpreted the deceptive advertising section of the Federal Trade Commission Act and determined that the simulation used by Colgate-Palmolive was deceptive.

The Court held that the FTC was expert in deceptive advertising and was often in a "better position than are courts" to make a determination. The Court also held that the FTC's order to the company was specific and not too broad when it included all the company's products. The Court went on to say that if the company had questions, it could ask them of the FTC.

Citizens to Preserve Overton Park v. Volpe (p. 188)

This case is a second example of judicial review of an administrative agency decision. The Court quoted from the Administrative Procedure Act, which set the standards to setting aside agency actions.

The first standard cited by the Court is a determination of whether the action was within the scope of the agency's authority. The second standard is whether the decision was reasonable. The third standard is whether the correct procedure was followed.

The appellate court held that these determinations had not been made by the trial court and sent the case back to be reviewed.

Forging Industry Association v. Secretary of Labor (p. 191)

The issue in this case is whether an administrative agency, OSHA, had exceeded its authority in the passage of a hearing-conservation amendment which reduced the noise exposure standard from the 90 db (decibels) to 85 db.

The court held that this standard was outside the authority of OSHA because it could penalize employers for nonworkplace hazards. An employee might suffer a hearing loss from activities done outside the workplace such as listening to loud music. OSHA was established to correct workplace hazards, not hazards that might occur outside the workplace. For this reason OSHA had to create a more valid standard.

Federal Security Administration v. Quaker Oats Co. (p. 192)

This is an example of a challenge by a business that an administrative agency regulation is not reasonable. The regulation in question established standards for products, including the standard "enriched" on the label for products that contained vitamins.

The Court held that the agency had followed the correct procedures and requirements in enacting this regulation. The Court also held that the regulation was reasonable, because overall it increased the protection of consumers.

Home Box Office, Inc. v. Federal Communications Commission (p. 194)

This is a second example of a case that deals with the issue of whether a rule made by an administrative agency is reasonable. The FCC regulation prohibited certain items from being shown on cable television because it was felt that the free television would be unable to compete.

The court disagreed. It first pointed out that the maxim that the judgment of the court could not override the judgment of the FCC, the experts in this area. However, it noted that the courts do have the power to determine whether a judgment is supported by evidence. The court held that this regulation was not supported by enough evidence that siphoning was harmful and was therefore unreasonable.

State Farm Mutual Automobile Insurance
Company v. Department of Transportation (p. 196)

This case is a challenge to an attempt of an administrative agency to rescind or revoke a regulation requiring certain cars to contain airbags as a safety precaution. The court held that NHTSA had to show why the recission of the rule was reasonable. The court felt that the agency's rationale was inadequate and that the agency was not acting according to its congressional charge to assure safety for the public.

SELF-TEST QUESTIONS

True/False

_F_ 1. Administrative agencies exist only at the federal level. (p. 177)

_F_ 2. Enabling acts of administrative agencies must include the specific implementation procedures the agency will use. (p. 178)

_I_ 3. An important feature of an administrative agency is that it has the ability to constantly monitor regulatory programs. (p. 179)

_I_ 4. In general, administrative agencies are capable of performing all three functions of the branches of government. (p. 179)

_F_ 5. Agencies cannot require information by the use of a subpoena; all information must be voluntarily given. (p. 181)

_F_ 6. Businesses often complain about the amount of recordkeeping and reporting an administrative agency demands. (p. 181)

_F_ 7. Once an employee of an administrative agency has given advice to an individual concerning compliance with the agency's rules and regulations, the agency is legally bound by the advice given. (p. 183)

_F_ 8. Unlike judicial proceedings, an agency hearing is not open to the public. (p. 185)

_F_ 9. Like judicial proceedings, agency hearings may or may not be heard by a jury. (p. 185)

_I_ 10. Some administrative agencies use the adjudicative process more as a rule-making than a dispute-settling mechanism. (p. 186)

_F_ 11. All agency regulations must be published in order that those affected may have the opportunity to comment. (p. 190)

_F_ 12. An administrative agency's rules and regulations have the same force and effect as a statute enacted by the legislature. (p. 190)

_T_ 13. The ultra vires limitation on agency power means that no regulation may be made arbitrarily. (p. 190)

_T_ 14. When reviewing an agency regulation, courts most often defer to the agency's expertise. (p. 192)

_F_ 15. Once an administrative agency creates a rule or regulation, only a court can abolish it. (p. 196)

Multiple Choice

1. Administrative agencies have the power to:
   a. control various substantive areas of law such as pollution and product safety.
   b. exist at all levels of government - federal, state, and local.
   c. combine the rule-making, the enforcement, and the adjudication functions in each agency.
   d. all of the above. (p. 177)

2. The best example of an agency that uses the adjudicative process more as a rule-making than as a dispute-settling mechanism is the:
   a. Environmental Protection Agency (EPA).
   b. Occupational Health and Safety Administration (OSHA).
   c. National Labor Relations Board (NLRB).
   d. Securities and Exchange Commission (SEC). (p. 179)

3. Which is *not* a criticism by business of administrative agencies regulations?
   a. Voters have no input into the activities of administrative agencies.
   b. After a certain time period, agencies become complacent and less innovative.
   c. Agencies are immune from the checks and balances of our structure of government.
   d. Agencies restrict business activities. (pp. 179-180)

4. Which of the following is *not* true concerning checks on agency power?
   a. The executive branch controls funding so subtle pressures can be exerted through financial withholding.
   b. The judicial branch has the power to review agency decisions.
   c. The legislative branch can abolish or change the agency in any way it sees fit.
   d. The Administrative Procedure Act provides standards and procedures which an agency must follow. (pp. 180-181)

5. Most of the information used by administrative agencies in their rule-making and adjudication processes is received:
   a. by subpoenaing witnesses and documents.
   b. through inspection of business records.
   c. voluntarily from individuals and businesses.
   d. through recordkeeping and reporting requirements. (p. 181)

6. In the *Marshall* case, the Supreme Court ruled that OSHA agents may inspect an employer's work area without his consent:
   a. without a warrant, because the warrant requirement would place too heavy a burden on the agency's inspection system.
   b. when they can demonstrate probable cause to believe that conditions in violation of OSHA exist on the premises.
   c. when they can show that reasonable legislative or administrative standards for conducting an inspection are satisfied.
   d. both b and c. (pp. 182-183)

7. Smith Manufacturing Company requests an advisory opinion from OSHA concerning the safety of one of the chemicals it uses in its plant. Smith later discovers, at great financial cost, that the advisory opinion was incorrect. Smith may:
   a. not sue OSHA because even an expert opinion can be wrong.
   b. not sue OSHA because the regulation was printed in the Federal Register and Smith is held to that knowledge.
   c. not sue OSHA because government agencies are immune to suit to save the public tax dollars.
   d. sue OSHA because Smith lost money without due process of law. (pp. 183-184)

8. Edward Smith has been served with a summons and a copy of a complaint against him by a federal administrative agency. At the subsequent agency hearing, Smith may reasonably expect:
   a. an opportunity to call witnesses and cross examine the agency's witnesses.
   b. an informal, closed hearing before a hearing examiner.
   c. the rules of evidence to be strictly adhered to.
   d. both a and c. (pp. 185-186)

9. Acme Corp. is asking the court to review an agency hearing. During such a review, the court is *least* likely to question:
   a. the agency's interpretation of the law.
   b. whether the agency exceeded its authority.
   c. the agency's findings of fact.
   d. whether the agency acted arbitrarily or unreasonably. (p. 186)

10. In the case where the Federal Trade Commission (FTC) accused Colgate-Palmolive of deceptive advertising, the Supreme Court held:
    a. The FTC did not have jurisdiction over Colgate-Palmolive.
    b. The FTC's order to Colgate-Palmolive was too vague.
    c. The use of undisclosed props is not a material deception.
    d. The FTC order was upheld by the court. (pp. 186-187)

11. An advantage to regulations created by administrative agencies is:
    a. once a rule has been made it must be published.
    b. it is uniform and thus flexible.
    c. the regulations are simply stated so there is no difficulty in following them.
    d. a and b only. (pp. 189-190)

12. A federal administrative agency has invited interested parties to file written comments and make oral presentations at a rule-making hearing. The major purpose of these public-participation procedures is:
    a.   to limit the agency's discretion in rule-making.
    b.   to give interested parties some voice in the rule-making process.
    c.   to provide public notice of the rule's provisions.
    d.   to allow those who will be affected by the rule to understand its provisions.

    (p. 190)

13. In the *Home Box Office* case where the Federal Communication Commission (FCC) set forth regulations to prevent competitive bidding for popular program material currently on free television, the court held that this siphoning:
    a.   is harmful to the public.
    b.   was accurately portrayed as a danger by the FCC.
    c.   will lead to loss of programming for those unable to purchase cable television.
    d.   none of the above.   (pp. 194-195)

14. The same standards of judicial review that apply to the formation of agency rules apply to:
    a.   both amendment and recission of agency rules
    b.   amendment, but not recission, of agency rules.
    c.   recission, but not amendment, of agency rules.
    d.   neither amendment nor recission of agency rules.

    (pp. 195-196)

15. In the *State Farm* case, where the Department of National Highway Traffic rescinded the regulation requiring airbags in automobiles, the court held:
    a.   an agency can never repeal a regulation without a given basis for the recission.
    b.   the agency's recission was arbitrary and unreasonable.
    c.   the agency exceeded its ultra vires limitation.
    d.   both a and b.   (pp. 196-197)

Essay Questions

1. Discuss the powers and limitations of administrative agencies.

2. Describe the similarities and differences between a courtroom trial and an administrative hearing.

Chapter 8

Ethics: Its Relationship with the Legal Environment and Business Decision Making

The study of ethics is a study of what is right or wrong. Managers can be confronted by difficult issues, such as whether to manufacture an abortion pill. The first part of this chapter focuses upon the argument that ethically based business decisions are not only right, but are in the business's self-interest. These decisions can affect the application of legal principles and/or affect damage awards.

The second part of the chapter uses an ethically-based decision model as the means to arrive at ethically reasoned business decisions. There is rarely one answer to an ethical problem, but by using such a decision model managers can insure they have considered all the factors necessary to make an ethical decision.

CHAPTER OBJECTIVES

After reading Chapter 8 of the text and studying the related materials in this chapter of the *Study Guide*, you will be able to fulfill the following objectives:

1. Understand the concept of business ethics.

2. Discuss the advantages of long-term and short-term business ethics.

3. Identify and analyze the factors that corporations should use in arriving at socially responsible decisions:
    a. Reflection on the problem.
    b. Consideration of the alternatives.
    c. Desire to act in a socially responsible manner.

MAJOR POINTS TO REMEMBER

What Is Business Ethics or Socially Responsible Decision Making?

1. There are several widely used definitions of business ethics. The first is earning a profit while inflicting the least possible harm on society. The second is voluntary activity undertaken for non-business reasons. The third is any activity that does not raise criticism. Note that each of these definitions lacks both guidance and operational methodology for achieving social responsibility. The authors' preferred definition is that business ethics is a search for the good.

Critiques of Common Misconceptions

2. There are two common misconceptions about ethics. The first is that ethics is simply a question of a person's personal values. This belief is a fallacy because ethics is the process of making a decision. It is not the answer; it is the way of reaching an answer.

3. The second misconception about ethics is that there is no way to choose the right answer if there are differing opinions. It is believed that this is especially difficult if both opinions are legal and if both have popular public support. This belief is a fallacy because it confuses an ethical analysis with a legal analysis or a popular analysis. This misconception also fails to account for subsidiary ethical questions.

4. Although there is rarely one right or wrong answer in social-responsibility or ethical questions, a decision-making process has proven to be advantageous in developing a course of conduct. Note the course of conduct adopted by Tylenol after capsules were tampered with by an unknown party.

Why Should a Business Seek to Act Ethically?

5. There are a few laws which require companies to act in an ethical manner. Early corporations imposed social responsibility on themselves by writing it into their charters. During the Industrial Revolution, this concept was replaced by the goal of strictly making profits. Today many businesses are voluntarily undertaking the role of ethical behavior because society expects behavior which goes beyond the law and because the market requires ethical conduct.

The Role of Ethics in the Legal Environment

6. There are two long term reasons for companies to voluntarily act in an ethically correct manner. The first is that such behavior is expected by both the market and by society in general. Recall the importance reliance plays in the making and the performing of contracts.

7. A second long term reason for companies to act ethically is that ethical behavior is a substitute for government regulation of businesses. The Truth-in-lending Act and environmental regulations are two examples of government regulations imposed upon business because of previous unethical activities. Although ethical business behavior can be expensive, compliance with government regulations can also be expensive.

8. There are three short term reasons for companies to act in an ethically correct manner. The first is that legal rules themselves often have an ethical component. Promissory estoppel and laws prohibiting the spreading of malicious lies are examples.

9. A second short term reason for companies to act ethically is rooted in the "doing what is right" factor in judicial decision making. Either unethical or ethical conduct may influence a decision maker's holding in a case. This is especially true in tort law, but can be found in other areas of law such as contract law as shown by the Pennzoil example.

10. A third short term reason for companies to act ethically is that unethical or ethical business behavior may affect monetary awards or fines. In the previously mentioned contract case, the jury awarded the wronged party three billion dollars in punitive damages. Under the Federal Sentencing Guidelines for business crimes, a business could have damages reduced if it has a strong in-house ethical program.

11. *Tennant Company v. Advance Machine Company* and *Millison v. E.I. du Pont de Nemours & Company* are two cases which emphasize the importance of ethical behavior in business.

**An Analytical Model for Making Ethically-
Based Decisions**

12. A model which can be used in making ethically-based decisions is important for managers to reduce their legal risk. The following model is not the only one which can be used, but is offered as an example of a workable approach to ethical decision making.

13. The threshold question in any ethical consideration is whether the activity is legal. Because most laws are really a reflection of society's ethics, an illegal action is generally inherently illegal.

14. The second question in any ethical consideration is whether the activity is opposed to any unwritten laws of society. These are the norms of social behavior.

15. The third question in any ethical consideration is whether the behavior is socially responsible. Three factors are involved in this inquiry. They are:
    a. Desire to act in a socially responsible manner. This is most likely to occur with management endorsement.
    b. Thorough reflection on the problem including the understanding of the problem's components.
    c. Consideration of the alternatives and how they might affect the corporation and its environment.

16. Consideration of the alternative ways of acting involves deliberation upon the effects on the corporation's external environment. This environment includes:
    a. The corporate entity -- Any alternative must consider the existence of the corporation itself. If the corporation is no longer in existence, it cannot act in a socially responsible manner in the future.
    b. The members of the organization -- Any alternative must consider the effects upon the corporate members, primarily the shareholders and employees. The corporation is financially obligated to these people. *A.P. Smith Mfg. Co. v. Barlow* is a case in which the shareholders challenged certain corporate decisions.
    c. The customers of the organization -- Any alternative must consider the health and safety of the users of the corporate products. *Toole v. Richardson-Merrell, Inc.*, deals with this issue.
    d. The community -- Any alternative must consider the effect upon the community where the corporation is located or upon which it has a significant economic effect.

MAJOR POINTS OF CASES

Tennant Company v. Advance Machine Company (p. 215)

The issues in this case are whether the principal (Advance) could be assessed punitive damages, and was responsible for the acts of its agent (McIntosh). McIntosh illegally went through the trash of a competing company and discovered confidential sales information. He conveyed this information to his superior, who conveyed the information to Pond, the president of Advance. McIntosh was in no way reprimanded for his activities until this lawsuit was brought. At that time, Pond fired McIntosh.

The lower court found for the plaintiff and held the defendant company liable for compensatory and punitive damages. The company appealed.

The appellate court held that punitive damages were permissible because top management should be ethical. Advance was liable for the acts of its agents because the top management did not reprimand or discharge the employee when they discovered his illegal activities. Therefore, the principal ratified or approved the agent's actions. Ratification may be done expressly or, as in this case, by implication.

Millison v. E.I. du Pont de Nemours & Company (p. 216)

The plaintiffs alleged that Du Pont fraudulently concealed the fact that they had asbestos-related diseases. As employees, they were required to have a yearly medical by Du Pont's doctors. They were not told they had the disease; in fact they were sent back to work which caused their conditions to be worsened by additional exposure to asbestos. If the plaintiffs' allegations could be proven, they would be entitled to recover under the Workers' Compensation Act. The issue in the case is whether the legislative intent was that Workers' Compensation be the employees' only remedy in situations like this.

The appellate court held that the plaintiffs' allegations against Du Pont went far beyond failure to warn of potentially dangerous conditions or intentionally exposing workers to the risks of disease. The court found a great deal of difference between these types of allegations and one alleging the fraudulent concealment of an existing disease. Had the plaintiffs known the facts, they could have minimized the risks to themselves.

The court held that the legislative intent did not prohibit plaintiffs in cases like this from other remedies under the law. However, the court pointed out that the plaintiffs must prove fraudulent concealment, not just negligence.

A.P. Smith Mfg. Co. v. Barlow (p. 222)

This is an example of a shareholder claim of wrongful use of funds by a corporation. The court balanced the corporate interests with the community interests and held that a corporate donation for maintenance of a university is permissible.

The court documented the value of educated individuals both to society in general and to businesses in particular. In addition to directly aiding private colleges and universities, corporations are indirectly aiding themselves by assuring the quality of the future members of the organization.

Toole v. Richardson-Merrell, Inc. (p. 224)

This case focuses upon the corporation's responsibility to its customers.

The issue is whether a manufacturer should be held liable for injuries suffered by customers as a result of use of the product. The court held that the manufacturer is liable.

In this instance, the corporation falsified both the lab tests and the drug application to the FDA. When permission was given by the FDA to put the drug on the market, the corporate sales staff was told that the drug was safe. It was only after the FDA seized the corporate records that the falsifications were discovered and the drug was removed from the market. Any injuries inflicted upon the users of the drug are the company's responsibility.

SELF-TEST QUESTIONS

True/False

____ 1. A goal of studying business ethics is to appreciate and understand the problems facing business managers. (p. 204)

____ 2. The best definition of business ethics is "earning a profit in one's business while inflicting the least possible harm to society." (p. 205)

____ 3. An unsolvable problem with business ethics is that there are many different ethical opinions and no way to choose among them. (p. 207)

____ 4. The market requires overall acceptance of ethical conduct by its participants. (p. 210)

____ 5. An advantage to corporate social responsibility is that it is an alternative to additional government regulations. (p. 211)

____ 6. Legal rules themselves often have an ethics component. (p. 212)

____ 7. Only civil damages awards may be reduced for companies showing a commitment to ethical behavior. (p. 214)

____ 8. The initial question in ethical analysis should be whether the firm has followed the law. (p. 218)

____ 9. Obeying legal rules and customs can sometimes lead to socially irresponsible conduct. (p. 219)

____ 10. Social scientists have discovered that an organization's ethics may determine whether its employees' behavior will be ethical. (p. 219)

____ 11. Since all business activities affect the surrounding environment, a firm is responsible for all the implications of its decisions. (p. 220)

_____ 12. Decisions that involve the profitability of the firm generally have few ethical implications. (p. 221)

_____ 13. The legal system has little responsibility for a firm's relationship with its customers. (p. 223)

_____ 14. Consideration of the community in a business's decision-making process generally includes the entire world. (p. 225)

_____ 15. A growing number of investors are solely interested in investing in socially responsible corporations. (p. 226)

Multiple Choice

1. A business should make a commitment to act as a responsible citizen because:
   a. morality of an issue can be easily agreed upon.
   b. unethical conduct can bring about legal consequences.
   c. it is a management ideal.
   d. it is always in a firm's best financial interest to do.

   (pp. 203-204)

2. Ethical business decision making is oftentimes difficult because:
   a. it is merely a question of personal values.
   b. there are many equally valid moral principles and no way to choose among them.
   c. it is frequently difficult to assess public opinion which should always be a firm's main concern.
   d. there are a number of factors to be weighed including an informed analysis of the proposed activity. (pp. 207-209)

3. During the Industrial Revolution, corporations maintained that their only accountability was to:
   a. the shareholders.
   b. the corporation itself.
   c. a very limited environment including the neighborhood where the corporation was located.
   d. no one. (p. 209)

4. Many businesses choose to act in an ethical manner because:
   a. the shareholders require it.
   b. the public expects it.
   c. it seldom takes away from the main goal of a corporation, i.e. making profits.
   d. if corporations do not act ethically, they are breaking the law.

   (pp. 210-211)

66

5. Which of the following is *not* a short term reason for business to act in an ethical fashion?
    a. Ethical behavior may be required by certain legal rules.
    b. Ethical behavior may prevent the government from regulating a certain business practice.
    c. Ethical behavior may affect the outcome of a legal decision.
    d. Ethical behavior may affect the assessment of fines.   (pp. 212-214)

6. In the *Tennant* case, the court held the executives liable for their employee's actions of going through a competitor's trash. The court's reasoning of this holding was:
    a. the executives ordered the employee to perform the act.
    b. the executives approved of the act by not reprimanding the employee for nearly one year.
    c. executives are always responsible for whatever occurs in their corporations.
    d. none of the above.   (pp. 215-216)

7. In the *Millison* case when the plaintiff alleged du Pont had concealed their illnesses from them, the court held:
    a. du Pont was guilty of fraudulent concealment.
    b. the plaintiffs had no legal recourse outside of Workers' Compensation.
    c. the plaintiffs should have dealt at arms length with their employer and used their own physicians as well as the company physicians.
    d. none of the above.   (pp. 216-218)

8. As a result of ethical corporate decision making, a company:
    a. will discover one definite, correct answer.
    b. will reduce the chances of corporate liability.
    c. will always be found to have acted within the law.
    d. will never have to pay legal damages.   (p. 218)

9. Which of the following statements concerning the relationship between business ethics and legal rules is correct?
    a. As long as a company obeys the law, it is generally considered to be socially responsible.
    b. By limiting activities that society considers to be wrong, the law can compel corporate responsibility.
    c. A company that does not obey the law is not generally considered to be acting in a socially irresponsible manner.
    d. Legal rules generally set a minimum standard for socially responsible conduct.
                                                                                 (p. 219)

10. Ethical decision making involves a thinking process which includes first a thorough examination of the problem and second:
    a. an instinctive reaction to the problem.
    b. a weighing of alternatives.
    c. merely following the dictates of law.
    d. adhering to corporate policy.   (p. 220)

11. The core of the relevant business environment which must be considered when making ethical decisions includes:
   a. the business itself.
   b. the shareholders only.
   c. the external environment which is unlimited.
   d. none of the above. (pp. 220-221)

12. In the *A.P. Smith Mfg. Co.* case, where the issue was whether Smith could legally donate funds to Princeton University, the court held:
   a. the corporation could not donate funds because it had no immediate need to recruit recent science graduates.
   b. the corporation could not donate funds because the shareholders had no input into the decision.
   c. the corporation could donate funds because it had agreed to hire only Princeton graduates in the future.
   d. the corporation could donate funds because scientists are needed for both the public and the corporate welfare. (pp. 222-223)

13. In the example of the Beech-Nut fraud, the corporation:
   a. saved money in the long run.
   b. merely did what other baby food companies were doing.
   c. lost credibility and market share.
   d. fired the executives responsible and therefore had no legal liability.
   (p. 223)

14. The environmental factor that is least related to the traditional operation of a business is:
   a. the continued existence of the company.
   b. the needs of the company's customers.
   c. the needs of the community in which the company operates.
   d. the needs of the employees and shareholders of the company.
   (p. 225)

15. Focusing on community interest when making an ethically responsible decision:
   a. often involves compromise as in the example of whether or not to play night baseball games in Chicago.
   b. could involve inclusion in "social interest" stock portfolios.
   c. could affect investors who wish to encourage socially responsible corporations.
   d. all of the above. (pp. 225-226)

Essay Questions

1. The law encourages ethical behavior. Discuss several ways in which this occurs.

2. Why must the business first consider the business entity when making a socially responsible decision?

68

Chapter 9

The Legal Basis of Enforceable Bargains: Contracts - The Essential Elements

Contract law has its roots in the common law or court-made law. Since the Industrial Revolution brought about changes in the marketplace, contract law dealing with the sale of goods has been codified in the Uniform Commercial Code.

This chapter gives an overview of traditional contract law and some of the modifications made by the UCC. In addition, this chapter explores nonlegal strategies to consider when negotiating a contract. The chapter focuses upon the requirements for a legal contract and concludes with a discussion of two legal theories which may cause courts to refuse to enforce a legal contract.

CHAPTER OBJECTIVES

After reading Chapter 9 of the text and studying the related materials in this chapter of the *Study Guide*, you will be able to fulfill the following objectives:

1. Describe the sources and historical background of the law of contracts.

2. Understand the nonlegal considerations when negotiating a contract.

3. Identify the requirements for a legal contract:
   a. Offer.
   b. Acceptance.
   c. Consideration.
   d. Capacity.
   e. Legality.

4. Recognize the doctrines of public policy and unconscionability.

MAJOR POINTS TO REMEMBER

Meaning of the Word Contract

1. A *contract* is an agreement which consists of a promise or set of promises that creates legal rights and obligations. A contract may be made through a formal written agreement or an informal written agreement. In many cases an oral contract or a contract made through the actions of a person is enforceable.

Sources of the Rules of Contracts

2. The traditional rules of contract law are found in the common law or legal cases. Traditional contract law is still applied in contracts involving real estate, employment, services, and other contracts which do not involve the sale of goods. If the contract is for a sale of goods (moveable personal property) some traditional contract laws have been modified by a statute known as the Uniform Commercial Code. Article Two of this statute governs contracts for the sale of goods.

3. One of the changes in contract law under the UCC is in the definition of contracts for goods. The UCC definition includes not only the words of a promise, but also actions, past dealings between parties, and custom in that particular area of business.

4. If Article Two of the UCC does not change a certain contract law for the sale of goods, then the traditional law still applies.

Historical Look at Contract Law Development

5. Historically, courts would require correction only of a poor contractual performance. They did nothing to remedy a refusal to perform a promise. Today, failure to perform and inadequate performance are both grounds for a breach of contract action and the appropriate legal remedies.

6. John Stuart Mill and other advocates of laissez-faire economics believed that the government should only interfere with free trade when necessary since they believed in the individual freedom of contracts. There has never been freedom to contract for illegal activities. Otherwise freedom to contract was common in the United States through the doctrine of caveat emptor, or "let the buyer beware." *Lochner v. New York* is a case in point.

7. In the twentieth century, courts began to recognize some limits to freedom of contract because of unequal bargaining power between the parties. This is especially true in contracts between businesses and consumers.

Nonlegal Considerations

8. There are some negotiating factors which influence the parties' behavior during the bargaining procedure. They are the parties' experience in the bargaining process, the parties' bargaining strategies, and the parties' expertise in the actual writing of the contract.

9. Repeat players are those parties who frequently make contracts of the same nature. These parties have the advantage of knowing and understanding the law better than their opponents. Repeat players often attempt to influence legislation and to litigate issues which will benefit their position in the long run. An experienced player makes fewer contracts than a repeat player, but has the advantage of prior dealings to aid him or her in the bargaining process.

10. A second factor in the bargaining process is the strategies each party may employ. The first of these strategies relates to the bargaining power of each side. Both sides should assess their bargaining positions and that of their opponent. Although a party in a weak position may have to make concessions, oftentimes he or she does so in the hopes of better terms in a future

contract. Sometimes a strong bargaining position will result in a grossly unfair one-sided contract as in the *Buchwald* example. In these rare cases, the courts may intervene.

11. There are other strategies which can be used in negotiating a contract. One is to employ an unemotional, experienced third party to act as a negotiator on a party's behalf. Another strategy is to use psychology when bargaining with an opponent. Lying is still another commonly used, though perhaps unethical, technique. A last strategy is a win-win approach in which each party to the contract feels he or she has won something of value.

12. A good negotiator attempts to force the opponent to make the opening offer. If this can be achieved, the negotiator has the advantage of knowing the opponent's position. A good negotiator has also acquired the skill of knowing when to press the opponent and when to back off.

13. One of the benefits of hiring an attorney to put the negotiations in writing is that an attorney knows the judicial interpretations of contract terminology. A second benefit is less understood by managers. Attorneys often think of situations which were not included in the negotiations. Managers sometimes argue that these situations are unlikely to occur and the inclusion of these provisions might reopen the negotiating process. Lawyers respond that unlikely situations do occur and that a contracting party takes a risk by not providing for them.

Contract Requirements - The Essential Elements

14. The requirements for a valid or legally enforceable contract are:
    a. Offer.
    b. Acceptance.
    c. Consideration.
    d. Capacity.
    e. Legality.
    In addition, there are two related areas which are discussed in Chapter 10. They are the requirement that there must be genuine assent by both parties and the requirement that some kinds of contracts must be written.

15. An *offer* is an indication of a desire to enter a contract. The person making the offer is called the *offeror* and the person to whom the offer is made is called the *offeree*. There are three requirements for a valid offer. They are the intent to make a contract, certain and definite terms, and that the offer be communicated to the offeree.

16. The requirement of intent to contract is determined by an objective reasonable person test. The question to be asked is whether a reasonable person would believe that the offeror intended to make a contract.

17. The requirement that the offer be clear and definite is applied differently to common law contracts than to contracts for the sale of goods. Common law contracts must be more precise than sales of goods contracts. This is so because Article Two of the UCC has fill in provisions for areas which are unmentioned by the offeror. All an offeror of goods needs to be is clear and definite about the quantity of goods he or she is offering to sell.

18. Most advertisements do not meet the requirement of being clear and definite as to the terms of a sale. For this reason most advertisements are not considered offers, but as an invitation

to make an offer. *Chang v. First Colonial Savings Bank* focuses upon when an advertisement is considered an offer and when an advertisement is considered an invitation to make an offer.

19. The third requirement for a valid offer is that the offer be communicated to the offeree. A person cannot accept an offer he or she does not know about.

20. An offer can be terminated by:
    a. The offeror -- The person who makes the offer can usually revoke (take back) the offer at any time before the offeree accepts. There are three exceptions to this general rule:
       1. Option contract -- If the offeree has given something of value to keep the offer open for a period of time, the offeror cannot revoke the offer until the time is ended.
       2. UCC option contract -- If the contract is for a sale of goods and a merchant signs a writing promising to keep the offer open for a period of time, this must be done. If no time is stated, a reasonable time, not exceeding three months, is implied.
       3. Promissory estoppel -- In this situation, a party is stopped from revoking the offer. This situation is covered in more detail later in the chapter.
    b. The offeree -- The person to whom the offer is directed can terminate the offer in three ways:
       1. Rejection (refusal) of the offer.
       2. Counter-offer -- This changes the terms of the offer and has the effect of a rejection. (Under certain circumstances, the UCC does view a counter-offer as an acceptance.)
       3. Automatic termination -- When a definite time is given for an offer to end, it terminates automatically if not accepted.
    c. Operation of law -- An offer can also terminate automatically if the offeror is silent on the matter. If no time is given for an offer to end, it terminates automatically after a reasonable time if not accepted.

21. The second element for a valid contract is acceptance or agreement to terms of the offer. In a common law contract, if the acceptance changes the terms of the offer, it is considered a counteroffer and terminates the offer. If the offeror has specified the manner of acceptance, the offeree must comply. Otherwise, acceptance can be made in any reasonable manner. Unless the offeror has specified that the acceptance is not effective until he or she receives it, an acceptance is valid when sent by the same or a faster manner than was used by the offeror. This is the implied agency rule or mailbox rule. If an acceptance is sent by a different or slower manner than was used by the offeror, the acceptance is not effective until received by the offeror.

22. The third element for a legally enforceable contract is consideration. It must be a bargained-for exchange in the offer and acceptance. In addition the person to whom the promise is made must incur a legal detriment or the person making the promise must receive a legal benefit. A promisee takes on a legal detriment by promising to do something which he or she had no prior obligation to do. To put it another way, the promisee had no preexisting duty to perform. A promisor gains a legal benefit by receiving something he or she had no prior right to obtain. *Jennings v. Radio Station KSCS* deals with the issue of whether there was a legal detriment to the promisee and a legal benefit to the promisor.

23. The exchanges which are bargained for by the promisor and the promisee do not have to be of equal value. In general parties have the freedom to decide the worth of the legal detriment

and the legal benefit of the contract. Courts will usually not get involved in determining whether there is adequacy of consideration or fair exchange by the parties. However, note that promissory estoppel is a related topic which will be discussed in Chapter 10.

24. The fourth element is capacity to make a contract. Two groups of parties are judged incapable of making a contract:

    a. Insane persons -- If declared legally insane by the courts, their contracts are considered void or unenforceable. If they are insane, but not yet declared so by the courts, their contracts are voidable or can be avoided by the party without capacity to contract.

    b. Minors -- People who have not reached the age of majority (usually age eighteen) can make contracts, but they are voidable by the minor. The exception to this rule is that minors may not avoid contracts for necessaries, or items needed for survival. Note the problem Chaplin had contracting with a minor.

25. The fifth element in a legal contract is legality. A contract must be for a lawful purpose to be enforced by the courts. *Dorado Beach Hotel Corporation v. Jernigan* is a case where the issue is the legality of gambling. Another type of illegal contract is a contract of adhesion. This is a one-sided contract by a party with a strong bargaining position who refuses to negotiate with a much weaker party.

26. In addition to the illegal contracts previously discussed, courts are refusing to enforce contracts in the following instances:

    a. Public policy -- If a contract is legal but goes against the public concept of fairness, a court will refuse to enforce it.

    b. Unconscionability -- This is a concept under which courts may refuse to enforce all or part of a one-sided contract for the sale of goods. *Frostifresh Corp. v. Reynoso* gives the rationale for applying the doctrine of unconscionability to a consumer, whereas *Potomac Electric Power Co. v. Westinghouse Electric Corp.* gives the rationale for *not* applying this doctrine to a business.

    Note however the modern legal approach to cohabitation contracts.

27. Usually a restraint of trade is illegal. However a covenant not to compete, though restraining trade, is legally enforceable if it is reasonable in protecting a legitimate interest of one of the parties. These covenants, or promises, not to compete are customary in contracts of employment and contracts for the sale of a business. The reasonableness of a covenant not to compete is judged by the time and the geographic restraints. Note the *H&R Block* example.

MAJOR POINTS OF CASES

Lochner v. New York (p. 238)

This historic case is an example of the traditional tendency of the courts to find in favor of freedom of contract. The New York labor law was designed to protect the health of employees. The Court held that the law interfered with both the employee's and the employer's rights to contract for mutually agreeable terms.

The dissent argued that the decision reached by the majority of the court was based on *laissez faire* economics (nongovernmental intervention in business) with which many citizens did not agree. He pointed out that the Constitution should protect the citizens and that various laws have regulated the lives and freedoms of others. He argued that the health of the employees was at stake here and that the contract should be set aside.

Chang v. First Colonial Savings Bank (p. 248)

Upon seeing First Colonial Savings Bank's advertisement the Changs deposited $14,000 in order to receive free gifts and a certain rate of interest for a three-and-one-half-year period. They received the gifts, but when they attempted to cash in the CD they were informed that there was an error in the advertisement and that they should have deposited $15,000 to receive the rate of interest. The Changs had not been told of this error at the time of their deposit, although there were pamphlets in the bank lobby with the correct figures. The Changs sued claiming that the advertisement was clear and definite and by their acceptance they entered into a binding contract with the bank. The trial court found for the bank.

The appellate court reversed. It stated that in most states, including Virginia, newspaper advertisements are invitations to bargain. However the exception to the rule are cases where the advertisement is clear and definite as in this case. The court held that under the exception, the advertisement was an offer which was accepted by the Changs and which created a binding contract.

As to the typographical error in the advertisement, the court held that the mistake did not invalidate the offer as it generally would. The court's reasoning was that in this particular case, the bank did not inform the Changs of this error until it had the benefit of the use of the Changs' money for three-and-one-half years.

Jennings v. Radio Station KSCS (p. 253)

The issue in this case is whether there was bargained-for consideration by both parties. The defendant radio station had promised to pay anyone $25,000 if it failed to play three songs in a row. When the plaintiff tried to collect, the radio station argued that the plaintiff had not provided consideration and therefore that there was no contract.

The appellate court disagreed, stating that the plaintiff's consideration was giving up his right to listen to other radio stations because he hoped to win the money. Thus the plaintiff relied on the defendant's promise to his detriment. The court also pointed out that the radio station benefitted by its promise because it attracted new listeners.

Dorado Beach Hotel Corporation v. Jernigan (p. 256)

The issue in this case is whether a gambling debt created in Puerto Rico where gambling is legal, will be enforced in Florida, where only certain types of gambling are legal.

The court held that the gambling debt would not be enforced in Florida. The rationale was that public policy condones only certain types of gambling in Florida, i.e., those involving spectator sports. The state will not encourage other types of gambling by assisting in the collection of monies owed.

Frostifresh Corp. v. Reynoso (p. 259)

This is an example of an unconscionable contract under the Uniform Commercial Code. Several elements of one-sidedness and unfairness are present. First, the plaintiffs were orally told things that were not in the written contract. Second, the plaintiffs had no opportunity to read the contract because they did not read English.

The issue was whether the court had the power to refuse to enforce the contract under the unconscionability section of the UCC. The court held that it did and rescinded the unfair portion of the contract.

Potomac Electric Power Co. v.
Westinghouse Electric Corp. (p. 260)

This case is an example of the court's reluctance to find unconscionability in a contract between two businesspeople.

The clause in question excepted Westinghouse from any liability except for repair of the unit. The court held that the clause was clear and that PEPCO did not have to deal with Westinghouse if it felt that the clause was unconscionable.

The rationale for holding businesspeople to a higher standard in this area is that the courts feel that most businesspeople are sophisticated enough to handle contract negotiations.

SELF-TEST QUESTIONS

True/False

_F_ 1. A contract can only result from a written or spoken agreement. (p. 234)

_T_ 2. Under the UCC prior understandings between the parties, industry customs, and the manner in which the parties perform the contract are relevant in determining the terms of an agreement. (p. 236)

_F_ 3. Historically there was unlimited freedom of contract, even for illegal contracts. (pp. 237-238)

_T_ 4. By the beginning of the twentieth century, the courts were becoming more receptive to social legislation regarding contractual powers. (p. 239)

_F_ 5. A repeat player is one who has experience in making contracts of differing types. (p. 240)

_F_ 6. As a general rule, the party who makes the initial offer is in the stronger position. (p. 243)

_T_ 7. The test used by the courts to determine the offeror's intent is the reasonable person test. (p. 246)

_F_ 8. One cannot accept an offer one does not know about unless it is an offer made to the general public. (p. 249)

_F_ 9. A termination of an offer by an offeree is called a revocation. (p. 250)

_F_ 10. Under the implied agency rule an acceptance is effective when it is received by the offeror. (p. 251)

_F_ 11. In judging whether consideration exists, the court looks for a bargained-for exchange of equal value. (p. 252)

<u>T</u> 12. People who have been declared insane in a court of law have no capacity to contract. (p. 255)

<u>T</u> 13. A contract of adhesion is an illegal contract. (p. 257)

<u>T</u> 14. Generally the party in the best position to assert the doctrine of unconscionability is a consumer. (p. 258).

<u>F</u> 15. In determining whether to uphold a covenant not to compete, courts rarely enforce a time restriction of over one year. (p. 262).

Multiple Choice

1. Article Two of the Uniform Commercial Code governs:
   a. contracts for the sale of goods.
   b. real estate contracts.
   c. contracts for the sale of services.
   d. employment contracts. (p. 235)

2. Historically, freedom of contract:
   a. was influenced by laissez-faire economics which originated in the United States.
   b. was embodied in the United States by the doctrine of caveat emptor.
   c. was struck down by the courts shortly after the Civil War.
   d. all of the above. (p. 237)

3. Advocates of the assessment of a party's bargaining position:
   a. advise assessing the bargaining position prior, during, and after negotiations.
   b. suggest a refusal to bargain at all if a party has a weak position.
   c. agree that miscalculations can do serious damage to both parties in some cases.
   d. point out that most one-sided contracts are amended by the courts. (pp. 240-242)

4. It is beneficial to have an attorney write up the terms of an agreement because:
   a. this lowers the risk that the agreement will have to be renegotiated.
   b. lawyers only suggest provisions to the agreement which are more likely than not to occur.
   c. this lowers the risk of things going wrong in the future.
   d. lawyers rarely write in a complex, archaic style. (p. 244)

5. For an offer to be considered clear and definite under common law:
   a. it must include precise terms such as price and delivery date.
   b. it must be in writing.
   c. only the quantity of goods to be sold must be stated.
   d. the UCC contains provision for any omitted terms. (pp. 246-247)

6. In the *Chang* case where the issue was whether the bank's advertisement was an offer or an invitation to make an offer, the court held the advertisement:
    a.   was an offer because it was clear and definite.
    b.   was an offer but was invalid because of the error in the advertisement.
    c.   was an invitation to make an offer because the general rule in most states is that advertisements can only be invitations.
    d.   was an invitation to make an offer which would have not been accepted by the bank because of the error in the advertisement. (pp. 248-249)

7. Kathy wrote Patrick and offered to sell to him her 1982 Chevy Nova, for $2000. Patrick wrote back and asked if he could have 3 days to think about the offer for the consideration of the enclosed check of $50.00. Kathy replied, via telegram, "Yes." The following day Kathy sold her car to Bill for $1500 cash. Based on these facts:
    a.   Kathy is in breach of contract because she sold the car to Bill at a lesser price.
    b.   Kathy is in breach of contract because she and Patrick had a valid option contract.
    c.   Kathy is not in breach of contract because an offeror may revoke an offer at any time.
    d.   Kathy is not in breach of contract because Patrick never agreed to buy the car. (p. 250)

8. A counteroffer:
    a.   is another name for the mirror image rule.
    b.   terminates the power of acceptance by the offeree.
    c.   is an attempted acceptance by the offeree which must be negotiated with the offeror.
    d.   occurs when the offeree fails to take any action. (p. 250)

9. Anne sends Maude a letter offering to employ her as a private secretary at $350 a week. The letter states that if Maude wishes to accept, Anne must hear from her by noon on September 1. Maude's acceptance:
    a.   can only be made by letter.
    b.   is effective when dispatched.
    c.   is effective when received.
    d.   both a and b. (pp. 251-252)

10. Larry saved Carolyn from drowning. He then told her that she owed him $1000 for his trouble. Carolyn does not have to pay Larry because:
    a.   there is no adequacy of consideration.
    b.   Larry had a preexisting duty to save Carolyn.
    c.   there was no bargaining before the act was performed.
    d.   there was no legal detriment to Larry. (pp. 252-254)

11. Jack turned 16 in July. In August he bought a 1990 Corvette and in September he wrecked the car. When he took the scraps of metal (which were once his car) back to the car dealer, the car dealer refused to give Jack his money back. The dealer:
    a.   must return Jack's money.
    b.   does not have to return Jack's money because the car was a necessary.
    c.   does not have to return Jack's money because the car was wrecked.
    d.   does not have to return Jack's money until Jack reaches the age of majority. (p. 255)

12. In the *Dorado* case, where the Florida court was asked to enforce gambling debts incurred in Puerto Rico, the court held:
   a. it would never enforce gambling debts because gambling is immoral.
   b. it would enforce the gambling debts if it was the type of gambling which was legal in Florida.
   c. it would enforce the gambling debts if it was not against public policy.
   d. b and c. (pp. 256-257)

13. Unconscionability is a doctrine:
   a. which gives judges discretion to tamper with contracts.
   b. which only applies to contracts governed by the UCC.
   c. is defined by the UCC as one where a party with superior bargaining power takes advantage of a party with lesser bargaining power.
   d. applies to events both prior to and after the contract is made. (p. 257)

14. In the *Potomac Electric Power Co.* case where Potomac alleged it had signed an unconscionable contract, the court held the contract was:
   a. unconscionable because the clause in question was inconspicuously printed on the back of the contract.
   b. unconscionable because Potomac did not want to contract with foreign manufacturers and Westinghouse was its only domestic choice.
   c. not unconscionable because negotiations, though rushed, were between two sophisticated corporations.
   d. not unconscionable because there was no indication that Potomac was forced to yield to any of the terms in the contract. (pp. 260-261)

15. A covenant not to compete:
   a. must be part of a larger agreement.
   b. is not considered a restraint of trade.
   c. must protect the legitimate interest of both parties.
   d. will be enforced if the territorial restriction covers a small, but not a large, area. (p. 262)

Essay Questions

1. What nonlegal considerations apply to the bargaining process?

2. Discuss the ways an offer may be terminated by the offeror.

Chapter 10

The Legal Basis of Enforceable Bargains: Contracts - Other Important Considerations

Chapter 9 focused upon the elements which are required to have a valid contract. This chapter gives two other instances in which courts will refuse to enforce a contract. They are the requirement of genuine assent to a contract and the requirement under the statute of frauds that some contracts be in writing.

The chapter continues with an overview of the contracts rights of some third parties. It analyzes the ways in which a contract is terminated and the types of damages an injured party may receive.

The chapter concludes with a discussion of circumstances in which courts impose contractual liabilities on parties even though no contract exists.

CHAPTER OBJECTIVES

After reading Chapter 10 of the text and studying the related materials in this chapter of the *Study Guide*, you will be able to fulfill the following objectives:

1. Recognize the different situations where there is lack of real assent to a contract.

2. Describe the principles of the statute of frauds and the parol evidence rule.

3. Understand the rights of a third party who has an intended interest in a contract.

4. Discuss the ways a contract may end and the conditions and degrees of performance.

5. Describe the types of monetary damages and equitable remedies which can be awarded for breach of contract.

6. Understand the circumstances and rationale for court enforcement of a contract when none exists.

MAJOR POINTS TO REMEMBER

Genuine Assent

1. Courts may refuse to enforce a contract having all five elements if one party can prove that there was not genuine assent. There are five typical situations in which no genuine assent is given:

a. Mistake -- If both parties made a material or crucial mistake, the contract is usually voidable. If only one party made a material mistake, courts generally enforce the contract. Note the example of the mismarked baseball card.

b. Fraud -- If a party relies on a false material fact and is thereby injured, the courts will set the contract aside. Note that generally an opinion is an exception unless given by an expert. *Blane v. Alabama Commercial College* is a case where fraud was the issue. Since fraud has been so prevalent in real estate cases, many real estate brokers are requiring sellers to disclose all known defects in their property.

c. Misrepresentation -- This course of action is like fraud except that the person making the false material statement did so unknowingly. *Vokes v. Arthur Murray, Inc.* is a case dealing with fraud and undue misrepresentation.

d. Undue influence -- If one party is strongly influenced by another and this second party benefits, the contract is set aside.

e. Duress -- If a party enters into a contract because of an economic or physical threat, the contract is set aside.

The Statute of Frauds

2. Many oral contracts are enforceable by the courts. The statute of frauds requires that four types of contract *must* be in writing, or they are unenforceable unless both parties have fully performed. These are:
   a. Contracts to be liable for another person's debts.
   b. Contracts involving real property.
   c. Contracts that cannot be performed within one year from the date that the contract was entered into by the parties.
   d. Contracts under the UCC statute of frauds for sales of goods over $500.

3. As with most statutes, there are some exceptions to this rule. In some instances partial performances of a contract will make the contract enforceable even though the contract was not in writing. The UCC statute of frauds makes an exception to the requirement of a writing if a party admits in court that there was a contract.

4. Under the statute of frauds any writing is legally enforceable if it states the basic terms of the contract and if it is signed by the party who is refusing to fully perform.

5. The parol evidence rule is another factor that must be considered by the courts. This rule states that oral testimony that changes the content of a final and complete writing is not admissible in court. The writing is the evidence of the parties' agreement. However, oral evidence about any further agreements made after the contract was signed are admissible unless these modifications need to be in writing under the statute of frauds.

6. Like the statute of frauds, there are exceptions to the parol evidence rule. If the written contract is incomplete, ambiguous (unclear), or contains an obvious clerical error, oral testimony is allowed to correct the contract. If a party alleges lack of genuine assent through one of the means discussed earlier in this chapter, this oral testimony is also allowed.

7. As a general rule, parties to a contract have a duty to read the contract before signing it. A party is bound to the terms of a signed contract to ensure the predictability of contracts. There are some exceptions to this rule. The first exception occurs if there is an illegal contract. As discussed in Chapter 9, courts will never enforce an illegal contract. Another exception made

by some, but not all courts, occurs when a party did not have the opportunity to read the contract, study its provisions, or have an opportunity to accept or reject the contract before signing it.

Interpretation of Contractual Provisions

8. A contract is an agreement which is negotiated by two parties with or without the assistance of attorneys. Most of the time the parties themselves interpret the terms of the contract. Occasionally a party refuses to comply with the contract, or there are either genuine or intentional misunderstandings between the parties. These occurrences are much less likely if the contract is as precise as possible. If a party is in doubt about the interpretation of a part or all of a contract, he or she should consult an attorney before signing the contract.

9. In some circumstances, parties must go to court to resolve their different interpretations of a contract. *Burroughs v. Metro-Goldyn-Mayer, Inc.* is a case in point. Because of the death of Burroughs, the court could not ask each party about their intent regarding the phrase in question. If the contract had been more explicit, this problem could have been avoided.

10. There are ethical questions which arise in the making of contracts. One such dilemma is whether manufacturers of weapons should be allowed to sell weapons to other governments.

Rights of Third Parties

11. Usually only the parties who made the contract have rights in the contract. However there are two circumstances where a third party has an interest in the contract. This occurs if there is an assignment to a third party or if there is a third party beneficiary.

12. An assignment is a transfer of rights by an assignor (an original party to the contract) to the assignee (the third party who is to receive the rights). A party can assign all of his or her rights to the contract, but the assignee takes these rights subject to any defenses against the validity of the contract. In other words if the contract is unenforceable, the assignee's rights are unenforceable.

13. There are several instances in which a party cannot assign his or her rights to a contract. The first is if the contract is one of a highly personal nature. The second instance is if the assignment would place an extra burden or risk on the party performing the contract. Although some contracts have clauses which prohibit assignments, most courts will uphold assignments if neither of the above instances apply.

14. An assignee should notify the other original party to the contract that the rights of the contract have been assigned to him or her. Otherwise, the assignor may wrongfully receive the rights assigned, or assign these rights to another party.

15. An original party to a contract may delegate his or her duties to a third party. This is not possible if the contract is one of a highly personal nature or if the contract prohibits delegation. Courts will uphold provisions against delegation. However, note that the original party to the contract is still responsible for the performance and can be sued if the third party does not perform adequately.

16. The second type of contract which affects a third party is a third party beneficiary contract. A beneficiary may be intended or incidental.

17. An intended beneficiary is one who was meant to benefit from a contract because the benefit was one of the main purposes of the contract. There are two types of intended beneficiaries. The first type is a donee beneficiary. In this instance a major purpose of the contract was to give a gift to this party. The second type of beneficiary is a creditor beneficiary. In this instance a major purpose of the contract was to repay a debt or duty to this person. Intended beneficiaries can sue if the benefits are not received.

18. An incidental beneficiary is one who will benefit if the contract is performed, but benefitting this third party was not a major purpose of the contract. Incidental beneficiaries cannot sue if the contract is not performed because there was no intent to benefit them.

Termination of a Contract

19. There are three ways that a contract may be concluded.
   a. Performance - The majority of contracts are ended by both parties performing their promises.
   b. Agreement - Both parties mutually agree and given consideration to cancel the contract.
   c. Operation of Law - Legal rules apply in certain instances which terminate a contract. One example is when the subject matter of the contract becomes illegal.

20. An obligation to perform under a contract may be ended by the fulfillment or nonfulfillment of a condition if the performance of the contract is dependent upon this condition. There are three types of conditions.
   a. Conditions Precedent - This type of stipulation requires that a certain event must occur before there is a duty of performance.
   b. Conditions subsequent - This type of a stipulation provides for a termination of a duty of performance after a certain event occurs.
   c. Concurrent Conditions - This type of stipulation provides that each party's duty to perform is dependent on the other party's performance.

21. There are three categories of contract performance.
   a. Complete Performance - This occurs when each party has fully performed. Their duties are discharged and they are entitled to their rights under the contract.
   b. Substantial Performance - This occurs when one or both parties has performed the fundamental part of their duties with minor variations. Although this is technically a breach of contract, a party's obligation will usually not be discharged because of a minor breach. In most cases, the obligation under the contract would be lessened by any damages the minor breach may have incurred.
   c. Material Breach - This occurs when one of the parties has failed to perform a major part of the contract. The nonbreaching party is discharged from any duties under the contract and has a right to damages from the party who has breached.

22. A contract may also be terminated if it is physically or legally impossible for one of the parties to perform and his or her personal performance is essential. In this case, each of the parties is excused from the contract.

Damages

23. When one of the parties fails to substantially perform, there is a breach of contract and the nonbreaching party may sue for damages. There are four types of damages in a breach of contract suit.
    a. Compensatory Damages - These are damages which pay the nonbreaching party for injuries resulting directly by the breach of contract.
    b. Consequential Damages - These are damages which are indirectly caused by the breach of contract. These damages are awarded only in instances where a reasonable person could have foreseen that they would occur if the contract was breached.
    c. Nominal Damages - These are minor damages awarded to a nonbreaching party who has suffered no great monetary loss.
    d. Punitive Damages - These are damages which are assessed to punish the breaching party. These are usually not found in breach of contract cases unless there is some serious intentional tort accompanying the breach.

24. Even though the contract has been breached, the injured party has a duty to keep the losses as reasonable as possible. *Parker v. Twentieth Century-Fox Film Corp.* deals with this concept of the duty to mitigate damages and to what extent it is required.

25. Parties to a contract may include a liquidated damages clause which specifies the damages either party must pay if there is a breach. Courts will enforce a liquidated damages clause if the damages at the time the contract was made would be difficult to estimate and if the damages clause is reasonable. Courts will not enforce a liquidated damages clause which is considered to be an unreasonable penalty.

Remedies

26. The usual remedy in breach of contract cases is monetary damages in an attempt to put the injured party in the same position he or she would have been in had the contract not been breached. If monetary damages are not sufficient, equitable damages can be awarded. There are two types of equitable remedies used in breach of contract cases.
    a. Specific performance - This remedy requires the breaching party to fulfill his or her promises under the contract. It is usually applied to sales of unique goods or to the sales of real estate.
    b. Injunction - This remedy requires a party to discontinue an act or activity for a certain period of time.

Enforcing a Contract When None Exists

27. In some situations, a court imposes contractual obligations when there is no contract. Two such situations are:
    a. Quasi contract -- In this instance, although a party had no intent to make a contract, the court finds that there was an implied contract. In order to ensure fairness, the party must pay for the reasonable value of the contract. *County of Champaign v. Hanks* is a case in point.
    b. Promissory estoppel -- In this situation, one party relies on a promise given by another. Typically there is no consideration given, so the contract is unenforceable. If the courts find that the relying party has changed his or her position and suffered damages, they

enforce the promise under this doctrine. *Hoffman v. Red Owl Stores* is an example of the use of the promissory estoppel.

MAJOR POINTS OF CASES

Blane v. Alabama Commercial College, Inc. (P. 269)

Blane spoke with a representative of the Riley Business College about her inability to type. The representative assured her that no student received a diploma unless he or she could type thirty-five words per minute. The representative added that the college had this policy to ensure their students were qualified to compete in the job market. Blane enrolled in the college and successfully met the typing requirement. After receiving her diploma, Blane was unable to find a job. She sued the college for fraud.

The court found for the college. After discussing the elements needed for fraud, the court concluded that none of the elements were present in this instance. The college representative had only promised to provide Blane with certain skills to compete for a job, but had never guaranteed her a job.

Vokes v. Arthur Murray, Inc. (p. 272)

The issue in this case is whether the plaintiff has a cause of action to enable her to present her case in court. The plaintiff was attempting to rescind several contracts under the defense of fraud or misrepresentation. The defendants claimed that their statements to her were merely opinion and therefore that she had no legal cause of action.

The appellate court held that although the statements made by the defendants might be classified as opinions, they were expert opinions, as it was felt that the defendants had superior knowledge. In addition, even though there is no duty to speak, once silence is broken the whole truth must be disclosed. With this rationale, the court held that the plaintiff was entitled to bring her case to court.

Burroughs v. Metro-Goldwyn-Mayer (p. 279)

Burroughs has sold the rights to the characters in his *Tarzan of the Apes* book to MGM. The contract stated that all remakes of the movie made by MGM would be "based substantially" on the first movie version. When a second remake was to be released, Burroughs's heirs tried to stop the release of the movie, claiming that the contract had been breached.

The court reviewed the story line of both films and held that they were similar. As to the charge that the later version was unfit for children, the court held that children were more sophisticated than in the past. The court also pointed out that the original version had scenes that were quite suggestive for the time period in which it was made.

Parker v. Twentieth Century-Fox Film Corp. (p. 291)

Shirley MacLaine Parker agreed to star in a musical for the defendant studio, which subsequently decided not to make the film. The defendant offered MacLaine the lead in a western. She refused and sued the studio for breach of contract. The defendant argued that she had refused to mitigate damages.

The court reviewed the general rule on wrongful discharge, which states that the employee is entitled to the salary that would be earned during the specified period of time less any monies

84

earned by other employment. An employee has the duty to mitigate damages by accepting other employment but not different or inferior employment. The court held that the western movie was both different and inferior and thus that MacLaine had not breached her duty to mitigate damages.

County of Champaign v. Hanks (p. 294)

Hanks was provided with a free attorney by the state because he was accused of a crime and stated that he could not afford an attorney. When it was later discovered that Hanks had sufficient assets to pay an attorney, the state sued to recover the cost of the state-appointed attorney. Hanks argued that there was no contract.

The court held that there was a contract implied in law. The essential question in a contract implied in law is whether the party received a benefit for which he or she should pay. In this case the defendant received free legal counsel valued at $2,000. He was thus unjustly enriched and had to pay the full value of the service.

Hoffman v. Red Owl Stores (p. 296)

This is an example of the doctrine of promissory estoppel. The standards for application are whether the promisor reasonably expected action, whether the action was induced, and whether justice requires enforcing the promise.

The facts illustrate these concepts. The promise to establish the plaintiff in a higher-paying situation induced to sell his existing business. The court held that if justice were to be done, the defendant had to be stopped from denying his promise. If the promise could not be kept, then the plaintiff should receive money damages.

SELF-TEST QUESTIONS

True/False

_____ 1. In most instances, silence is not considered fraud. (p. 269)

_____ 2. If a person is under duress, he or she agrees to the terms of a contract due to fear. (p. 274)

_____ 3. A contract that has been fully performed by one party is not subject to the statute of frauds. (p. 275)

_____ 4. The general rule regarding the duty to read before signing a contract is that a person is bound by what he or she signs. (pp. 276-277)

_____ 5. In most situations, the parties themselves interpret the meaning of a contract. (p. 278)

_____ 6. An assignor may assign some, but not all, his or her rights under a contract. (p. 282)

_____ 7. A person may delegate duties under a contract even if the contract expressly prohibits it. (p. 284)

_____ 8. A contract can terminate through operation of law if a change in the law makes the contract illegal. (p. 286)

_____ 9. Under impossibility of performance, a person is excused from a contract only if he or she can't physically perform. (p. 289)

_____ 10. Punitive damages are quite common in breach of contract cases involving large corporations. (p. 290)

_____ 11. The party who breaches a contract has a duty to keep damages as low as possible through mitigation of damages. (p. 290)

_____ 12. A liquidated damages clause will be enforced by the courts unless the clause is considered a penalty. (p. 292)

_____ 13. Equitable remedies in contract law include injunctions and quasi-contracts. (pp. 292-293)

_____ 14. Quasi-contracts are not technically contracts. (p. 294)

_____ 15. Promissory estoppel can be applied to any promise where consideration is missing. (pp. 295-296)

Multiple Choice

1. Diana and Carlos had been negotiating the sale of a sports car valued at approximately $35,000 for several weeks when Diana decided to offer the sports car to Carlos for $30,000. Diana's secretary, however, accidentally omitted a zero while typing the letter. When Carlos received the $3,000 offer, he was delighted and immediately accepted. Diana and Carlos:
   a. have a contract, because all of the necessary elements are present.
   b. have a contract, because Diana made an unilateral mistake and must live with it.
   c. do not have a contract, because Carlos knew of Diana's mistake and cannot take advantage of it.
   d. do not have a contract, because both parties were mistaken about the purchase price.
   (p. 268)

2. The difference between fraud and misrepresentation is that a person suing for misrepresentation need not show:
   a. intent.
   b. presence of a material fact.
   c. reliance.
   d. injury.
   (pp. 268-274)

3. Steven, an expert in antiques, persuaded David to purchase an oak table by telling him, "I predict this table is sure to become a collector's item." Based on these facts, if the table goes down in value, David:
   a. can avoid the contract on the grounds of fraud.
   b. can avoid the contract on the grounds of misrepresentation.
   c. can avoid the contract on the grounds of mistake.
   d. cannot avoid the contract because Steven was merely giving his opinion.
   (pp. 268-270)

4. Which of the following statements concerning the statute of frauds is correct?
   a. The statute of frauds requires certain types of contracts to be in writing.
   b. The statute of frauds defines certain acts that make a contract voidable on the grounds of fraud.
   c. The statute of frauds applies to fully performed contracts as well as to those that have not yet been performed.
   d. Both a and c. (pp. 274-275)

5. The parol evidence rule:
   a. requires modifications of certain types of contracts to be in writing.
   b. does not allow oral testimony about a detailed and complete written contract.
   c. focuses upon promises made before and after the writing of a contract.
   d. deals with written evidence of genuineness of assent. (pp. 276-277)

6. The modern trend of the courts concerning the duty to read rule has resulted in:
   a. the majority of courts searching for proof of assent rather than just a mere signature.
   b. an attempt by the courts to ensure more certainty in business contractual relationships.
   c. a determination of whether the party understood what he or she was signing.
   d. all of the above. (pp. 277-278)

7. In the *Burroughs* case where the issue was whether MGM had breached the contract by remaking the film in a way which was a material departure from the original film, the court held the remake:
   a. was a material departure because there were major changes in the sequencing of events.
   b. was a material departure because the remake was not suitable for young children.
   c. was not a material departure because there were insufficient changes in the elements of the story.
   d. was not a material departure because the earlier film was more suggestive and the changes in these scenes was due to a shift in social values. (pp. 279-281)

8. The Smith Mfg. Co. agreed to pay Saundra Gardner $1500 to repaint their managerial offices. Saundra had represented herself as an experienced painter, but in fact this was her first painting job. Saundra assigned the $1500 to her brother Roy in exchange for his used truck. Which of the following statements is true?
   a. If Roy does not notify Smith of the assignment, Roy cannot sue Saundra for nonpayment if she refuses to pay him.
   b. If Smith discovers Saundra's fraud and discharges the contract, Roy cannot sue Smith for breach.
   c. Saundra cannot assign these rights because she is performing a personal service contract.
   d. Saundra cannot assign these rights if there is a clause in her contract with Smith prohibiting such an assignment. (pp. 283-284)

9. A donee beneficiary:
   a. has rights under a contract because a major purpose of the contract was to discharge a preexisting debt.
   b. has rights under a contract because a major purpose of the contract was to make a gift to him or her.
   c. has no rights under a contract because he or she was not an intended beneficiary.
   d. has no rights under a contract because the modern trend in most states is to eliminate third party beneficiaries. (pp. 284-285)

10. Phyllis promised to pay her son Dom $2000 if he graduated with honors from the business school. This provision is known as a:
    a. condition precedent.
    b. condition subsequent.
    c. concurrent condition.
    d. implied condition. (pp. 286-287)

11. If a party substantially performs his or her contractual obligation, he or she:
    a. has fully performed the duties under the contract.
    b. has breached the contract and may be sued.
    c. has breached the contract, but the other party is still obligated to perform.
    d. has breached the contract and the other party has no recourse against him or her. (pp. 287-288)

12. In the *Parker* case, which dealt with mitigation of damages, the court held that Shirley MacLaine:
    a. was wrongfully discharged and did not have to mitigate damages.
    b. was wrongfully discharged and had to mitigate damages by agreeing to perform in any picture the studio wished.
    c. was wrongfully discharged and had to mitigate damages by accepting comparable work.
    d. was not wrongfully discharged and was therefore under a legal obligation to mitigate damages. (p. 291)

13. Specific performance:
    a. is applied only in sales of unique goods.
    b. requires a party to refrain from performing a certain action or actions.
    c. is a court order which, if disobeyed, can lead to the assessment of punitive money damages.
    d. is available only when money damages are not adequate. (pp. 292-293)

14. In the *Hanks* case, where the man accused of a crime stated he had no money to hire an attorney, the court held:
    a. Hanks had to pay for the attorney because of promissory estoppel.
    b. Hanks had to pay for the attorney because there was an implied in law contract.
    c. Hanks did not have to pay for the attorney because he did not agree to do so.
    d. Hanks did not have to pay for the attorney, but was liable for fraud. (pp. 294-295)

15. During a fund-raising campaign, Pat promised to donate $10,000 to First Church toward the purchase of a new pipe organ. On the basis of Pat's promise, First Church entered into a contract with Heavenly Tunes, Inc., for the manufacture and installation of the new organ. If Pat now refuses to pay the $10,000 and First Church sues, it probably will recover:
    a. $10,000, because all the necessary elements of a contract are present.
    b. nothing, because Pat's statement lacked consideration.
    c. the reasonable value of the organ, because the law will imply a quasi-contract.
    d. $10,000, because the law will apply the doctrine of promissory estoppel.

(pp. 295-296)

Essay Questions

1. Discuss each of the situations when the courts may refuse to enforce a contract because one of the parties has not genuinely assented to the agreement.

2. Discuss each of the situations when the courts may find a contract even though all the requirements for a contract are not present.

Chapter 11

Assessing External Costs of Doing Business: Tort Liability

Torts, except for breaches of contract, are civil wrongs. The policies that underlie this body of law are society's attempt to compensate the victim and deter the wrongdoer, thus influencing people's behavior.

This chapter gives an overview of torts and explores the rationales for tort law in the past and the evolving tort law of the present.

CHAPTER OBJECTIVES

After reading Chapter 11 of the text and studying the related materials in this chapter of the *Study Guide*, you will be able to fulfill the following objectives:

1. Describe the principles that underlie the law of torts.

2. Identify the elements needed to prove a tort and the exceptions to this general rule.

3. Describe two basic areas of tort law:
   a. Intentional torts.
   b. Negligence.

4. Identify tort defenses and their historical treatment.

5. Discuss new developments in tort law and the modern rationale for them.

MAJOR POINTS TO REMEMBER

What Is Tort Liability?

1. The common law legal environment requires of all businesses a duty to act reasonably in all their functions. If this duty is breached, businesses may have to pay any damages arising from their acts. The tenant of tort liability encourages careful decision making by managers. Tort law endeavors to shift the cost of harm from those injured to those causing the injury.

2. Tort law is a certain body of civil (noncriminal) law covering civil wrongs other than breaches of contract. The usual remedy is to require the defendant to pay the plaintiff's tangible and intangible damages.

90

3. Three principles underlie the law of torts:
   a. Victim compensation - The aim is to restore the injured party, as much as possible, to his or her position before the injury occurred. To be compensated, a victim must show that the injury was caused by the defendant, not his or her own actions. In addition if the defendant has no ability to pay, the victim cannot be compensated.
   b. Allocation of risk and loss between the parties - This allocation often varies depending on the potential effect upon society as a whole.
   c. Regulation of conduct - Individuals and businesses tend to modify their behavior if the economic cost of nonmodification are too great.

4. The three major goals of torts are aided by insurance. Both individuals and businesses may purchase liability insurance, which will pay any damages for which a defendant might be found liable. Insurance therefore has assured that injured parties are compensated for their injuries. In addition, insurance companies may require businesses to adopt safety procedures that prevent torts from occurring.

5. Because of the increased cost of insurance, some businesses were to afford less coverage and some businesses were able to afford none at all. As a result, legislative tort reforms have been enacted which limit damage awards, modify tort law, and more strictly regulate insurance companies. Note also the differences between the cost of American and European tort recoveries.

Tort Law Classifications: Focusing on the Nature of the Conduct

6. There are two types of torts: intentional torts and torts of negligence. The difference between these torts is the defendant's intent. An action designed to cause harm would be considered an intentional tort, while a thoughtless act which caused harm would be considered negligence. Note that for tort liability to be present, a breach of duty must occur.

7. In intentional torts, as the name implies, the issue is whether the defendant's act was intended to cause injury. Since establishing a person's intent with certainty is difficult, the courts apply the reasonable-person test. If a reasonable person would believe that the act in question would result in injury, the act is held to be an intentional tort. The defendant is liable to the injured party for the actual damages caused. In some cases, the defendant is assessed punitive damages in addition as a punishment. *Hackbart v. Cincinnati Bengals* is a case that further explains this concept.

Examples of Intentional Torts

8. There are a number of intentional torts. Three examples are battery, defamation, and intentional interference with a contract. All torts require the showing of causation and injury. The torts discussed below require the showing of additional elements.

9. Battery is a purposeful (intentional) touching of a person without his or her permission. A battery consists of a voluntary act, intent, and indignity or physical harm. The circumstances, time, and place of the act are also taken into account.

10. Defamation is an intentional tort where the defendant's words injure the plaintiff's reputation. No physical damages occur. A defamation consists of words communicated to a third party which are understood to be disparaging about the plaintiff.

11. Interference with a contractual relationship is a wrongful infringement with another's business activity. Because competition is vital in a capitalist society, establishing this tort is complicated. An intentional interference with a contract consists of a valid contract with the defendant's intent to disrupt.

12. The tort of negligence or unintentional injury does not carry the same ethical implications as the intentional tort. The plaintiff must prove four elements in both types of torts:
    a. A legal duty for a certain standard of care exists.
    b. The defendant breached that duty.
    c. This breach was the cause of an injury to the plaintiff.
    d. This injury resulted in actual damage to the plaintiff.

13. The standard of care (a above) is based on a fictitious person known as the reasonable person. The behavior in question is measured against what a reasonable person would or would not have done. *Weirum v. RKO General, Inc.* focuses upon when a duty of care is owed.

14. Causation, or proximate cause (c above) requires that the injury caused by the defendant must have been foreseeable. If the injury is too far removed from the action by probability standards, the defendant is not liable or responsible. *Palsgraf v. Long Island R. Co.* is a famous case that further explains this concept. *Crankshaw v. Piedmont Driving Club, Inc.* is a second case which focuses upon proximate cause.

Tort Law and History

15. During the nineteenth century, courts were sympathetic to business problems. Accordingly, three doctrines were developed that made it more difficult for an injured party to collect damages. These doctrines are:
    a. Contributory negligence -- If the defendant could show that the plaintiff was also negligent, the plaintiff received *no* damages. *Haring v. New York and Erie Railroad* is a case in point.
    b. Assumption of the risk -- If the plaintiff was voluntarily in a situation where there was a risk of injury, the plaintiff received *no* damages.
    c. Fellow servant rule -- If the plaintiff was injured by a fellow employee in a job-related incident, the employer could not be sued. *Farwell v. Boston and Worcester Railroad* is a case dealing with assumption of the risk and the fellow servant rule.

16. Note that these doctrines were denounced by some at the time and have been modified somewhat today.

Developments in Tort Law

17. As in all other areas of law, tort law changes to reflect public policy. One such development in the early twentieth century was statutory compensation of injured workers. This system virtually eliminated tort claims of injured workers by providing money from a workers' compensation fund paid into by all employers. Although benefits

have been sharply increased by many states, many critics argue that employees would be financially better off suing their employers. *Blankenship v. Cincinnati Milacron Chemicals* is a recent case that explores this development. Fraud on behalf of both employees and employers is also a major concern. Employers are concerned about the rising costs of workers' compensation. They are also troubled by attempts to expand coverage to include not only negligent torts, but those in which an employer failed to correct unsafe working conditions.

18.   A second recent development in tort law is the concept of comparative negligence, aimed at offsetting the sometimes harsh result of contributory negligence. Under this doctrine, the plaintiff's negligence is compared to the defendant's. The plaintiff then receives a proportion of the damages instead of no damages, which would be the case under contributory negligence. However some courts are giving no awards even if both parties were negligent, if the plaintiff assumed the risk.

19.   A third recent development in tort law is the introduction of new torts. One new tort is the concept of wrongful discharge of employees who have no contractual protection and can be fired without cause. These are at-will employees. *Wagenseller v. Scottsdale Memorial Hospital* is an example of some legal arguments involved in establishing this new tort. A second new tort is the appropriation of the property right in performance styles as in the case of *Midler v. Ford Motor Company*. However, keep in mind that the result in the *Midler* case has not been uniformly followed by all courts.

MAJOR POINTS OF CASES

Hackbart v. Cincinnati Bengals, Inc. (p. 307)

The issue in this case is whether an intentional striking of one football player by another can be considered an intentional tort. The court held that it could.

The court justified this decision by noting that this conduct was outside the rules of the game. Whether the extent of the injury was intentional or not, a reasonable person would have been able to foresee the likelihood of this type of injury from his action. Therefore, the defendant was liable.

Weirum v. RKO General, Inc. (p. 314)

A radio station ran a contest in which the disc jockey awarded prizes to the first contestant who spotted him. The disc jockey gave clues to his next destination over the radio. As two teenage drivers were racing to locate the disc jockey, Weirum's car was pushed off the road and Weirum was killed.

The issue in this case is whether the risk of physical harm to the plaintiff was foreseeable by the defendant radio station. The court held that it was.

Although every action may involve some danger, the set up of this contest encouraged dangerous activities. The radio station could have had a different type of contest without such a risky situation.

Palsgraf v. Long Island R. Co. (p. 316)

The issue in this famous case is whether the defendant's act of negligence was the proximate cause of the plaintiff's injury.

The court held that it was not and that the defendant was therefore not liable. The court held that while knocking the package to the ground was a negligent act, the fact that the unmarked package contained firecrackers, which might injure a distant passenger, was not foreseeable. A duty of care was owed only to any passenger who might have been standing near the train.

The dissent argued against the concept of foreseeability in proximate cause. The rationale was that a negligent act was committed and that the defendant should be liable for the consequences, whether foreseeable or not.

Crankshaw v. Piedmont Driving Club, Inc. (p. 318)

When Harris became ill while eating shrimp at the Piedmont Driving Club, she went to the rest room. A short time later, her friend Crankshaw entered the rest room to see if Harris was all right. Crankshaw slipped on some of Harris's vomit which was right inside the door. Crankshaw fell down and broke her hip. She claims that the restaurant's serving of unwholesome foods was the proximate cause of her injury. Write the opinion.

Haring v. New York and Erie Railroad (p. 320)

This case centers on the doctrine of contributory negligence, which holds that if a plaintiff contributes to an injury by his or her own negligence, the plaintiff cannot recover damages.

The issue is whether the question of negligence was a question for the jury to decide. The court held that it was not, for two reasons. First, the plaintiff's negligence was never in question. Second, the court felt that the jury's compassion for the individual rather than a corporation could influence this decision. (Note the year of this case.)

Farwell v. Boston and Worcester Railroad (p. 321)

This is another historic case, which focuses upon the fellow servant rule and assumption of the risk. The issue is whether an employee, injured through the action of a fellow employee, may sue the employer. The court held that he may not, under the fellow servant rule and assumption of the risk.

The court expanded upon the rationale for this doctrine. The first reason given was that the employee was receiving compensation for his duties and thus assumed the risks associated with his employment. The second reason was that under the fellow service rule, an employee is in a position to observe and report any misconduct of other employees to the employer. If nothing is corrected by the employer, the employee is free to quit.

Blankenship v. Cincinnati Milacron Chemicals (p. 324)

In this case the court was called upon to interpret a statute. The issue is whether the Workers' Compensation Act covers workers injured by their employers' intentional torts. If it does, then the plaintiffs have no tort claim and would receive payments out of the workers' compensation fund.

The court held that the act did not include intentional torts. It was felt that an intentional tort is not expected from one's employer and that coverage under the act might encourage such torts. If one occurs, the employees should have the right to a court hearing.

The dissent argued that the language in the act did not specify compensation only for negligence and that if intentional torts were to be excluded, the act would have stated this. The dissent argued that this decision would encourage more workers to sue their employers, which defeats the intent of the Workers' Compensation Act.

Wagenseller v. Scottsdale Memorial Hospital (p. 329)

This case involves the termination of an at-will employee who brought a cause of action for wrongful discharge.

The court reviewed the history of at-will employment or the hiring for an unspecified period of time. In the past, employers had the right to discharge an at-will employee for any reason.

Today three-fifths of the states have adopted causes of action for wrongful discharge. The change in thinking has been brought about by the public policy of equating to some degree the power between an employer and an employee. Employers may still fire at-will employees for good cause or no cause but no longer for bad cause.

In this case, the court held that the plaintiff was fired for bad cause because she had refused to participate with her supervisor and others in "mooning" during a raft trip. The court pointed out that mooning might have violated an indecent exposure statute in the state. Even if it did not, the plaintiff had the right of privacy.

Midler v. Ford Motor Company (p. 332)

The issue in this case is whether the defendant took something which was not theirs and thus committed a tort when an imitator of Bette Midler sang in a Ford commercial. The company defended its actions by saying that unlike a song, a voice is not protected by copyright law.

The court held that Ford had committed a tort. The fact that Midler's voice was unusual and that Ford had hired a sound-alike indicated that Midler's voice had value and should be protected. However, the court stated that their ruling would not apply to all voices, only those which were distinctive.

SELF-TEST QUESTIONS

True/False

_____ 1. The scope of risk for tort liability is far greater than the risk for contract liability. (p. 302)

_____ 2. Damages in tort attempt to restore the injured party to his or her condition before the injury to the extent that money can do so. (p. 302)

_____ 3. Tort law provides a system of social insurance whereby people who receive an injury to their interests are automatically compensated for it. (p. 302)

_____ 4. Tort law and insurance operate together to further the major goals of tort doctrine. (p. 304)

_____ 5. A defendant who commits a tort of negligence may be assessed punitive damages as well as actual damages. (p. 306)

_____ 6. A person may be held liable for an intentional tort only if he or she acted maliciously. (p. 307)

_____ 7. A battery requires physical damage either to the plaintiff or to his or her property. (p. 309)

_____ 8. The plaintiff must establish all four elements in both torts of intent and negligence. (p. 312)

_____ 9. Proximate cause is an unforeseen event which results in negligence. (p. 315)

_____ 10. To a large extent, the law of negligence grew out of changes brought about by the Industrial Revolution. (p. 318)

_____ 11. Today, employers usually raise the assumption of the risk defense against injured employees. (pp. 320-321)

_____ 12. Workers' compensation statutes have removed the compensation of injured employees from the tort law system. (p. 323)

_____ 13. Today, most states have substituted a system of comparative negligence for the old contributory negligence doctrine. (p. 327)

_____ 14. The at-will employment doctrine is a federal doctrine which insures uniformity in wrongful discharge cases. (p. 328)

_____ 15. The doctrines of tort law apply to property rights as well as personal injuries. (p. 331)

Multiple Choice

1. Which is *not* a general purpose of tort liability?
   a. To create an incentive for careful decision making by managers.
   b. To shift the risk of injury from those harmed to those who create the risk of harm.
   c. To provide a general insurance system for injured members of society.
   d. To reflect trends in society. (pp. 301-302)

2. As a result of the increasing costs of tort liability insurance:
   a. tort law reforms which limited awards for damages were enacted.
   b. insurance companies were deregulated by the government.
   c. more social entitlement programs were enacted to encourage lower tort awards as in Europe.
   d. all of the above. (pp. 304-305)

3. An intentional tort:
   a. can only occur if the defendant had intent to harm.
   b. focuses upon the conduct itself and not the frame of mind of the defendant.
   c. only provides punitive damages.
   d. must involve violation of a duty.   (pp. 306-307)

4. Which of the following situations is *most* likely to be considered an intentional tort?
   a. A football player steps on an opposing player's hand during a tackle.
   b. A peanut vendor drops his tray on a spectator's head when the strap breaks.
   c. A spectator slips on a hot dog wrapper and knocks down a little old lady.
   d. A practical joker pulls the stadium seat out from under his friend, causing him to break a wrist.   (pp. 306-307)

5. The tort of negligence:
   a. creates an unreasonable risk of injury.
   b. rarely occurs in a business environment.
   c. may cause criminal charges to be filed against the defendant.
   d. applies the reasonable person standard to establish intent.
                                                       (p. 312)

6. While she was adjusting her seat belt, Polly's eyes strayed from the road and her car cut across the corner of a playground. None of the children was hit. Nellie observed Polly's car leave the road and in her hurry to get a better view of what was happening, fell and broke a leg. If Nellie sues Polly for the tort of negligence, she will probably:
   a. not win, because Polly was acting as a reasonable person would act under the circumstances.
   b. not win, because Polly did not intend to harm her.
   c. not win, because Polly's conduct was not the proximate cause of her injury.
   d. not win, because her injury was not serious enough.
                                                       (pp. 312-315)

7. Which of the following is *not* a necessary element of the tort of negligence?
   a. breach of duty.
   b. injury.
   c. proximate cause.
   d. intent.   (pp. 313-315)

8. Proximate cause involves:
   a. the reasonable person standard of care.
   b. foreseeability.
   c. actual loss or injury.
   d. negligence only.   (p. 315)

9. In *Palsgraf v. Long Island R. Co.*, where fireworks exploded indirectly injuring a passenger, the majority held that:
   a. the plaintiff was negligent for carrying fireworks in a railway station.
   b. the explosion was not the proximate cause of Palsgraf's injury.
   c. the railroad workers were responsible for Palsgraf's injury.
   d. Palsgraf contributed to the accident by standing where she did.
                                                       (pp. 316-317)

10. In the nineteenth century, courts limited the ability of the plaintiff to collect damages. This can best be seen in the doctrine of:
    a. comparative negligence.
    b. wrongful discharge.
    c. fellow servant rule.
    d. workers' compensation. (pp. 318-322)

11. While feeding the chimpanzees at the zoo, Roger was severely bitten on the hand. The evidence indicates that Roger ignored conspicuously posted signs asking visitors not to feed the animals. Roger will probably be barred from collecting damages from the zoo under the theory of:
    a. contributory negligence.
    b. assumption of risk.
    c. comparative negligence.
    d. the fellow servant rule. (pp. 320-322)

12. In the historical *Haring* case, where the plaintiff was hit by a train, the court held that the question of negligence could not be submitted to the jury because:
    a. the plaintiff had defeated his claim of negligence through his own acts of negligence.
    b. when a person has contributed to his own injury, he cannot recover any amount of money.
    c. juries tend to be more sympathetic to individuals than to corporations.
    d. all of the above. (p. 320)

13. Which of the following statements concerning workers' compensation is correct?
    a. Under most workers' compensation statutes, the employee is barred from bringing a common law tort action against the employer.
    b. Generally, the statutory amount awarded for a work-related injury is quite high.
    c. The fellow servant doctrine bars recovery in a workers' compensation claim.
    d. Workers' compensation statutes provide the major form of government control over safety in the workplace. (pp. 323-324)

14. In the *Blankenship* case which deals with employees who seek to sue their employer for an intentional tort under the Workers Compensation Act, the court held:
    a. The workers may sue under the Act because it covers an employer's intentional torts.
    b. The workers cannot sue under the Act because an intentional tort is a natural risk of employment.
    c. The workers can't sue under the Act because the Act gives employers immunity from civil liability involving intentional torts.
    d. The workers can't sue under the Act, but have a cause of action under intentional tort law. (pp. 324-325)

15. The at-will employment doctrine:
    a. is a recent development in tort law.
    b. gives employees the right to quit at any time without legal liability unless this is breach of contract.
    c. gives employers the right to fire employees at any time for good cause even if a contract to the contrary exists.
    d. makes it unlawful to fire an employee who engages in union activities.

(pp. 328-329)

Essay Questions

1. Discuss the three principles which underlie the law of torts.

2. Discuss the advantages and disadvantages of workers' compensation statutes.

Chapter 12

Property Rights

This chapter focuses upon the nature and classifications of property as well as the balance of property owners' rights with individual and governmental rights. The basis of all business proceedings is the acquisition, use, and transfer of property.

Property law is one of the oldest areas of law and is basically concerned with the rights of ownership. Traditionally, a property owner's rights were superior to the individual rights of others. As society has changed, the balance has moved such that individual rights, in many instances, are superior to property rights.

CHAPTER OBJECTIVES

After reading Chapter 12 of the text and studying the related materials in this chapter of the *Study Guide*, you will be able to fulfill the following objectives:

1. Discuss the nature of property as a relationship between individuals that a government must enforce.

2. Identify the classifications of property:
   a. Real or personal.
   b. Tangible or intangible.

3. Define a fixture and discuss the four guidelines courts use in determining when it becomes a part of real estate.

4. Describe the tension between property rights and individual rights.

MAJOR POINTS TO REMEMBER

The Nature of Property

1. Property has two elements. The first is a relationship between a property owner and all others such as individuals, business, or government. The second element is a series of laws which recognize, adjust, and enforce property rights. In capitalistic countries, property rights are considered to be natural rights, not defined rights granted by the government.

2. People who own property usually own the right to control the property in certain ways. Their rights are both limited by the government and supported by the government against others. For example, a person who wishes to build on his or her property has the right to do so, but there may be a local ordinance or law against building too close to another's structure. *Williams v. Weisser* is a case that shows an individual's property rights of an unusual nature. Note also the copyright violation by 2 Live Crew.

Where Does a Rule of Property Come From?

3. In capitalist countries property owners have freedom of choice unless there is a conflict with the freedom of choice of another property owner. Then it is up to the law to resolve the controversy.

4. Property rights and property laws historically have involved consideration of four factors:
   a. Contribution to the economy.
   b. Certainty and ease of application.
   c. Enforceability.
   d. Fairness.

Predictability of Property Rights and Business

5. *Moore v. Regents of the University of California* is an example of the application of these factors to today's technology. The results of this case underscore the importance of predictability in law as discussed in Chapter 1.

6. Property is classified in two ways:
   a. Real property -- Land and fixtures thereon, such as a house.
   b. Personal property which is further subdivided:
      1. Tangible personal property or chattels -- Movable property that has physical characteristics, like a book.
      2. Intangible personal property -- Moveable property that has no physical characteristics, like an idea.
   Differing legal rules or procedures apply depending on the classification of the property.

7. *Fixtures* are items of personal property that because of their use become classified as either real or personal property. Courts use several tests to determine how the property should be classified. These tests include:
   a. A written agreement or the parties' intent as to the use.
   b. The difficulty of moving the property without causing damage.
   c. The appropriateness of the use of the property.
   Sigrol Realty Corp. v. Valcich is a case that further explores the concept of fixtures.

8. As discussed earlier, intangible personal property has no physical characteristics, but can be considered among a business's assets. Traditionally accounts receivable and goodwill have been of great value to businesses. In today's economy, intellectual property such as patents, trademarks, copyrights, and trade secrets are becoming increasingly important. In 1982, Congress established a special federal court to deal with intellectual property cases. *Midway Mfg. Co. v. Artic International, Inc.* is a case which deals with intellectual property.

9. With the onset of new technology such as genetically engineered life forms and digital technology, courts are endeavoring to balance the interests of the investors with the difficulties of enforcing these rights.

The Use of Property: Scope and Conflicts

10. When a property owner's rights conflict with an individual's rights, the courts must decide whose right is more substantial. Just as in cases of one person's individual rights as opposed to the individual rights of the majority, property rights have been limited by the courts. This happened through pressures by labor unions, populists, grange movements, and the passage of antitrust and New Deal legislation. Today, the courts generally favor individual's rights over property rights. *State of New Jersey v. Shack and Tejeras* and *Katko v. Briney* are examples of recent court cases.

11. When the property rights of individuals conflict, the law endeavors to decide these conflicts through the common law and through land use planning and environmental regulations.

12. The common law allows a property owner to use his or her land in any manner unless these decisions affect an adjoining land holder's enjoyment of his or her property. Trespass is a common law doctrine which forbids unauthorized, intentional entry on another's land. It can be a physical presence, or use of another's airspace by a plane or an aroma. Nuisance is a second common law doctrine which forbids acts which annoy or disturb the adjoining landowner. Use of another's airspace could be adjudged a nuisance as well as a trespass.

13. In applying the common law, courts attempt to balance the uses of the property against the rights of society in general. One problem with the application of common law doctrine is its ineffectiveness over some environmental hazards. *Boomer v. Atlantic Cement Co.* illustrates the limitations of common law regulation of the effects of pollution.

14. A second problem with balancing conflicting uses of land is that property rights do not cover some aspects of property ownership such as a view. *Fontainebleau Hotel Corp. v. Forty-Five Twenty-Five, Inc.* deals with the issue of sunlight.

MAJOR POINTS OF CASES

Williams v. Weisser (p. 339)

The issue in this case is whether the plaintiff can restrain the publication of his lecture notes under his common law copyright rights. The court held that he could.

The rationale for this decision is that the intangible goods (oral delivery of the lectures) could be used by students in any way but publishing them. Only the creator and owner of the notes can publish them.

Moore v. Regents of the University of California (p. 342)

Moore was told by his doctor, Golde, that Moore's spleen needed to be removed. Unknown to Moore, Golde, and Quan, a researcher employed by the medical center, planned to use Moore's spleen to conduct research. After the operation, Moore was instructed by Golde to come in for follow-up visits because Golde wanted to have exclusive access to the cells by way of a doctor-patient relationship. When Golde established a cell line from Moore's cells, the University Regents applied for a patent listing Golde and Quan as inventors. The Regents, Golde, and Quan would all share in royalties from the patent.

Moore sued for conversion arguing that he had continued to own the cells and that the defendants had unauthorized use of his property.

The appellate court disagreed. It held that Moore had no expectation of continued possession of his cells after surgery. The court discussed the difficult balancing of interests in this case. On the one hand is the policy of the fiduciary duty of a doctor and the policy of informed consent. On the other hand there is the policy of protecting parties who are engaged in important research which would benefit the public in general. The court determined that if the legal theory of conversion was extended to cells removed from a person during surgery, this could impede investment in medical research. Therefore, the court held Moore's complaint was limited to an action for breach of fiduciary duty or lack of informed consent.

The dissent argued that there were two other policies to be considered in this case. The first is a legal prohibition against abuse of the body for the economic benefit of another person. The second consideration is the lack of fundamental fairness in this case and the unjust enrichment of those holding the patent. The dissent believed that Moore's contribution was vital and he should share in the profits.

Sigrol Realty Corp. v. Valcich (p. 347)

The issue in this case is whether certain chattels or tangible personal property that are annexed to real property should be considered real property (fixtures).

The court held that they are not real property, because of the intent of parties. The court reviewed the three classifications of chattels: those that, though annexed, remained movable; those that became a part of the real property; and those that can be either, depending upon the agreement between the chattels' owner and the landowner.

In this case, there was no agreement that would have made the chattels real property. Also, the method of annexation on the land indicates an intent that they were to remain movable chattels.

Midway Mfg. Co. v. Artic International, Inc. (p. 349)

Midway manufactures video games which contain printed circuit boards which cause images and sounds to appear to the player. Artic manufactures circuit boards, one of which speeds up the rate of play of one of Midway's games. Another circuit board manufactured by Artic is an almost identical copy of Midway's game Pac-Man. Midway sued claiming that Artic's sales of these circuit boards infringe upon Midway's copyright in the two games.

The issue in the case is whether circuit boards are "audiovisual works" which are protected under the 1976 Copyright Act. The court held that they were because the player of a video game cannot create the images or the sequences. The most a player can do is choose among the sequences offered by the maker of the game. Therefore the creative ability of the game lies in the works of the inventor and can be protected under the Copyright Act. Due to this decision, Artic can no longer sell the circuit boards in question.

State of New Jersey v. Shack and Tejeras (p. 353)

This is a case involving trespass upon a landowner's property. However, the reasons for this trespass were to give medical and legal aid.

The court held that the landowner could not sue for trespass. The rationale for this decision is that traditionally a landholder could use his or her property in any legal manner if the rights of others were not violated. This leads to the current conclusion that accommodation between property rights of the landowner and the individual rights of others is necessary. In this instance, denying the fundamental rights of medical and legal aid was wrongful, and the landowner could not sue for trespass.

Katko v. Briney (p. 355)

This case is an example of the tension between property rights and individual rights. The issue is whether the property owner is liable to the individual who was seriously injured while entering an abandoned house.

The defendant property owner inherited a farmhouse and some farmland. Her husband tried to farm the land, but left no machinery about. Over time the buildings became run down and the house and farm appeared to be abandoned although there were "No Trespassing" signs posted.

Over a ten year period there was a series of breakins with some damage to the house and some loss of household items. In order to stop the damages, the defendant's husband set up a shotgun which was rigged so that it would fire if anyone opened the bedroom door.

The plaintiff had lived in the area several years and considered the house abandoned. He and a friend broke in through a boarded window with the intent to take anything of interest to them. When the plaintiff opened the bedroom door, the gun went off and he was seriously injured.

Boomer v. Atlantic Cement Co. (p. 357)

This case illustrates limitations on common-law pollution remedies. The nuisance doctrine in New York held that a nuisance must be abated no matter what the economic consequences. The majority of the court held that the only way to abate the nuisance in this case would be to close down the plant. It was felt by the court that this was too great a hardship. The majority held that the manufacturer should pay permanent damages, or an injunction would be issued to close the plant.

The dissent disagreed with this course of action upon two grounds. The first was the effect that this decision would have as a precedent or other nuisance cases. The second was concern for the environment.

Fontainebleau Hotel Corp. v. Forty-Five Twenty-Five, Inc. (p. 358)

In this case the issue is whether the court should issue an injunction or order prohibiting a certain action. This action in question was construction that would block sunlight on the plaintiff's property for a certain portion of each day.

This court held that a landowner has no right to the sunshine falling on his or her land. Since the defendant was using his land in a way that was legal, although obstructing the sunlight, the plaintiff was not entitled to any injunction forbidding this use.

SELF-TEST QUESTIONS

True/False

_____ 1. The foundation for all business activity is the idea of property. (p. 336)

_____ 2. Property may be defined as a relationship between its owner and the government. (p. 337)

_____ 3. In order for property rights to exist, there must be a system of laws to confer, adjust, and enforce the rights. (p. 338)

_____ 4. Because property rights reflect the major values of our society, these factors never conflict. (p. 341)

_____ 5. Without predictability of property law, business decisions would become extremely risky. (p. 344)

_____ 6. Whether property is classified as real or personal, a property owner's rights remain the same. (p. 345)

_____ 7. Real and personal property can be tangible or intangible. (p. 345)

_____ 8. The legal standard applied to fixtures is a reasonable person standard. (p. 346)

_____ 9. In determining whether property is a fixture, any written agreement is the conclusive factor. (p. 346)

_____ 10. Intellectual property laws are designed to protect original ideas. (p. 348)

_____ 11. Intangible personal property generally has less value than tangible personal property. (p. 348)

_____ 12. Historically, property and individual rights had a differing legal foundation. (p. 352)

_____ 13. In a conflict between individual rights and property rights, generally individual rights prevail. (p. 352)

_____ 14. Trespass, under the common law, can only occur through a person's physical presence on another's land. (p. 356)

_____ 15. Every important property value that is associated with the ownership of property is considered a property right. (p. 358)

Multiple Choice

1. Property rights of owners:
   a. allow them to do anything they wish if they have title to their property.
   b. have basically remained unchanged over the last century.
   c. are the government granting of specially defined rights.
   d. require a system of laws for enforcement. (pp. 336-337)

2. Capitalism is based upon the idea that ownership of property is given to individuals by:
   a. natural law.
   b. the state and local government.
   c. the courts.
   d. all of the above, depending on the situation. (p. 338)

3. When deciding property rights disputes today, courts balance all of the following considerations except:
   a. accordance with the laws of nature.
   b. contribution to the economy.
   c. certainty and ease of application.
   d. fairness. (p. 341)

4. Under the terms of a contract, John owes Martha $100. Martha has an ownership interest in:
   a. real property.
   b. tangible personal property.
   c. intangible personal property.
   d. a fixture. (p. 345)

5. Peter and Paul have a contract for sale of Peter's house. A dispute has arisen over whether an antique mantelpiece is included. The court is most likely to hold the mantelpiece to be a fixture if it finds:
   a. that the written contract is silent as to the mantelpiece.
   b. that the mantelpiece is unique and does not blend with the carpet, draperies, and woodwork in the room.
   c. that the mantelpiece is not fastened to the wall.
   d. that removing the mantelpiece would be difficult and would leave a large hole in the wall. (p. 346)

6. Which of the following is *not* true about fixtures?
   a. Fixtures are atypical types of property.
   b. The written agreement between the parties shows intent and is the conclusive factor regarding fixture removal.
   c. The standard the court uses in fixture disputes is the reasonable person standard.
   d. Any item easily removable from real property suggests the item is not a part of real property. (p. 346)

7. Intangible personal property includes:
   a. accounts receivable.
   b. intellectual property.
   c. business goodwill.
   d. all of the above. (p. 348)

8. A recent problem with intellectual property has been:
   a. there is less incentive for business to develop new ideas due to the decline of royalty payments.
   b. computer software is no longer subject to patent protection.
   c. protection of copyrights in artistic areas has decreased due to the creation of a new federal court dealing exclusively with intellectual property.
   d. the rise in the number of intellectual property lawsuits. (pp. 348-349)

9. In the *Midway* case, where the issue was whether computer circuit boards could be protected under the 1976 Copyright Act, the court held:
   a. they could be protected because the investor is the creator of the sequences.
   b. they could be protected in general, but not in this particular case because the boards were in the public domain.
   c. they could not be protected because the player has discretion as to how the sequences are chosen.
   d. they could not be protected because circuit boards are beyond the definition of items covered under the 1976 Copyright Act. (pp. 349-350)

10. Historically individual rights which clashed with great concentration of business powers:
    a. were upheld in the *Plessy* case when the courts ordered the integration of the railroads.
    b. were strengthened by the movement from farming communities to cities in the 1800s.
    c. were supported by the courts in the early days of the New Deal legislation.
    d. were strengthened by antitrust legislation. (pp. 351-352)

11. When comparing individual rights against property rights, generally the courts today:
    a. treat the conflicting rights equally.
    b. favor individual rights over property rights.
    c. insulate the individual from conforming to the norm of society.
    d. leave the power in the hands of the property owners. (p. 352)

12. In the *State of New Jersey* case, when a field worker and an attorney wanted to go on private property to attend to the health of an migrant worker, the court held:
    a. this was an illegal trespass.
    b. the property owner's right in his land was absolute.
    c. the property owner should have allowed the two men access to the migrant worker.
    d. the property owner should have allowed any individual access to the migrant worker. (pp. 353-354)

13. The common law doctrine of nuisance:
    a.   is balanced against the relative uses of each property.
    b.   has been the most effective means of controlling pollution.
    c.   forbids unauthorized intentional entry onto another's land.
    d.   is limited to acts which endanger health.   (p. 356)

14. When comparing conflicting property rights, generally the courts:
    a.   favor a small business over a large business.
    b.   have practically abandoned the common law doctrine of trespass.
    c.   attempt only to resolve these issues by means of land use planning.
    d.   allow any type of land use as long as it doesn't infringe on others' rights.
                                                                      (p. 356)

15. In the *Boomer* case where an injunction was to be imposed on a cement plant found guilty of nuisance, the court held that the injunction:
    a.   should not be permitted as closing down one plant would not solve the problem in the county.
    b.   should not be permitted because the plant's paying of permanent damages is a more reasonable solution.
    c.   should be permitted because it is the usual remedy for nuisance and the plant should not receive special treatment.
    d.   should be permitted or there is no incentive for the plant to alleviate the wrong permanently.   (pp. 357-358)

Essay Questions

1. Discuss the classifications of real property, tangible personal property, fixtures, and intangible personal property.

2. Give an overview of the legal philosophy in regard to conflicts between property rights and individual rights. How does this philosophy change in regard to conflicts between the rights of two or more property holders?

Chapter 13

Legal Aspects of Business Organizational Forms

This chapter discusses the five forms of business organization. All business organizations combine labor, capital, and management. The same type of business could be operated under any of the formats discussed in this chapter. However there are personal preferences by businesspersons and more importantly there are legal advantages and disadvantages to each. In selecting the appropriate form of business organization, managers should consider four factors. These factors are the principles of limited liability, profit sharing, management rights, and control.

This chapter discusses each of the five types of business organization in turn. There is a general overview and historical background for each. The four principles listed above are applied to each form of business organization.

CHAPTER OBJECTIVES

After reading Chapter 13 of the text and studying the related materials in this chapter of the *Study Guide*, you will be able to fulfill the following objectives:

1. Discuss five forms of business organization:
   a. sole proprietorship.
   b. partnership.
   c. limited partnership.
   d. corporation.
   e. limited liability company.

2. Understand the four principles which affect the selection of a type of business organization. They are the principles of:
   a. limited liability.
   b. profit shares.
   c. management rights.
   d. control.

3. Describe the differing types of corporate organization such as the parent-subsidiary enterprise and the close corporation.

4. Identify the special problems of corporations such as the piercing of the corporate veil and corporate squeeze outs.

MAJOR POINTS TO REMEMBER

A Focus on Business Organizational Forms: General Ideas

1.   The same type of business may be operated using any of the forms of business organization discussed in this chapter. The major consideration is the legal characteristics of each firm.

2.   All business organizations are comprised of capital from investors, individuals to make up the labor force, and individuals who manage the company. Each of these functions may have a different legal significance depending on the type of business organization selected. This chapter focuses on four of the more basic legal principles. The first is the limited liability principle which deals with the extent of personal liability of the members of the organization. The second is the legal right, if any, to share in profits. The third is the management rights principle which is the legal right, if any, to participate in management decisions. The fourth is the control principle which is the legal right, if any, to have some control in the business.

The Sole Proprietorship

3.   The sole proprietorship is the least complicated form of business organization. There are no legal formalities in creating a sole proprietorship which may be any size, although most are small.   It is the only form of business organization that need not have employees, although most do. The sole proprietorship has all the control and provides all the management of the business. He or she receives all the profits or losses as well as assumes the responsibility for any legal liabilities against the business. However the sole proprietor must follow all laws applying to business, such as contract or tort law. This includes agency law (discussed in the next chapter) if he or she has employees.

The Partnership

4.   A partnership is the sharing between two or more partners the control, management rights, profits or losses, and personal liability. This form of business organization has its own collection of laws. Historically partnership law goes back to Babylonian times. In the United States statutes controlling partnerships were passed by states in 1914 in the Uniform Partnership Act.   Both this act or its successor, the Revised Uniform Partnership Act (which amended parts of the UPA) still apply to partnerships today.

5.   The Uniform Partnership Act defines a partnership as "an association of two or more persons to carry on as co-owners of a business for profit." Since there are no formal procedures needed to form a partnership, this definition is the only test needed to determine whether a business organization is a partnership. Partnership contracts, while not required, are helpful in determining the rights and duties of each partner. If there is no partnership agreement, the Uniform Partnership Act states that each partner will have equal rights to profits, management, and control. *Zajac v. Harris* focuses on both the definition of a partnership and the equality of partners.

6.   The four business interests which apply to all business organizations apply to partnerships in the following ways. Under the limited liability principle, if neither the partnership itself nor its insurance is able to cover business losses, the partners must use their own

property. Note the impact this may have on partners of Price Waterhouse. As a result of the bankruptcy of Laventhol & Horwath, large partnerships are lobbying stage legislatures for changes in this rule. Under the profit share and management rights principles, partners have a right in a share of the profits and a right to share in the management of the partnership. Under the control principle, partners have the right to vote on issues affecting the firm. Unless there is a partnership agreement which states otherwise, all partners have an equal vote regardless of their contribution of capital or business experience.

The Limited Partnership

7.   The limited partnership form goes back to the Middle Ages. In the United States today limited partnership law in the states generally follows rules set out in the Uniform Limited Partnership Act or the Revised Uniform Limited Partnership Act.

8.   The limited partnership is a form of business organization designed for those who want to invest in a partnership. It consists of general partners who manage the business, and limited partners who invest in the business. The limited partnership contains elements of both the corporation and the partnership. Like a corporation, a limited partnership must be formed pursuant to a statute that requires certain formalities. Like corporate investors, investors in a limited partnership have limited liability. As in a partnership, the general partners are regulated by partnership law and all partners share in the profits of the partnership. *Holzman v. De Escamilla* is an example of loss of limited liability by limited partners who take part in the management of a business.

9.   The four business interests apply to a limited partnership in the following ways. Under the limited liability principle, limited partners have no personal liability for business losses which exceed the assets of the partnership or its insurance. The most the limited partner can lose is his or her investment in the business. However if limited partners manage the business, they lose this limited liability. Under the profit share principle, a limited partner has the right to share in the profits of the partnership. Under the management rights and control principles, a limited partner has no right to participate in either management or control except in a very limited way such as approval of new or limited partners joining the firm.

The Corporation

10.   A corporation is a fictitious legal person separate from any of its members. Legally, a corporation can do many of the things that a natural person can do. Early corporations go back to Roman times, although some historians place them even earlier. Corporations in the United States were most directly modeled after the English joint stock companies. The earliest American corporation was chartered in 1768. State corporate statutes today generally are much less restrictive. These statutes outline the procedures which must be followed in order for a business to incorporate. These procedures generally include filing articles of incorporation with the state, and if approved, adopting by-laws and electing directors and officers. In addition, shares of stock must be issued and regular meeting of corporate directors and shareholders must be held.

11. Since a corporation is a fictional person, its actions such as making contracts can only be carried out through persons acting as agents. The law of agency will be discussed in the following chapter. Two of the most important groups of members of a corporation are:

a. Shareholders -- These people are the owners of the corporation and control it indirectly through voting for a board of directors. If a shareholder wishes, he or she may authorize another to vote in his or her place as a proxy.

b. Directors -- These people are legally responsible as a group for the overall management of the corporation. They also have fiduciary duties which will be discussed in the next chapter.

12. Due to the limited liability principle, corporate investors rely on having their personal assets protected. For this reason, courts apply the piercing the corporate veil doctrine narrowly to individual investors. However, where there is a parent-subsidiary enterprise, the investors are other corporations. In these cases, courts broadly apply the piercing the corporate veil doctrine as seen in *Walkovszky v. Carlton*.

13. Under the profit share principle no investor has a right to a share of corporate profits. If the board of directors decides to invest the profits in the corporation, investors do not have to relinquish their right to profits as partners or limited partners do. Under the management rights principle, only the board of directors has the right to manage the corporation. Under the control principle, shareholders have the right to vote for members of the board of directors. Members with the most shares of stock have the most control.

14. A special type of corporation is the close corporation. It has few investors and its shares of stock cannot be bought or sold in any public market. Often a close corporation is a small family owned business, but it does not have to be. A close corporation, because of the few number of investors, is similar to a partnership since generally the investors manage the corporation. A problem in a close corporation is the corporate squeeze-out where majority shareholders make decisions which injure the minority shareholders. These shareholders have little recourse because there is no organized market to either appreciate or sell their shares. A recent trend is for courts to hold there is a duty owed by the majority shareholders to the minority shareholders. *Hagshenas v. Gaylord* focuses upon this trend.

15. The issue of corporate control is different in a publicly traded corporation where shares are bought and sold in an organized marketplace. The difference is that generally only majority stockholders vote. Since managers usually own most of the stock, they can elect themselves as board members. In other cases, management becomes allied with the board and assists in their election. Oftentimes, board members reward management with higher salaries than executives in other countries command. Corporate critics point out that these actions are unfair to the shareholders. Although shareholders always have had the option of selling their stock, a new trend is developing where small investors are joining together in mutual funds or pension plans. These larger entities are attempting to pressure corporations to become more responsive to the interest of all shareholders.

16. Each traditional form of business organization has negative features. A new form of business organization has been created by eight states with other states considering adoption. This form is called the limited liability company which combines the best features of the other forms of business. Owners are called members and in addition to limited liability, they share in the profits and, if they wish, can participate in the direct management of the business. They are treated in the same way as partnerships for income tax purposes. In the future this form of business could replace the partnership and, in some cases, the corporate forms of business organization.

MAJOR POINTS OF CASES

Zajac v. Harris (p. 370)

The issue in this case is whether a partnership or an employer-employee relationship existed.

Because no partnership agreement is required to form a partnership, the court looked at the actions of the parties. The two men went into business together without the express intent of entering into a partnership. There was no partnership agreement and the business did not file a partnership income tax return. The firm withheld taxes on Harris's behalf and carried workers' compensation for him. However, the court held that a partnership existed because the defendant had the right to share in the profits of the business. This is the primary test for the existence of a partnership.

Holzman v. De Escamilla (p. 374)

The issue in this case is whether the limited partners were acting as general partners by taking part in the management of the business. The court held that this was the case because the limited partners consulted on the types of crops to be planted. They also had control over the partnership. Therefore, the limited partners had lost their limited liability.

Walkovsky v. Carlton (p. 381)

Walkovszky was seriously injured when he was hit by a cab owned by Seon Cab Corporation. Carlton was a shareholder in ten cab corporations, each of which owned only two cabs and carried the minimum automobile liability insurance required by law. Walkovszky alleged that all ten cab companies were operated as a single unit and that he was entitled to hold the stockholders personally liable because of this fraud.

The court stated that it would pierce the corporate veil in cases of fraud. If a corporation is a part of a larger corporation, which actually conducts the business, then this larger corporation would be liable. To hold a shareholder individually liable it must be alleged and proven that the corporation was carrying on business in the individual's personal, rather than corporate, capacity. This was not the case here. The fact that the corporation had been split up to save on insurance costs was not enough to hold Carlton personally liable.

The dissent argued that the majority decision not to hold the shareholders personally liable was a violation of the public interest. It stated that the legislative intent for minimum insurance was to provide for some recovery from individuals and corporations who did not have the assets to purchase more than the minimum automobile insurance. It was not intended as a shield for corporate shareholders who organized schemes such as this in order to avoid public responsibility.

Hagshenas v. Gaylord (p. 385)

In the spring of 1982, Hagshenas filed for a dissolution of Imperial Travel Ltd. because of a corporate deadlock between himself as a 50% shareholder and the Gaylords, the other 50% shareholders. The Gaylords counterclaimed, alleging Hagshenas had breached his fiduciary duty. In the fall of 1982, Hagshenas resigned from the corporation, but did not give up his stock. He began a competing travel business with Imperial's former employees. The Gaylords sought a preliminary injunction to stop this competition. In the fall of 1987, the trial court held Hagshenas had breached his fiduciary duty and he appealed.

The appellate court upheld the lower court decision. The court stated that although a shareholder generally does not owe a fiduciary duty to a company, this does not hold true if the company is a close corporation such as this one was. In this instance the stock was equally split between Hagshenas and the Gaylords. The parties acted like partners in the running of the business.

In addition, shareholders in a close corporation do not sell their stock on the public market. For these reasons, there must be trust between the parties at the time the close corporation is formed. This duty of trust and confidence is a fiduciary duty. The proper course of action for Hagshenas was to refrain from competition with the close corporation until he sold his shares or an order for dissolution had been handed down.

SELF-TEST QUESTIONS

True/False

_____ 1.   The same type of business may be operated using any of the types of organization discussed in this chapter. (p. 365)

_____ 2.   All persons providing capital to a business organization have the same legal liabilities. (p. 366)

_____ 3.   There is no legal distinction between a sole proprietor and his or her business. (p. 368)

_____ 4.   No formal agreement is required to conduct a business as a partnership. (p. 369)

_____ 5.   A partnership agreement cannot be used to contradict rules under the Uniform Partnership Act. (p. 370)

_____ 6.   As a result of large damage awards against them, small partnerships are lobbying state legislatures for changes in partners' liability. (p. 371)

_____ 7.   A limited partner who participates in the management of the firm may lose his or her limited liability protection. (p. 374)

_____ 8. In order for a corporation to exist legally, it must follow the statutory procedure set out in the state corporate statute. (p. 377)

_____ 9. A corporation has many of the legal characteristics of a natural person including the ability to invest money. (p. 377)

_____ 10. Shareholders generally participate in the management and operation of a corporation. (p. 378)

_____ 11. The courts will pierce the corporate veil if managers mingle any corporate property with personal property. (p. 380)

_____ 12. In order for a corporation to refuse to pay dividends to its investors, the investors must agree to this decision. (p. 383)

_____ 13. A developing trend in law is the application of a fiduciary duty of majority shareholders to prevent them from squeezing out minority shareholders. (p. 385)

_____ 14. Unhappy shareholders in a publicly traded corporation can either sell their stock or try to pressure management to change certain policies. (p. 387)

_____ 15. Limited liability companies have been created by legislation in the majority of states. (p. 388)

Multiple Choice

1. Sheila wishes to start a business where she will have all the control. A sole proprietorship is a good choice for her because it:
   a. is not regulated by any body of law.
   b. need not have any employees.
   c. is limited to small businesses.
   d. has relatively few legal formalities in its creation. (pp. 367-368)

2. In the *Zajac* case where the issue was whether Harris was an employee or a partner of the business, the court held he was:
   a. an employee because no partnership income tax return was filed.
   b. an employee because his taxes were withheld and the business paid worker's compensation insurance for him.
   c. a partner because he received half the profits from the business.
   d. a partner because the court found *Zajac* had the intent of starting a partnership. (p. 370-371)

3. Under partnership law unless otherwise stated in a partnership agreement, partners have the right:
   a. of protection of their personal assets.
   b. to vote on issues affecting the firm.
   c. of an amount of control depending on their capital investment.
   d. to be compensated by a salary. (pp. 372-373)

4. Limited partnership law is different than partnership law because it:
   a. is a recent innovation of the courts.
   b. is controlled by federal, not state, statutes.
   c. is used primarily for investments in risky business.
   d. allows limited partners to only receive a fixed dollar return on their investment.
   (pp. 373-374)

5. In a limited partnership, both the limited partners and the general partners share:
   a. profits.
   b. management responsibilities.
   c. liability.
   d. both a and c.
   (pp. 375-376)

6. If Jerry, Ben, and Stacey wish to form a corporation, state statutes require:
   a. legislation approval of each application.
   b. a minimum number of shareholders.
   c. shares to be traded on the New York Stock Exchange.
   d. regular meetings of the board of directors.
   (p. 377)

7. Which of the following is *not* true about the limited liability of corporations?
   a. Directors may not be charged with financial corporate liability.
   b. Corporate shareholders can only lose the amount of their investment in the corporation.
   c. Limited liability was an integral part of corporate law since its inception.
   d. There are two standards of limited liability - one for individual investors and one for corporate investors.
   (p. 379)

8. An important characteristic of a corporation is its separate legal identity. Occasionally, however, the courts "pierce the corporate veil" and impose personal liability. This is *most* likely to occur when:
   a. the corporation was formed to limit the personal liability of shareholders.
   b. the business has been unsuccessful and the corporation is insolvent.
   c. corporate creditors can no longer collect from the corporation.
   d. members of the corporation have failed to treat it as a separate legal entity.
   (p. 380)

9. A parent-subsidiary enterprise is:
   a. less likely to have the piercing the corporate veil doctrine applied by the courts
   b. an unusual type of corporation.
   c. limited to short term ventures.
   d. defined by the types of owners of the enterprise.
   (p. 381)

10. In the *Walkovszky* case where the plaintiff wanted to hold the shareholders personally liable for his injuries, the court disagreed because:
    a. there were no allegations the shareholder conducted business in their individual capacity.
    b. there were no allegations that the defendant controlled the larger corporation.
    c. there was no fraud in the setting up of a fragmented corporate entity.
    d. the legislative intent in posing a minimum insurance law was to shield drivers.
    (pp. 381-383)

11. The legal responsibility for managing a corporation is vested in its:
   a. shareholders.
   b. board of directors.
   c. officers.
   d. president. (p. 383)

12. A close corporation:
   a. must be a small and/or family owned company.
   b. does not allow the trading of shares.
   c. is similar to a partnership in management style.
   d. has no majority shareholders (p. 384)

13. In the *Hagshenas* case, where Hagshenas was accused of breaking his fiduciary duty to the corporation, the court held:
   a. he had breached his duty because he still owned shares of stock when he opened a competing business.
   b. he had breached his duty because shareholders owe duties to the corporation unless it is a close corporation.
   c. he had not breached his duty because there was no trust and confidence between the parties at the time of his leaving.
   d. he had not breached his duty because he had filed for dissolution of the corporation before he resigned. (pp. 385-386)

14. Due to the issue of corporate control in large publicly traded corporations:
   a. shareholders now elect both the boards of directors and the officers of the corporation.
   b. shared ownership through mutual funds is pressuring management to be more responsive to all shareholders.
   c. has affected the laws on the fiduciary duty of majority shareholders not to elect themselves as board members.
   d. has required minority shareholders planning to sell stock to notify the majority shareholders so that they might rectify the situation if they choose. (pp. 386-387)

15. A limited liability company gives limited liability to its members, but does *not* give them:
   a. the duty to manage.
   b. favorable tax treatment.
   c. the right of control.
   d. the right to profits. (p. 388)

Essay Questions

1. Discuss the four principles which affect a person's choice of a business organization and how these principles apply to each of the five forms of a business.

2. Describe the doctrine of piercing the corporate veil.

Chapter 14

Members of Business Organizations: Regulation of Their Activities through Agency and Fiduciary Duty Principles

No matter what type of business organization a manager chooses, the business is actually managed and operated through the work of individuals. Two areas of law which cover the business relationship with its employees are discussed in this chapter. The first legal area involves the law of agency which applies certain rules that determine when the firm will be responsible for the actions of its agents in the areas of contracts and torts. The second legal area involves the principles of fiduciary duty which impose duties of care and loyalty to certain individuals.

CHAPTER OBJECTIVES

After reading Chapter 14 of the text and studying the related materials in this chapter of the *Study Guide*, you will be able to fulfill the following objectives:

1. Describe the agent-principal relationship and identify the agents and principals in each of the five types of business organizations.

2. Describe the doctrine of vicarious liability.

3. Discuss the three ways an agent can bind a principal to a contract:
    a. Actual authority
    b. Apparent authority
    c. Ratification

4. Describe the fiduciary duties of care and loyalty and to whom they apply.

5. Discuss the business judgement rule and the corporate opportunity doctrine.

MAJOR POINTS TO REMEMBER

Business Concerns Arising from an Organization Member's Actions

1. A basic concern of the legal environment relates to the legal roles and duties of persons who work for business organizations. This chapter focuses upon laws concerning fiduciary relationships, authority principles under agency law, and the doctrine of vicarious liability under agency law.

118

The Law of Agency: Who Are the Agents?

2. An agent-principal relationship is formed by the consent of the two parties and gives the agent the power to act on behalf of the principal. The principal has the right to control the activities of the agent. In addition, once this relationship is formed, the principal is liable for any injuries caused by the agent in the course of employment. *Hurla v. Capper Publications, Inc.*, is a case that involves the identification of an agent-principal relationship.

3. The law of agency applies to all types of businesses which have employees. Except for a sole proprietorship, each of the other types of business organizations have other agency laws which apply solely to them. In a partnership, partners are held to be both principle and agents of each other. In a limited partnership general partners are principals and agents of each other and the limited partners. Limited partners are principals, but not agents. In a corporation, only the officers are agents of the corporation which is the principal. In a limited liability company, members are agents if they are managing the firm. The company is the principal.

Business Consequences of the Agency Relationship

4. The doctrine of vicarious liability is also known as the doctrine of respondent superior. It has been a part of American common law and European law for hundreds of years. It holds that the principal is liable for any tort committed by an agent within the course and scope of the principal's business. An agent is also liable for his or her torts. It is not always easy to determine what is and what is not within the course and scope of the principal's business. Some factors considered by the court are:
    a. Were the agent's actions common among other employees?
    b. Was the agent's action unexpected by the employer?
    c. When and how did the act occur?
    d. If physical violence by the agent was involved, was it fully unexpected by the employer? *Williams v. Community Drive-In Theater, Inc.* and *Harris v. Trojan Fire Works Company* are cases that involve torts committed by agents that raised the issue of respondent superior.

5. Agency law also holds that the principal is bound to any contract that an agent makes if the agent has the authority to do so. Generally the agent is not bound to the contract. There are three doctrines that regulate the agent's power to make a contract. They are:
    a. Actual authority -- The principal has expressly or by implication given the agent specific powers to make a contract.
    b. Apparent authority -- The principal must create the impression that the agent can make a contract and third parties must have reasonably relied on this apparent authority.
    c. Ratification -- The principal, while not authorizing the agent's authority, affirms the contract in some way, such as accepting the benefits of the contract.
    Managers should limit or define carefully an agent's authority to prevent occurrences as in *Lind v. Schenley Industries Inc.*

Principles of Fiduciary Duties

6. A fiduciary relationship is one of power and trust. A fiduciary has the power to manage another's property and is trusted to manage that property for the benefit of the other party. In an agent-principal relationship, the agent is the fiduciary and has two duties. The first is the duty of care which requires the agent to be watchful of the principal's interest. The second is the duty of loyalty which requires the agent to put the principal's interests first, even above his or her own.

7. All organizations require fiduciary duties from agents to principals. Again, except for a sole proprietorship, each of the other types of business organizations have special duties arising from the nature of the firms. In a partnership, partners owe fiduciary duties to each other. In a limited partnership, the general partners owe fiduciary duties to each other and to the general partners. In a limited liability company, managing members of the firm owe fiduciary duties to all other members of the firm whether they are managers or not. In a corporation the board of directors and officers owe a fiduciary duty to the shareholders.

The Fiduciary Duty and Director - Shareholder Relationships

8. The fiduciary duty standard goes beyond the reasonable person standard and focuses on the way people should act. It imposes a higher level of care and loyalty than is ordinarily required by law. There are many persons who act as fiduciaries such as trustees, attorneys and accountants. This section will examine the fiduciary duties of a corporate director.

9. The law imposes a fiduciary duty upon the directors of a corporation in order to diminish their powers. This duty includes the duty of care and the duty of loyalty. For the duty of care, the standard applied by the courts is the amount of care that a prudent person would apply. *Bates v. Dresser* is a case that further explains this standard. A defense to this duty is the business judgment rule, which provides that the directors are not liable for an alleged duty of care breach unless fraud or bad faith can be proved. *Shlensky v. Wrigley et al.* is an example of this defense.

10. For the duty of loyalty, the goal of the courts is to protect the corporation's interests from the directors' interests. A director cannot benefit by taking something away from the corporation or by taking advantage of the corporation. Note that a director may have dealings with the corporation if there is full disclosure to an independent board of directors or if the dealings are fair and reasonable. *Globe Woolen Co. v. Utica Gas & Electric Co.* centers upon this duty.

11. Under the corporate opportunity doctrine, two more loyalty standards are required of directors. This doctrine prohibits two acts. The first is competition with the corporation. The second is taking advantage of an opportunity of interest to the corporation without giving the corporation the right of first refusal.

MAJOR POINTS OF CASES

Hurla v. Capper Publications, Inc. (p. 394)

The issue in this case is whether the principal had the right to control the agent's actions and can therefore be held liable for the agent's tort. The general rule is that if the principal does not have control or the right to control, the employee is considered an independent contractor and solely responsible for his or her own torts.

The court held, due to the lack of control by the employer, that the employee was an independent contractor.

Williams v. Community Drive-In Theater, Inc. (p. 398)

The issue in this case was whether the trial court erred in granting summary judgment. The appellate court held that it did.

The court stated that there was a genuine issue of fact for a jury to determine. The issue was whether McKenna was acting within the scope of her employment when she shot the plaintiff for an unauthorized entry on the company property. McKenna's duties usually consisted of working at the concession stand. On the night of the incident, she was asked by her supervisor to help close up the theater. This duty involved the prevention of unauthorized entry. The court held that the issue of the drive-in's liability should be determined by a jury.

Harris v. Trojan Fireworks Company (p. 399)

This case deals with the doctrine of vicarious liability, or respondent superior. The general rule is that a principal is liable for the acts of an agent as long as the acts are within the scope of the agent's employment.

The issue in the case is whether the principal is liable for an intoxicated agent's driving accident, which killed one man and injured two other people.

The Christmas party was held on company time, employees were expected to attend, and alcohol was supplied by the principal. On the other hand, the defendant made the decision to drive home. He was not on company time or on company property when he hit the plaintiff.

Lind v. Schenley Industries Inc. (p. 402)

The issue in this case is whether the agent had the apparent authority to bind the principal. In the case, an agent of the company had made a contract with a third party who relied on it. The company then claimed that the agent did not have the authority to make the contract. The court held that under the apparent authority doctrine, if it was reasonable for the third party to believe that the agent had the authority to make such a contract, the agent has the authority to bind the principal.

Bates v. Dresser (p. 407)

This case illustrates the issue of the fiduciary duty of care. The Court held that the board of directors had not violated that duty but that the president had.

In determining whether this duty has been breached, the courts apply the prudent person standard. The facts show that a prudent board of directors would not have detected the novel fraud. A prudent president should have detected the fraud because of his involvement in the daily running of the business and the number of suspicious events.

Shlensky v. Wrigley et al. (p. 409)

The business judgment rule is the focus of this case, in which a shareholder challenged a decision of the board of directors as being detrimental to the business.

The court held that the board of directors has the right to exercise its own business judgment as long as no fraud, illegality, or conflict of interest is involved. A board of directors does not have to follow the lead of others in the same business. Whether the judgment is correct or incorrect is not for the courts to speculate upon.

Globe Woolen Co. v. Utica Gas & Electric Co. (p. 412)

This case centers on the fiduciary duty of loyalty, in which a director must approve only fair contracts that benefit the corporation. Note that the director may personally benefit as well. In this case, the defendant was a director of both corporations who had created a contract that was grossly unfair to one of the corporations. The court held that the defendant had breached his duty of loyalty even though he did not actually vote to accept the contract. The rationale of the court was that the defendant had a dominating influence on the acceptance of such a one-sided contract.

SELF-TEST QUESTIONS

True/False

_____ 1. In order for an agency relationship to be formed, the agent must have written power to act for the principal. (p. 394)

_____ 2. In a limited partnership, all partners are agents of each other. (p. 396)

_____ 3. Under the doctrine of vicarious liability, a tort is imposed on someone who has done no wrong. (p. 396)

_____ 4. Since the trend in tort law is victim compensation, the scope of the principal's liability for actions of an agent are narrowly interpreted by the courts. (p. 398)

_____ 5. If an agent has actual authority to make a contract, the agent is not a legal party to the contract. (p. 400)

_____ 6. For apparent authority to occur, it must be reasonable for the third party to rely on the agent's statements. (p. 401)

_____ 7. A principal cannot be bound to the contract unless he or she expressly grants his or her agent the power to bind him or her. (pp. 401-402)

_____ 8. Ratification is assumed by an agent when the principal's directions are general or vague. (p. 402)

_____ 9. All employers owe fiduciary duties to their employees. (p. 405)

_____ 10. Because shareholders vote directly for the board of directors, shareholders have a fiduciary duty to the corporation. (p. 406)

_____ 11. A fiduciary duty imposes a level of care and loyalty based upon the prudent person standard. (p. 407)

_____ 12. The business judgment rule is the best defense to the accusation of a breach of fiduciary duty of loyalty. (p. 409)

_____ 13. In evaluating the business judgment rule defense, courts reflect upon the correctness of the director's decision. (p. 409)

_____ 14. The fiduciary duty of loyalty prohibits individual directors from taking advantage of their position for personal gain. (p. 411)

_____ 15. The corporate opportunity doctrine imposes two more loyalty standards upon directors of corporations. (p. 414)

Multiple Choice

1. In order for an agency relationship to be formed:
   a. there must be a consensual relationship between any two parties.
   b. the principal must have the right to control the activities of the agent.
   c. the principal must owe special legal duties to the agent.
   d. both a and b.   (p. 394)

2. Agents of a corporation include:
   a. officers.
   b. board of director members.
   c. shareholders.
   d. all of the above.   (p. 396)

3. In a limited liability company, all members who:
   a. receive salaries are considered agents.
   b. manage the business are considered agents.
   c. control the company are considered principals.
   d. receive profits are considered principals.   (p. 396)

4. Under the doctrine of vicarious liability:
   a. an agent is not liable for his or her torts.
   b. the tort must have occurred while the agent was performing the principal's business.
   c. it only applies if the agent committed the tort with the principal's knowledge.
   d. it is increasingly being interpreted more narrowly by the court.

   (pp. 396-397)

5. The rationale behind the doctrine of vicarious liability is:
   a. unique to English and American common law.
   b. to make employers liable for unexpected actions of their agents.
   c. to hold employers liable because they get better insurance rates than individuals.
   d. the deep pocket theory.

   (p. 397)

6. Jeff has been hired by Sanjeev to sell Sanjeev's car "for no less than $1,000." If Jeff gets a neighborhood service station to wash the car and fix its two flat tires so that it will be easier to sell, Sanjeev will probably:
   a. be responsible for the bill, since Jeff had express authority to do this.
   b. be responsible for the bill, since Jeff had implied authority to do this.
   c. not be responsible for the bill, since Jeff had no authority to do this.
   d. not be responsible for the bill unless he ratifies Jeff's act.

   (pp. 400-402)

7. For a principal to be held liable under apparent authority:
   a. a third party must have reasonably relied on the agent's authority.
   b. the agent must have received express instructions which were vague.
   c. the principal must have given the agent the impression he or she had the right to enter into this type of contract.
   d. the principal must have benefitted from the agent's action.

   (pp. 401-402)

8. The *Lind* case which dealt with the man who accepted a sales position because of the incentive plan is an example of the court's finding of:
   a. apparent authority.
   b. actual authority.
   c. ratification.
   d. none of these since the position was that of an independent contractor.

   (pp. 402-403)

9. In a limited partnership, the general partners and the limited partners:
   a. are both principals and agents to each other.
   b. owe *fiduciary* duties to the partnership, but not to each other.
   c. are liable for the torts of their agents.
   d. none of the above.

   (pp. 405-406)

10. The fiduciary duty of care standard is:
    a. the reasonable person standard.
    b. only applied to fraud.
    c. only applied when a decision causes monetary loss.
    d. a standard of hindsight.

    (p. 407)

11. A minority shareholder is suing the directors of XYZ Corporation for breach of fiduciary duty, alleging that certain decisions made by the board have resulted in operating losses to the corporation. Under the business judgment rule:
   a. a director who failed to attend directors' meetings and therefore knew nothing about the decisions has not breached the duty of care.
   b. a director who made no attempt to gather information concerning the decisions, but merely voted with the majority, has not breached the duty of care.
   c. a director who honestly and reasonably believed the decisions to be correct has not breached the duty of care.
   d. both a and c. (p. 409)

12. In the *Shlensky* case which dealt with the refusal of the major stockholder of the Chicago Cubs to install lights in the ballpark, the court held the stockholder:
   a. had the right to make this decision due to the business judgment rule.
   b. had the right to make this decision because he was, in effect, the owner of the corporation.
   c. did not have the right to make this decision because he breached his fiduciary duty of loyalty.
   d. did not have the right to make this decision because he breached his fiduciary duty of care. (pp. 409-411)

13. The fiduciary duty of loyalty:
   a. prohibits a director from engaging in business deals with the corporation.
   b. regulates a director's decision-making process.
   c. requires full disclosure if a director has a personal interest in a corporate decision.
   d. prohibits a director from making a profit due to his or her status. (pp. 411-412)

14. In the *Globe* case where Maynard was a director of both the electric company and the woolen mill, the court held he breached his fiduciary duty of loyalty because he:
   a. refused to vote on the contract.
   b. was looked upon as a representative of the electric company.
   c. knew how great the mill's loss would be.
   d. had a dominating influence. (pp. 412-414)

15. The corporate opportunity doctrine:
   a. is a defense to the fiduciary duty of loyalty.
   b. does not allow a corporate director to take advantage of opportunities he or she hears of while serving on the board.
   c. requires a corporate director to give the corporation the right of first refusal.
   d. forbids a corporate director to enter into business dealings with the corporation. (pp. 414-415)

Essay Questions

1. Describe the duties and rights of parties in an agent-principal relationship.

2. Discuss the fiduciary duties of care and loyalty and to whom they apply.

Chapter 15

White-Collar and Business Crime: Regulation of Business through the Criminal Process

Crimes have always presented a serious threat to society. This chapter discusses the classification of crimes and criminal court procedures. The constitutional protection guaranteed to individuals accused of crimes is also detailed.

Recently, society and the courts have become more alarmed about the prevalence and the cost of white-collar crimes. The latter part of this chapter deals with some of the more common crimes committed against and by businesses.

CHAPTER OBJECTIVES

After reading Chapter 15 of the text and studying the related materials in this chapter of the *Study Guide*, you will be able to fulfill the following objectives:

1.   Identify the classifications of crime.

2.   Recognize the differences between criminal and civil procedures.

3.   Understand the constitutional rights of those accused of crimes.

4.   Identify major white-collar crimes.

MAJOR POINTS TO REMEMBER

Classes of Crimes

1.   A *crime* is an act or omission against society for which the government imposes a fine or a jail or prison sentence. A *felony* is a more serious crime, which is punishable by a fine or a sentence of over a year in a penitentiary. A *misdemeanor* is a less serious crime punishable by a fine or a sentence of less than a year in jail. Violations of city and county laws are generally called *petty crimes*. Note that some crimes, like murders, are classified in only one category, while with others, like theft, the classification depends on the seriousness of the crime.

Prosecution of Cases

2.   There are two types of litigation under the American legal system -- civil and criminal. There are instances in which an act may be tried in either system. For example, a battery

is both an intentional tort and a crime. Most often, an action is either a civil or criminal offense.

3.   A civil case is brought by one individual against another, and the usual remedy is money damages to make the plaintiff "whole." A criminal case is brought by the government against an individual, and the usual remedy is a fine or imprisonment. The goal of criminal law is to punish the criminal, not to make the victim of the crime whole.

4.   In a typical felony proceeding, the following steps are taken:
   a.   Arraignment or appearance -- This is the first appearance before the judge in order to determine the pleas of the accused. A lawyer will be appointed by the court if the accused cannot afford one, and bail may be set.
   b.   The preliminary hearing -- If a grand jury is not required, a preliminary hearing is held. The prosecution must present some evidence at this point that shows that a crime was committed and that shows reason to believe that the accused committed the crime. If the judge concurs, the person is bound over for trial.
   c.   Grand jury -- If a grand jury is required, that body decides whether there is enough evidence to bind the accused for trial. It does this by handing down an indictment known as a true bill. The Constitution requires an indictment for a capital crime.
   d.   Arraignment -- the accused is entitled to hear the evidence against him or her and enter a plea of guilty or not guilty. The trial date is set at this point. It is at this stage that plea bargaining often occurs. The government agrees to drop or reduce the charges if the defendant pleads guilty. Plea bargaining has advantages for both sides: the government does not have to proceed with the expense of a trial, and the accused receives a lesser sentence. Of course, the accused has the right to a trial and does not have to plea bargain.
   e.   The trial -- The standards for proof are more stringent than in a civil case. The prosecution must prove beyond a reasonable doubt that the accused committed a crime. Constitutional provisions provide the right to be tried in the district where the crime was committed and a speedy and impartial jury trial.
   f.   Sentencing -- A recommendation for sentencing is made to the judge on the basis of the person's history. The judge considers the information but is not bound by it. The length of the sentence is governed by statute, which usually provides some flexibility.
   g.   Appeal -- A convicted person may appeal to a higher court or file a writ of habeas corpus asking for release, claiming that his or her due process rights were violated.

Constitutional Protection

5.   The Constitution provides guarantees for a fair trial. The amendments that provide this guarantee are:
   a.   The Fourteenth Amendment -- This has been used to extend some of the requirements of the Bill of Rights of the United States Constitution to the states.
   b.   The Fourth Amendment -- This prohibits the government from conducting unreasonable searches and seizures. A warrant for probable cause must be acquired from the court before a person or property may be searched. The warrant must specify what items may be seized. A warrant may also be issued for

a person's arrest. This amendment applies to businesses as well. *G.M. Leasing Corp. v. United States* is a case that deals with search and seizure.

    c.   The Fifth Amendment -- This requires a grand jury indictment in certain cases and protects individuals from double jeopardy, or being tried twice for the same offense. It also prohibits compelling a person to testify against himself or herself. A confession may be admitted into evidence only if a person knowingly and voluntarily gave it. This privilege or right applies only to testimony and not to physical evidence such as blood samples. Business records may be appropriated by the government when in the possession of the owners or when in the possession of their attorney or accountant.

    d.   The Sixth Amendment -- This provides for a fair trial by requiring a speedy, public trial by an impartial jury. A defendant has a right to be informed of the charges against him or her, to answer them, and to subpoena witnesses if necessary. The right to require the government to provide counsel if the defendant cannot afford a lawyer is also provided.

White-Collar Crime

6.   This type of crime is a nonviolent method of acquiring money, property, or a business for personal advantage. White-collar crime can be committed against business and by business.

7.   Mail and wire fraud statutes prohibit the use of the mail, the telephone, or other devices to transmit any fraudulent schemes to swindle the average person. This is applied to both essential elements and elements incident to a scheme to defraud as shown in *Schmuck v. United States*. The penalties are a fine and/or imprisonment. A person or business can be found liable as well under RICO, as explained in the next section.

8.   The Racketeer Influenced Corrupt Organization Act (RICO) prohibits using money gained by two or more racketeering activities within a ten-year period to:

    a.   gain or maintain control of an enterprise.
    b.   invest in an enterprise.
    c.   participate in the conduct or affairs of an enterprise.

Racketeering activities include many white-collar crimes such as mail, wire, securities, or bankruptcy fraud. The government may bring suit under RICO with the penalties being an extremely high fine and/or a lengthy prison sentence. Private parties may bring a civil suit under RICO. In addition, a judge may order the defendant to forfeit certain property which deprives him or her of its use. This law can affect an owner of a business or a lender such as a bank, as well.

9.   Many states have passed their own version of RICO. These, like the federal law, provide both criminal and civil penalties as well as forfeiture provisions which allow pretrial forfeiture of the accused's property. *Caplin and Drysdale v. United States* deals with the issue of whether these forfeiture provisions infringe upon a person's Sixth Amendment right to an attorney.

10.   Civil RICO allows private parties to sue for treble damages and attorney fees. The Supreme Court has held that a civil suit can be brought against a defendant who has not been convicted of a crime and no injury need be shown except that the defendant

committed the action. In another case, the Court added the requirement that the plaintiff must prove he or she was directly harmed by the alleged wrongdoing.

11. The number of civil RICO cases has risen dramatically in recent years. Although outsiders may be liable, *Reves v. Ernst & Young* is a case which discusses the extent of involvement needed for liability under RICO.

12. A growing trend has been for courts to hold executives more accountable to the public than they have been in the past. *United States v. Park* is a case in which an executive was held criminally liable for a failure to comply with regulations.

MAJOR POINTS OF CASES

G.M. Leasing Corp. v. United States (p. 424)

This case involves the warrantless seizure of corporation property. The Court held that this action was a violation of the Fourth Amendment. The Court also recognized that there are occasions on which businesses are to be treated differently from individuals. The Court also recognized that there are occasions in which a warrantless search is permissible. However, this instance was no more than an attempt to enforce tax laws, and in this case there was no justification for treating corporations differently from individuals.

Schmuck v. United States (p. 428)

Schmuck turned back odometers on cars and then sold them to dealers who resold them. As part of the resale process, the dealers sent title applications to the Wisconsin Department of Transportation. The issue in this case is whether Schmuck can be convicted of mail fraud.

The Supreme Court held that Schmuck was guilty of mail fraud even though he didn't personally use the mails to precipitate the fraud and even though the use of the mails was not an essential part of the fraud. A mailing which is incidental or even innocent which is part of the execution of a fraud is sufficient to find the perpetrator of the fraud guilty.

Caplin & Drysdale v. United States (p. 436)

The issue in this case is whether the RICO forfeiture statute violates the Sixth Amendment of the Constitution which provides that defendants have the right to choose their counsel in a criminal case.

The Supreme Court held that it did not. First of all defendants with no money do not have the right to choose counsel; they only have the right to be adequately represented by court-appointed attorneys. Secondly, the forfeiture statute does not prevent a defendant from retaining counsel of choice with any money which is not forfeitable. Third, like the proceeds from robbery, the forfeited money does not really belong to the defendant. The purpose of the forfeiture statute is to "lessen the economic power of organized crime and drug enterprises." Thus this statute justifiably penalizes defendants with no other assets than wrongfully acquired ones.

Reves v. Ernst & Young (p. 439)

In 1981, the Co-Op was audited by Russell Brown which merged with Arthur Young and eventually became part of Ernst & Young. The auditor overvalued the assets of the Co-Op. A condensed version of this audit was distributed to the Co-Op's members in 1982. In 1984 the Co-Op filed for bankruptcy. The trustees in bankruptcy filed suit against Arthur Young. The Court of Appeals found for Young and Reves appealed.

The Supreme Court upheld the lower court decision. It looked to the meaning of the words in the applicable statute and determined that "conduct" and "participate" indicated that a company must have taken part in directing the affairs of the other business. In this case Arthur Young had relied on the Co-Op's records and indicated this reliance to the Co-Op's Board. Arthur Young did not participate in the operation or management of the Co-Op and therefore was not liable.

Unites States v. Park (p. 441)

This case focuses upon the liability of an executive under the Food, Drug, and Cosmetic Act of 1938. Note that executives in these types of businesses are held to an extremely high standard because of the nature of their products, which may endanger public health.

The Court relied on precedent that held that an executive could be criminally liable for a wrongful act of the corporation. This is true even if the executive was not directly responsible or even if the executive did not have the intent to commit a crime. The court restated the legislative purpose of the act, which is to require a duty to "insure that violations will not occur."

SELF-TEST QUESTIONS

True/False

____ 1. Businesses today suffer very little from the effects of nonviolent crime. (p. 418)

____ 2. Fines may be imposed on defendants convicted of felonies, but not on those convicted of misdemeanors. (pp. 418-419)

____ 3. Victims of crimes are rarely compensated for damages. (p. 419)

____ 4. A grand jury determines the guilt or innocence of a defendant. (p. 421)

____ 5. A defendant who pleads not guilty at the arraignment may not change the plea to guilty later on. (p. 421)

____ 6. Generally, the state may not appeal when the defendant is found not guilty at the trial level. (p. 422)

____ 7. Today, most of the provisions of the Bill of Rights apply to state as well as federal proceedings. (p. 423)

_____ 8. The Fifth Amendment privilege of not compelling persons to be a witness against themselves has not been extended to businesses. (pp. 425-426)

_____ 9. White-collar crimes are only those which are committed by a person in the course of his or her occupation. (p. 427)

_____ 10. In mail and wire fraud cases, courts have interpreted the term "defraud" very narrowly. (p. 427)

_____ 11. The main purpose of RICO is to attack the economic base of organized crime. (p. 430)

_____ 12. White-collar crimes are exempt from RICO. (p. 431)

_____ 13. RICO permits an accused party to retain enough funds to hire the attorney of his or her choice. (p. 435)

_____ 14. A civil RICO suit may proceed even if the defendant has not been convicted of a crime. (p. 438)

_____ 15. There is a growing trend toward imposing criminal sentences on chief executive officers. (p. 441)

Multiple Choice

1. The major purpose of a criminal suit is:
   a. to compensate the victim for the damages done to him or her.
   b. to return the injured party to the position that he or she occupied before the defendant's wrongful act.
   c. to compensate the state for the defendant's wrongful act.
   d. to punish the defendant for violating state or federal law.
   (p. 419)

2. A grand jury:
   a. does not have to be required by the states.
   b. is guaranteed in federal cases only for the crime of murder.
   c. consists of fewer members than a trial jury.
   d. has, as its major purpose, the determination that a crime has been committed.
   (p. 421)

3. In a criminal case:
   a. the prosecution must prove its case by a preponderance of the evidence.
   b. the case must be held in the district where the crime was committed.
   c. the judge uses precedent from past cases to determine the length of the sentence.
   d. the double jeopardy clause of the Constitution prohibits a new trial for any reason. (pp. 421-422)

4. The police suspect that Walter has committed a crime and think that a search of his house and business would yield enough evidence to convict him. For the search to be valid, a warrant is required:
   a. for both Walter's house and his business.
   b. for Walter's house but not for his business.
   c. for Walter's business but not for his house.
   d. for neither Walter's house nor his business. (pp. 423-424)

5. A person may assert his or her Fifth Amendment privilege not to be a witness against himself or herself by:
   a. refusing to give a blood sample.
   b. refusing to turn over business records no longer in his or her possession.
   c. refusing to testify in court.
   d. all of the above. (p. 426)

6. The right of an accused to confront witnesses against him or her is included in the:
   a. Fourth Amendment.
   b. Fifth Amendment.
   c. Sixth Amendment.
   d. Fourteenth Amendment. (p. 426)

7. Henry has been charged with a misdemeanor. If he is convicted, he could be sentenced to a ninety-day term in the county jail. Henry cannot afford an attorney and is demanding that the county provide one for him. Under current interpretation of the Sixth Amendment, the county:
   a. must provide Henry with counsel because his conviction could result in a jail sentence.
   b. must provide Henry with counsel because indigent people are entitled to representation in all cases.
   c. need not provide Henry with counsel because he is not being tried for a felony.
   d. need not provide Henry with counsel because he is not being tried for a federal crime. (p. 426)

8. Which of the following is *not* true regarding white-collar crime?
   a. It is nonviolent.
   b. It is committed against businesses not by businesses.
   c. It usually involves fraud.
   d. It is difficult to detect. (p. 427)

9. In the *Schmuck* case where the defendant was accused of mail fraud, the court held that the defendant:
   a. was not guilty because he never used the mail to send for the titles.
   b. was not guilty because the use of the mails was not an essential part of his scheme.
   c. was not guilty because the mailings occurred after the fraud had been committed.
   d. was guilty because the success of his venture depended upon the receipt of the titles. (pp. 428-429)

10. A "pattern of racketeering activity" under RICO includes:
    a. misdemeanors and felonies under state law.
    b. any criminal violation under the United States Code.
    c. two or more predicate acts committed within a ten year period.
    d. any white-collar crime committed by an agent of a business.

    (pp. 430-431)

11. RICO was passed in order to make it illegal to:
    a. acquire control of a legitimate business in order to cleanse illegal monies.
    b. acquire control of a legitimate business with funds generated by criminal activities.
    c. collect an illegal debt.
    d. all of the above. (pp. 430-431)

12. State versions of RICO
    a. apply civil penalties only.
    b. contain forfeiture provisions permitting the seizure of property.
    c. only apply to persons convicted of a crime.
    d. are modeled after the federal act. (pp. 432-433)

13. In a civil RICO case:
    a. a private party can sue RICO if the defendant has already been convicted of a crime.
    b. a private party can sue under RICO if an injury is shown.
    c. the government must prove both elements in order to file a case under RICO.
    d. none of the above. (pp. 438-439)

14. In the *Reves* case where the issue was whether the accounting firm was liable for fraud under RICO, the court held that the firm:
    a. was liable because the auditor overvalued Co-Op's assets.
    b. was liable because it ommitted pertinent information in the annual report.
    c. was not liable because it was an "outsider."
    d. was not liable because it did not participate in the management of the Co-Op.

    (pp. 439-440)

15. In *United States v. Park*, the Supreme Court ruled that an executive could be criminally liable under the Food, Drug, and Cosmetic Act:
    a. unless he or she properly delegated the responsibility for compliance to a dependable subordinate.
    b. only when he or she had personal knowledge of noncompliance with the act.
    c. only when he or she had personal knowledge of noncompliance and a culpable state of mind.
    d. if he or she had the authority to make the corporation comply with the act and failed to do so. (pp. 441-442)

Essay Questions

1. What are the major differences between civil procedure and criminal procedure?

2. What is RICO and what are the penalties if a defendant is found guilty of such an act?

Chapter 16

Products Liability

This chapter discusses the law of products liability, which refers to individuals' injuries caused by products. The negligence theory discussed in Chapter 11 is reviewed in this chapter as well as an introduction to other theories of liability. Products liability law is drawn in part from the law of torts and in part from the law of contracts. This law has evolved over the years and is now a major concern of business because of the number and cost of the suits.

CHAPTER OBJECTIVES

After reading Chapter 16 of the text and studying the related materials in this chapter of the *Study Guide*, you will be able to fulfill the following objectives:

1. Identify the four causes of action for product injury of individuals:
   a. Negligence.
   b. Warranty.
   c. Misrepresentation.
   d. Strict liability.

2. Recognize the different groups of businesses that may be liable for injury under products liability law.

3. Recognize when a manufacturer does and does not have a duty to warn.

4. Understand the evolving nature of products liability law.

MAJOR POINTS TO REMEMBER

Products Liability and History

1. Before the Industrial Revolution, courts followed the doctrine of *caveat emptor* or let the buyer beware. This was a reflection of the society at a time when buyers dealt directly with sellers, and products were less complex than today. Courts reasoned that buyers had the opportunity for inspection and if they bought a defective product, they had to absorb the loss. As businesses grew larger and as products became more sophisticated, courts, again reflecting society's views, began to hold the seller responsible for defective products.

2. Historically, the injured plaintiff had to be in privity of contract with the defendant. This means that the plaintiff could only sue the person from whom he or she had bought the product, which in most cases was the retailer. Often the retailer did not have the funds to meet the judgment against the business. Because public policy demanded that these injured parties be allowed to fully recover, privity was abolished from negligence law by

134

the landmark case of *MacPherson v. Buick Motor Co.* Since that case occurred, courts have removed the privity requirement in most product liability suits.

Negligence

3. In a negligence suit, the plaintiff must prove that the defendant breached a duty of care, which was the proximate cause of the plaintiff's injury. Although the law of negligence varies from state to state, the *Restatement (Second) of Torts* has recommended that certain rules be adopted. Many judges have followed these suggested rules, which then become law in that particular state.

4. Some of the laws suggested by the *Restatement* are:
    a. A manufacturer is liable for physical injuries caused by a product with poor design, improper construction, or improper assembly.
    b. A manufacturer must use due care to inspect and test the safety of the product. The manufacturer must also warn of any foreseeable dangers associated with the use or misuse of the product.
    c. A manufacturer must use reasonable care throughout the manufacturing process. This duty of care is owed to any person who uses or is endangered by the use of the product.

Warranty

5. In a breach of warranty suit, the plaintiff must prove that a warranty was part of the basis of the bargain and that the breach of the warranty resulted in an injury to the plaintiff. There are three types of warranties:
    a. Express -- This type of warranty is expressly stated by speech, writing, picture, sample, or model. *Drayton v. Jiffee Chemical Corp.* is an example of a case involving an express warranty.
    b. Implied warranty of merchantability -- This type of warranty is created by law, and the implication is that goods are fit for their ordinary use. Only merchants are liable for this type of warranty.
    c. Implied warranty of fitness for a particular purpose -- This type of warranty is also created by law. In these cases, the buyer must rely on the seller's judgment that the product is fit for a particular purpose.

6. There are several valid defenses to a breach of warranty action. The defendant may have disclaimed all warranties, as Lotus did with its computer software. The plaintiff may not have given the defendant timely notice of the breach. If the defendant is not a merchant, he or she is not liable for a breach of the implied warranty of merchantability. Finally, some states still hold that there must be privity of contract in warranty actions.

Misrepresentation

7. In a misrepresentation suit, the plaintiff must establish that the defendant has misrepresented the product and that the plaintiff was injured as a result of a reliance on the misrepresentation. Even if the misrepresentation is innocent or unintended, the defendant is liable. Privity of contract is not a defense. *Klages v. General Ordnance Equipment Corporation* is a case in point.

8. Strict liability is a tort action suggested by the *Restatement (Second) of Torts* that has been widely adopted. It was a response to the tort belief that if one of two innocent parties must bear the loss because of a defective product, it should be the manufacturer, who is in a better position to absorb the loss. Note that fault is not an issue here. Strict liability has become the most widely used theory of recovery.

9. For strict liability to apply, there must be the following conditions:
    a. A product must be in a defective condition unreasonably dangerous to the user or his or her property.
    b. The seller must be in the regular business of selling such a product.
    c. The product is expected to and does reach the user without substantial change in its condition.
    d. The law applies even though the seller has used all possible care.
    e. Privity of contract is not a defense.

10. In strict liability, as in negligence, the seller must provide adequate warnings with his or her products. Note the liability that the manufacturer had when its failure to warn made the product unreasonably dangerous. When sellers provide adequate warnings the court finds in their favor as demonstrated in *Felix v. Hoffman-LaRoche, Inc.*

11. Manufacturers do not have to warn consumers of obvious dangers, such as danger associated with steroids or alcohol. However, there are some nonobvious dangers of alcohol which may not be apparent. *Brune v. Brown Forman Corp.* discusses the duty to warn in these instances. Note that in 1989 the Alcoholic Beverage Labeling Act requires a warning on all containers with alcohol.

12. The hardest strict liability requirement for the courts to define is the requirement that the product be in a "defective condition unreasonably dangerous." *Fraust v. Swift and Company* deals with this problem.

13. Historically, courts did not permit people to recover for mental injuries. Today, there is a trend for courts to permit recovery for emotional injuries. *Sease v. Taylor's Pets, Inc.* discusses the issue.

14. The increase of products liability suits and the amount of awards to injured parties have created new concerns for business. One concern is the courts' acceptance of new theories of recovery such as market share liability. This allows plaintiffs who do not know which manufacturer produced the drug which injured them to recover from all such manufacturers based on their market share. A second concern is the high cost of products liability insurance. A third is the number of businesses which have declared bankruptcy because of large liability awards to plaintiffs.

15. Businesses have responded to these concerns by unsuccessful lobbying for a uniform products liability act and for the abolishment of lawyer's contingency fees in products liability cases. Other efforts have been successful in some states in limiting liability to products on the market for ten years or less and the restriction of punitive damage amounts. Businesses have also responded to strict liability suits by discontinuing production of certain products and by limiting changes in existing products. A more positive business response for the consumer is the manufacture of better and safer products.

MAJOR POINTS OF CASES

MacPherson v. Buick Motor Co. (p. 451)

The defendant manufacturer sold a car to a retail dealer, who sold the car to the plaintiff. While operating the car, the plaintiff was injured due to defective wheels, which the manufacturer had purchased from a wheel manufacturer. The plaintiff sued the car manufacturer for negligence for failing to inspect the wheels. The defendant argued that there was no privity of contract between him and the plaintiff.

The court held that if a product could be dangerous and if the manufacturer knew that the product was to be used by one other than the direct buyer (the retailer), the manufacturer had a duty to manufacture the product carefully. This would include inspecting parts bought from other manufacturers. Privity of contract was not a defense in this case.

Drayton v. Jiffee Chemical Corp. (p. 455)

The issue in this case is whether an advertisement stating that a "liquid-plumber" was safe in an express warranty.

The court held that an express warranty may be given through an advertisement if the buyer had relied on the statement. In addition, the court held that it was foreseeable that the product might cause an injury and thus it was the duty of the manufacturer to warn buyers of the dangers associated with this type of product.

Klages v. General Ordnance Equipment Corporation (p. 458)

The first issue in this case is whether innocent misrepresentation of a material fact should be a cause of action in this state. The court held that it should be, in the belief that adoption of this particular section of the *Restatement (Second) of Torts* is merited.

The second issue in this case is whether the statement that the plaintiff relied upon was material fact or merely the seller's opinion. The court held that the statement was a specific statement about the properties of the product and thus was a material fact that the plaintiff was justified in relying upon.

Felix v. Hoffman-LaRoche, Inc. (p. 463)

As a result of a drug prescribed by her physician for acne, the plaintiff gave birth to a deformed child. She sued the drug manufacturer for damages.

The court found for the drug manufacturer which had adequately performed the two duties required by law. The first was a duty to warn physicians of any side effects of the drug. The second was that the warning need be adequate. As a result, the physician was totally knowledgeable about the damages associated with this drug and the drug manufacturer was not liable.

Brune v. Brown Forman Corp. (p. 465)

The issue in this case was whether tequila manufacturers had a duty to warn that an excessive amount of tequila could result in death. The defendant argued it was protected by *Restatement (Second) of Torts* Section 402A which states that alcoholic beverages properly made cannot be considered defective.

The court looked at the comments accompanying Section 402A. Comment h discusses warnings which need to given if the manufacturer knows of danger from abnormal consumption. Comment i discusses warnings which should be given if purchasers would be unaware of the danger while comment j reinforces this concept of general knowledge. The court stated that while some attributes of alcohol are general knowledge and need no warning, most people do not know that an excessive amount of alcohol can cause death.

Fraust v. Swift and Company (p. 468)

The issue in this case is whether peanut butter should be considered an "unreasonably dangerous product" under strict liability.

The court looked to the *Restatement (Second) of Torts* for guidance. The appropriate section stated that a substance was unreasonably dangerous if there were dangers unknown to the public. If the dangers were known to the public, no warning is required.

In this case, the dangers of a child choking on peanut butter are generally unknown. The court held that without a warning by the manufacturer, the product could be considered unreasonably dangerous, and strict liability law could apply.

Sease v. Taylor's Pets, Inc. (p. 469)

This case focuses upon the issue of emotional damages in a strict liability action. Normally, in an action under strict liability, the plaintiff can recover for physical damages only.

The plaintiff in this case argued that because they were exposed to rabies by a pet skunk, they had suffered emotional distress. The court held that the two plaintiffs who were able to receive rabies shots had suffered physical harm and could recover for that. As to the plaintiff who could not receive a rabies shot, he could not recover for any damages. The court stated that recovery for emotional distress is only valid in cases of intentional torts and declined to extend it to cases under strict liability.

SELF-TEST QUESTIONS

____ 1.   The doctrine of caveat emptor is still followed by courts today. (p. 450)

____ 2.   Historically buyers could only sue the immediate seller of the product. (p. 450)

____ 3.   Privity of contract means that the plaintiff can sue the retailer, the transporter, or the manufacturer. (pp. 450)

____ 4.   Strict liability has become the most favored theory of plaintiff's recovery under products liability law. (p. 452)

____ 5. The *Restatement (Second) of Torts* was passed by the legislatures of most of the states. (p. 452)

____ 6. All states require retailers to inform purchasers of any dangers in products if they could result from the proper use, but not misuse, of the product. (p. 453)

____ 7. An express warranty may be created by the seller through the use of a sample or model. (p. 454)

____ 8. Only a merchant seller can create the implied warranty of fitness for particular purpose. (p. 456)

____ 9. Implied warranties cannot be disclaimed by manufacturers. (p. 457)

____ 10. Strict liability theory maintains that if one of two innocent persons must bear the loss caused by a defective product it should be the seller. (pp. 460-461)

____ 11. There is virtually no defense to a strict liability suit. (p. 461)

____ 12. A strict liability suit can only be brought against a seller regularly engaged in selling that product. (p. 462)

____ 13. The requirement in strict liability cases which is the hardest for courts to determine is the "unreasonably dangerous" standard. (p. 467)

____ 14. In a products liability suit, the traditional view is that plaintiffs can only recover if they have received a physical injury. (pp. 469-470)

____ 15. Strict liability suits have dramatically raised the cost of insurance for businesses. (p. 471)

Multiple Choice

1. Product liability law:
   a. applies even if a seller has exercised the highest level of care.
   b. comes in part from tort law and in part from property law.
   c. has slowly evolved over time, but today seems settled.
   d. is still evolving, but the tendency today is to decrease the pool of defendants who are liable to injured parties. (p. 449)

2. Historically, in the products liability area:
   a. courts followed the doctrine of *caveat emptor.*
   b. courts allowed recovery based exclusively on tort law.
   c. the privity of contract doctrine was abolished.
   d. it was impossible to bring a suit against a retailer.
   (pp. 449-450)

3. In the *MacPherson* case, where the plaintiff sued the manufacturers of a defective wooden tire, the court held the plaintiff could only sue:
   a. the automobile dealer because he had made the contract with him.
   b. the automobile dealer because the manufacturer's duty was to him exclusively.
   c. the manufacturer because it was responsible for the finished product.
   d. the manufacturer because it bought the wheels from a disreputable manufacturer.
   (pp. 451-452)

4. Which of the following is *not* true about negligence?
   a. Courts apply *Restatement (Second) of Torts* doctrines in most cases.
   b. Duty to warn is a major issue under negligence law.
   c. Negligence is the most effective cause of action under products liability law.
   d. Plaintiffs must establish that the defendants did not use reasonable care.
   (pp. 452-454)

5. John Doe was harmed by a product manufactured by Acme, Inc. and is suing Acme for damages in a negligence action. Acme's best defense will be to show:
   a. that Doe purchased the product from a retailer, not directly from Acme.
   b. that the product was not unreasonably harmful.
   c. that Acme exercised reasonable care during the entire manufacturing and distributing process.
   d. that Acme had no direct contractual relationship with Doe.
   (pp. 452-454)

6. Tom purchased an electric knife manufactured by Super Blades, Inc., at a local discount store. When he attempted to use the knife to carve his Thanksgiving turkey, the blade snapped and badly cut Tom's hand. Tom is most likely to recover damages from Super Blades in an action based on:
   a. negligence.
   b. breach of express warranty.
   c. breach of implied warranty of merchantability.
   d. breach of implied warranty of fitness for particular purpose.
   (pp. 454-456)

7. An implied warranty of merchantability:
   a. is created by operation of law.
   b. must be in writing.
   c. can be created by any seller.
   d. all of the above.
   (p. 456)

8. To recover under an implied warranty of fitness for a particular purpose, the plaintiff:
   a. must prove a breach of duty of care.
   b. must prove reliance on the seller's judgment.
   c. must produce a written warranty.
   d. a and b.
   (p. 456)

9.   A seller may specifically disclaim or exclude:
     a.   all warranties.
     b.   only express warranties.
     c.   only implied warranties.
     d.   no warranties.   (pp. 456-457)

10. In the *Klages* case where the night auditor sued the mace company for misrepresentation, the plaintiff had to prove that his injury resulted from the company's misrepresentation of the character of quality of the product and:
     a.   that the manufacturer fraudulently or negligently misled the public.
     b.   that he relied upon the misrepresentation.
     c.   that he was in privity of contract with the manufacturer.
     d.   both a and b.   (pp. 458-460)

11. To recover under strict liability the plaintiff must prove:
     a.   unreasonable care.
     b.   privity of contract.
     c.   intent.
     d.   no change in condition after the product left the manufacturer.
                                                                   (pp. 461-462)

12. At a large supermarket, Tania purchased a can of hairspray manufactured by Coifs Control Company. The first time she sprayed her hair, vapor from the spray got into her eyes, causing a severe burn and decreased vision in her left eye. If Tania sued Coifs Control in an action based on strict liability, Coifs Control's best defense would be:
     a.   that it exercised extreme skill and care in the manufacture and sale of the hairspray.
     b.   that it had effectively disclaimed any and all warranties.
     c.   that it was not responsible for her harm, because she purchased the hairspray from the supermarket, not Coifs Control.
     d.   that the label on the can contained a clear and conspicuous warning concerning possible eye damage from improper use.   (pp. 461-463)

13. A manufacturer's duty to warn:
     a.   applies to all dangers associated with the product.
     b.   applies only to nonobvious dangers associated with the product.
     c.   must be given directly to the consumer.
     d.   does not apply to products which cannot be made safer.
                                                                   (pp. 464-465)

14. In the *Sease* case where the plaintiffs asked for emotional damages under strict liability, the plaintiffs:
     a.   lost because a live animal is not a product so strict liability does not apply.
     b.   lost because an essential element under strict liability is physical harm.
     c.   won because the court followed precedent of other states which allowed emotional damages.
     d.   won because one of the plaintiffs was allergic to rabies injections and should be compensated for his severe distress.   (pp. 469-470)

15. One effect of products liability on businesses today is:
    a. insurance coverage has expanded to cover business needs.
    b. businesses have ceased to produce certain products.
    c. a uniform products liability law has been passed.
    d. the contingency fee system of lawyers has been severely curtailed.

(pp. 471-473)

Essay Questions

1. Distinguish between the three different warranties under products liability law.

2. Discuss the manufacturer's duty to warn as applied in negligence and strict liability law.

Chapter 17

Consumer Law

Although freedom of contract has long been recognized as a basis of contract law, public policy has demanded specialized treatment for consumers. Generally, consumers have less power than businesses and may fail to understand complicated contracts.

A consumer is any person who buys or borrows for personal, family, or household purposes. Note that a businessperson may be a consumer in certain instances. The use of the product is the determining factor.

This chapter discusses some of the major consumer protection laws as they apply to the consumer as buyer and the consumer as borrower.

CHAPTER OBJECTIVES

After reading Chapter 17 of the text and studying the related materials in this chapter of the *Study Guide*, you will be able to fulfill the following objectives:

1.   Understand the purposes and regulations enacted by the FTC to protect the consumer as buyer. The regulations are discussed in the areas of advertising, warranties, and door-to-door sales.

2.   Understand the purposes and content of other federal legislation to protect the consumer as borrower. The acts discussed are:
      a.   The Truth-in-Lending Act
      b.   The Fair Credit Reporting Act
      c.   The Equal Credit Opportunity Act
      d.   The Fair Debt Collection Practices Act
      e.   The FTC modification of the Holder-in-Due-Course Doctrine
      f.   The Bankruptcy Act

MAJOR POINTS TO REMEMBER

Consumer Law and Business Behavior

1.   Because business practices did not reflect changes in society, a consumer movement grew in the 1960s and 1970s. This movement resulted in consumer protection legislation designed to protect the consumer as buyer and the consumer as borrower.

2.   Consumer protection laws have increased costs to businesses which must observe them and to the government which must enforce them. Businesses have lobbied for the reduction and simplification of consumer protection laws. In the 1980s fewer new consumer laws were passed in part because of business's influence and in part because the most urgent consumer problems had already been addressed.

The Consumer as Buyer

3.   As discussed in Chapters 15 and 16, the FTC was originally created to enforce the antitrust laws. In 1938, the Wheeler-Lea Amendment was enacted to enable the FTC to prohibit "unfair and deceptive acts" committed against competitors and consumers.

4.   The FTC has protected consumers against false advertising through:
      a.   Prohibiting the use of deceptive price advertising.
      b.   Requiring that advertising disclose the use of mockups.
      c.   Creating the remedy of corrective advertising, in which a company must create new advertising to explicitly correct previous deceptive advertising.
      Note that state statutes also prohibit deceptive advertising practices.

5.   Another important piece of consumer protection legislation is the Magnuson-Moss Warranty-Federal Trade Commission Improvement Act. Although the act does not require that warranties be given, any warranties on consumer products that are given must be conspicuous and in language that can be easily understood by consumers. The act also requires that a warranty for a product over ten dollars must specify whether a full warranty or a limited warranty is given. A full warranty basically allows the buyer to choose between a refund or replacement of the defective part for an unlimited period of time. A limited warranty provides fewer protections for a consumer than a full warranty. Class action suits may be brought under this act, as in the General Motors situation.

6.   The Federal Trade Commission also regulates door-to-door sales, which include contracts made at the consumer's home or at any place other than the seller's normal place of business. Any contract for most goods over twenty-five dollars must contain a conspicuous clause informing the consumer of his or her right to cancel the contract within three business days. Exceptions to this rule include real estate, insurance securities, and emergency home repairs.

The Consumer as Borrower

7.   Consumers borrow from such places as banks, credit unions, or by the use of credit cards. There are two types of credit available:
      a.   Open-end credit -- A credit card is an example of this type of credit, in which the borrower may make periodic charges up to a preestablished credit line. The loan may then be paid in full or in installments.
      b.   Closed-end credit -- A fixed mortgage is an example of this type of credit. A certain sum is borrowed for a specific period of time, with the loan to be repaid in a certain number of equal installments.

8.   The Truth-in-Lending Act was passed to provide consumer borrowers with full disclosure of the finance charge and the annual percentage rate. The act was amended in 1980 to make compliance simpler for lenders. The goal of the act is to enable consumers to compare the costs of borrowing money.

9.   Another right granted to consumers is the right to cancel contracts concerning loans on their homes or loans using their homes as security. A consumer has three days to cancel the contract from the time the Truth-in-Lending disclosures are given. *FDIC v. Hughes Development Co., Inc.* deals with this topic.

10. The Truth-in-Lending Act also limited the consumer's liability to fifty dollars in the case of unauthorized charges on credit cards. *Oclander v. First National Bank of Louisville* discusses when a charge is considered unauthorized.

11. The Fair Credit Reporting Act provides consumers who have been denied credit the right:
    a.   To receive the name and address of the agency which has the report.
    b.   To receive at least a summary of the information.
    c.   To demand that any important error be investigated and corrected.
    d.   To write a short statement of disagreement to be kept with the report.
    Pinner v. Schmidt contains a violation of this act.

12. The Equal Credit Opportunity Act prohibits credit discrimination on the basis of sex, race, marital status, national origin, religion, age, or receipt of public assistance. *United States v. American Future Systems, Inc.* is a case in point.

13. The Fair Debt Collection Practices Act prohibits third-party debt collectors from harassing debtors by threats of violence, obscenity, profanity, or repeated telephoning. It also prohibits false and misleading representations or publicizing communication. *Juras v. Amon Collection Services* is a case in point.

14. The Holder-in-Due-Course Doctrine allows any holder in due course of a promissory note to enforce the promissory note against the signer. A holder in due course is one who takes the note in good faith, for value, and without notice that there are any claims against it.

15. The FTC modified this doctrine in cases where the signer of a promissory note was a consumer. The rationale for this was that many sellers were discounting these notes to banks or financing companies. If there was a problem with the goods sold, the sellers had in effect already received payment and some refused to rectify the problem with the missing or defective goods. Thus, the consumer had to continue paying for unsatisfactory goods. The FTC modification exempts consumers from payment until the problem with the goods has been rectified. *Mahaffey v. Investor's National Security Co.* is an example of the application of this modification.

16. Bankruptcy law is designed to enable debtors to be discharged from their debts and to provide a fair distribution to creditors of equal standing. All creditor claims against the bankrupt are dealt with under bankruptcy laws.

17. Bankruptcy law is very old and originated under the Romans. The U.S. Constitution gave the U.S. Congress the power to enact federal bankruptcy law. There has been a federal bankruptcy law since 1898 although there have been revisions and amendments since that time.

18. There are two types of relief for debtors. If the debtor's assets are to be liquidated and distributed to the creditors, this is a Chapter 7 proceeding. If the debtor's affairs are to be restructured without liquidation, this is a Chapter 11 proceeding for partnerships and corporations. Individuals may file under Chapter 11 although this is rare. A Chapter 13 proceeding for most individuals, including sole proprietors, is another type of restructuring with different rules.

19. A Chapter 7 liquidation can be brought through a voluntary or involuntary petition. In a voluntary petition, the debtor asks for relief. The debtor does not have to be insolvent to file for bankruptcy. The court notifies the creditors and appoints a trustee who sells the assets of the bankruptcy estate. These assets consist of all property owned by the debtor except for exempt property which is determined by federal or state law. After a first meeting of the creditors, the trustee and the debtor, the case usually ends with the debtor being discharged from most of his or her debts. An involuntary bankruptcy is brought about by a creditor or creditors owed $5,000 petitioning the court to declare the debtor bankrupt. The debtor can be forced into bankruptcy if either he or she was not paying debts as they came due or if a custodian was appointed or took possession of most of the debtor's property. Involuntary bankruptcies are relatively rare.

20. A Chapter 11 reorganization is a restructuring of the debtor's financial affairs. This type of bankruptcy can also be voluntary or involuntary. Instead of a trustee the court appoints a creditors' committee to investigate and make recommendations. The debtor must submit a reorganization plan within 120 days after the court order for relief. If he or she does not do this, then anyone may file a plan. Regardless of who files the reorganization, it must be in the best interest of the creditors and approved by the creditors and the court.

21. In a Chapter 13 repayment, an individual with a regular income and a limited amount of debt may file a plan for repayment of a certain part of his or her obligations. Only the debtor can voluntarily enter into such a plan. The court will approve the plan if it was presented in good faith and if the debtor's secured creditors agree. If the debtor complies with the plan, the debtor will receive a discharge on those debts which are permitted by law.

MAJOR POINTS OF CASES

FDIC v. Hughes Development Co., Inc. (p. 486)

The plaintiffs notified the Guaranty Bank that they were canceling the loan on their house because the bank had failed to make certain disclosures required by the Truth-in-Lending Act. The bank went bankrupt and the FDIC was appointed its receiver. The FDIC argued that the plaintiffs could not rescind the loan agreement because the FDIC now held the mortgage.

The court held that the Hughes had the right to rescind the agreement. The purpose of the Truth-in-Lending Act is to allow comparison shopping and to return the parties to their original position if the act isn't observed. There is no valid policy reason to amend this law if the original creditor becomes insolvent and is taken over by a government agency like the FDIC.

Oclander v. First National Bank of Louisville (p. 488)

    Oclander opened a MasterCard account with Aparicio, from whom she later separated. She notified the bank that she had destroyed Aparicio's card. When he later charged items to the card, Oclander claimed she was not liable for Aparicio's charges.

    The court disagreed. A card holder's protection is against unauthorized charges which are defined as those made by a person who does not have actual, implied, or apparent authority. Since Aparicio had possession of an unexpired card with his name on it, he had apparent authority to use it.

Pinner v. Schmidt (p. 490)

    The issue in this case is whether the plaintiff, Pinner, could recover for violation of the Fair Credit Reporting Act. Pinner was refused credit and obtained his credit report. He disagreed with the charges and asked the agency to investigate. The second time he was refused credit, he notified the agency he was suing Schmidt, who was the creditor responsible for Pinner's negative credit rating. The agency noted that litigation was pending without specifying that Pinner was the plaintiff.

    The court held that Pinner could recover because the credit reporting agency has two duties. First it must use reasonable procedures when investigating a credit report, and second it must delete inaccurate materials. Neither of these was done satisfactorily in this case.

United States v. American Future Systems, Inc. (p. 493)

    The issue in this case is whether the defendant's two credit programs were discriminatory under the Equal Credit Opportunity Act. The preferred credit program was offered only to single, white, unmarried females. These applicants received immediate credit. The nonpreferred credit program was offered to all others. These applicants had to make three successive payments before they were entitled to receive the goods. In addition, if these payments were not received, the defendant kept both the goods and the money already paid.

    The court held that these two programs were discriminatory because the only criteria for placement were the sex, race, and marital status of the applicant.

Juras v. Amon Collection Service, Inc. (p. 495)

    When Juras defaulted on his student loans, the collection service withheld his transcripts. Juras sued, claiming this was a violation of the Fair Debt Collection Practices Act because loans are to be made without security.

    The court defined security as property of the debtor. The court held that the transcript was the property of the university that Juras had attended. In addition the court claimed that Congress wished diligent enforcement against debtors and that withholding the transcript was a reasonable manner of enforcing payment of the debt.

Mahaffey v. Investor's National Security. (p. 498)

    The Mahaffeys contracted with Five Star for home insulation. A promissory note with their house as security was signed. The note was sold to Mortgage Finance Co. The Mahaffeys refused to pay on the note because the insulation was never installed. Mortgage Finance sued on the note.

The court held that the Mahaffeys did not have to pay. The contract with the insulation company was fraudulently induced and since the contract was not performed the Mahaffeys had a second defense against the contract. Mortgage Finance Co. took a note which already stated it was subject to contract defenses. Therefore the finance company has no cause of action against the Mahaffeys.

SELF-TEST QUESTIONS

True/False

____ 1. Consumer protection laws sometimes infringe on businesses' freedom of contract. (p. 477)

____ 2. The consumer movement resulted in many new federal laws, but in no new state laws affecting consumers. (p. 479)

____ 3. When the FTC determines that a particular advertising campaign has deceived the public, it may order the company to undertake an advertising campaign to correct false impressions created by an earlier ad. (p. 480)

____ 4. Both written and oral warranties are covered by the Federal Warranty Act. (p. 480)

____ 5. The Federal Warranty Act requires that some form of warranty be given on all products sold for ten dollars or more. (pp. 480-481)

____ 6. One major purpose of the Truth-in-Lending Act is to enable borrowers to compare interest rates. (p. 484)

____ 7. Under the Truth-in-Lending laws, a person has the right to cancel the loan only three days after the signing of the agreement. (p. 487)

____ 8. The most one can be liable for as a result of unauthorized credit card use is fifty dollars. (p. 488)

____ 9. Any consumer bringing an action under the Fair Credit Reporting Act has the right to receive credit. (pp. 489-490)

____ 10. The Equal Credit Opportunity Act was initially aimed at race discrimination. (p. 492)

____ 11. A lender may legally refuse a loan to an otherwise qualified person because he or she receives public assistance income. (pp. 492-493)

____ 12. A creditor may not threaten the debtor with a civil or criminal action. (p. 496)

____ 13. A creditor cannot threaten a debtor with attachment of wages unless she or he has the intent to take this action. (p. 496)

_____ 14. To be a holder-in-due-course, a person or business must take the instrument in good faith. (p. 497)

_____ 15. Only consumers are allowed to reorganize their assets under a Chapter 13 bankruptcy. (p. 503)

Multiple Choice

1. Consumer law:
   a. upholds traditional freedom of contract rules.
   b. peaked in the 1970s.
   c. oftentimes is costly to businesses.
   d. was resisted by the courts originally.   (pp. 477-479)

2. Deceptive and unfair trade practices laws:
   a. are enforced by the Federal Trade Commission.
   b. can be remedied by punitive damages.
   c. forbids the use of mockups
   d. protects consumers but not business competitors.   (pp. 479-480)

3. Which of the following statements concerning the Magnuson-Moss Warranty Act is (are) correct?
   a. The act requires a written warranty to be designated as a "full" or a "limited" warranty.
   b. The act requires the seller of a consumer product that costs more than ten dollars to provide a warranty.
   c. The act is applicable to both written and oral warranties on consumer products.
   d. both a and b.   (pp. 480-481)

4. A full written warranty must provide:
   a. that the manufacturer will correct the defect with only a charge for labor.
   b. that the time period during which the warranty will be in effect will be reasonable.
   c. that consequential damages cannot be limited unless conspicuously stated on the warranty.
   d. that the consumer can be required to accept replacement of the defective product instead of a refund.   (pp. 480-481)

5. Door-to-door sales regulations:
   a. only apply to sales of over $50.00.
   b. only apply to sales made at consumer's home.
   c. only apply to sales of goods and insurance.
   d. is only regulated by the Federal Trade Commission.   (p. 482)

6. A major purpose of the Truth-in-Lending Act is to:
   a. regulate the rates that lenders may charge for lending money.
   b. give the borrower a three-day "cooling off" period in which to cancel a credit transaction.
   c. allow consumers to make meaningful comparisons between rates charged by different lenders.
   d. relieve consumers of all liability for the unauthorized use of lost or stolen credit cards. (pp. 484-486)

7. In the *Oclander* case where the woman was sued for her boyfriend's credit card charges, the court held Oclander:
   a. was not liable because she did not authorize the charges.
   b. was not liable because she was unaware of the charges.
   c. was liable because she had not surrendered her boyfriend's car to the bank.
   d. was liable because her boyfriend had apparent authority to use the card. (pp. 488-489)

8. In the *Pinner* case where the plaintiff sued alleging violations under the Fair Credit Reporting Act, the court held the act was violated because the credit reporting agency:
   a. was negligent.
   b. had a duty to use reasonable care.
   c. was obligated to reverify the accuracy of the delinquent entry.
   d. all of the above. (pp. 490-492)

9. The Equal Credit Opportunity Act was originally enacted to protect discrimination because of:
   a. sex and marital status.
   b. sex and race.
   c. sex and receipt of public assistance.
   d. sex, marital status, race, and receipt of public assistance. (pp. 492-493)

10. Which of the following is *not* correct about the Fair Debt Collection Practices Act?
    a. It is restricted to debts for person, family, or household purposes.
    b. It applies to creditors only.
    c. It applies to third party debt collectors only.
    d. It was passed, in part, to protect the debtor's right to privacy. (p. 495)

11. Which of the following actions is prohibited by the Fair Debt Collection Practices Act?
    a. Threatening to file a criminal charge.
    b. Communicating with the debtor at his or her workplace.
    c. Communicating with the debtor's attorney.
    d. All of the above are illegal. (p. 496)

12. The FTC modification of the Holder-in-Due-Course Doctrine means that consumers:
    a. may never be holders-in-due-course.
    b. have defenses against holders-in-due-course.
    c. must follow special regulations when dealing with holders-in-due-course.
    d. have greater access to certain types of businesses such as financing institutions. (pp. 496-497)

13. In the *Mahaffey* case where the consumers refused to pay the note held by the finance corporation, the courts held the finance corporation:
    a. was entitled to payment because it had no notice of possible claims and defenses.
    b. was entitled to payment because it was not responsible for the actions of the insulation company.
    c. was not entitled to payment because the contract was fraudulent.
    d. was not entitled to payment because it was not a holder-in-due-cause.

    (p. 498)

14. Bankruptcy law:
    a. is a uniquely American innovation.
    b. has been in existence since the Constitution was ratified.
    c. is revised every six years.
    d. protects creditors as well as debtors.

    (pp. 500-501)

15. In a Chapter 7 type of bankruptcy:
    a. the debtors' financial affairs are restructured.
    b. only federal exemptions are allowed.
    c. a committee of creditors is appointed by the court.
    d. the petition can be filed by a creditor.

    (pp. 501-502)

Essay Questions

1. What is the Holder-in-Due-Course Doctrine? How did the FTC modify this doctrine?

2. Discuss major types of bankruptcy.

Chapter 18

Employment Discrimination

Employment opportunities in the United States have evolved from those of an agrarian society to those of an industrial society. Other chapters trace the effects of industrialization upon trusts, consumers, and unions. This chapter deals with equal opportunity for members of racial and religious minority groups and women. Note how some aspects of contract law were changed by discrimination law and the ways in which a company can prevent discrimination practices.

The major focus of the chapter is the Civil Rights Act of 1964 and the classifications of people that it protects. The types of discrimination that are impermissible and permissible are discussed. The final section of the chapter covers recent developments in employment law.

CHAPTER OBJECTIVES

After reading Chapter 18 of the text and studying the related materials in this chapter of the *Study Guide*, you will be able to fulfill the following objectives:

1. Understand the need for acts prohibiting discrimination.

2. Identify the protected classifications.

3. Understand the effects of the Civil Right Act of 1964.

4. Recognize recent developments in employment law concerning affirmative action and sexual harassment.

MAJOR POINTS TO REMEMBER

Historical Background

1. After the Civil War, blacks were still victims of segregation in many areas, including the workplace. Many employers refused to hire blacks or only hired them for menial, low-paying positions. As women began to enter the workplace, they too felt the effects of discrimination. Women's wages were generally much lower than men's wages. In addition, there were sexual stereotypes about the types of work that women were believed capable of doing. *Bradwell v. The State of Illinois* is an example of sexual stereotyping.

2. The Civil Rights Act of 1964 was passed because of the public policy that discrimination in the workplace should be eliminated. The act attempts to balance the conflicting principles that all people should be treated as individuals and that all people should be free to associate with whomever they choose. Compare these attitudes with those of the Japanese.

3. The judicial branch has been instrumental in interpreting the general language of the Civil Rights Act of 1964. As the complexion of the Supreme Court has become more conservative, many Title VII precedents were reinterpreted. However, Congress enacted The Civil Rights Bill of 1991 which reversed six Supreme Court precedents that had made it more difficult for a worker to raise a Title VII claim.

Title VII: Civil Rights Act of 1964

4. Title VII of the Civil Rights Act of 1964 prohibits employment discrimination on the basis of race, color, sex, religion, or natural origin. There are other state and federal laws which prohibit employment discrimination on other grounds, such as age. However the focus of this chapter is only on the Civil Rights Act of 1964.

5. There are two major goals of Title VII. The first is to provide equal opportunity for all workers to compete for jobs or promotions without being stereotyped. The second goal of Title VII is to provide certain groups, such as racial minorities and women, entry into certain types of jobs.

6. The Equal Employment Opportunity Commission enforces the Civil Rights Act of 1964 on behalf of injured parties. The state or local agency investigates the claim. If there is no appropriate agency or the claim doesn't proceed in a timely manner, the EEOC processes the charges. The EEOC then investigates and attempts to reach a settlement. If a settlement is not reached, the EEOC may file a suit in federal district court. However, if the EEOC investigates and determines that the law has not been violated, the complaining party still has a right to bring a private action.

What Is Discrimination?

7. To *discriminate* means to choose or to differentiate. Title VII makes it illegal for employers to choose or to differentiate among people on the basis of race, color, sex, religion, or national origin in hiring or promotion practices. Note that other factors, such as work performance, can be used in determining which person to hire or to promote. *Ulane v. Eastern Airlines, Inc.* is a case in which an employee alleges discrimination because of sex.

8. There are four categories of employment discrimination under Title VII. The first is disparate treatment and occurs when a person is treated differently because of race, color, sex, religion, or national origin. Sometimes disparate issues are the result of stereotyping. *Price Waterhouse v. Hopkins* is a case in point.

9. The second category is neutral practices or policies that discriminate. The employer applies a standard that is seemingly neutral but has the effect of a disparate impact on a certain group or groups in the protected categories. In the *Griggs* case the Supreme Court held that neutral practices, such as job requirements, must be a business necessity related to job performance. Managers had to become very careful that their job selection requirements were job related. The standard of proof needed for a prima facie case of discrimination in this category is the issue in *Bradley v. Pizzaco of Nebraska, Inc. d/b/a Domino's Pizza.*

10. A third category is policies or practices that perpetuate the effects of past discrimination. Two major practices have been scrutinized by the courts:
   a. Seniority systems, which protect those workers who have been employed for a longer time in the company. Although the Civil Rights Act of 1964 included a provision protecting bona fide seniority systems, the issue arose whether a system which reflected employment discrimination before 1964 could be considered bona fide. The Supreme Court held that it could.
   b. Comparable worth, which evaluates wages on the basis of the worth of the work to the employer in comparison to people in all the other positions in the company. Advocates claim that comparable worth is less discriminatory than the market system. *American Federation of State, County, and Municipal Employees v. State of Washington* discusses these concepts in more detail.

11. The final theory of discrimination is the duty of reasonable accommodation. This only applies to discrimination against a person because of religious beliefs. Unless it would create an undue hardship on the employer, an employee's religious beliefs and practices must be accommodated. *Trans World Airlines v. Hardison* is a case in point.

Permitted Discrimination: The Bona Fide Occupational Qualification

12. The Title VII categories may be discriminated against if the employer can show a bona fide occupational qualification or a legitimate purpose for discrimination. A BFOQ is a requirement that is reasonably necessary for operating a business. Refusing to hire a non-Muslim to fly in the Mecca area is one example. BFOQs are rare because an employer has to establish three elements:
   a. The connection between the requirement and job performance.
   b. The necessity of the requirement for the successful performance of the job. Note that this is not to be based on employee or customer preferences.
   c. The job performance affected by the requirements must be the essence of the employer's business. Note the court's analysis of these elements in *Diaz v. Pan American World Airways, Inc.*

Developments in Equal Employment Law

13. The goals of affirmative action plans are to counteract the effects of discrimination over the years by providing employment advantages to the protected classifications. Businesses can voluntarily adopt affirmative action plans in order to ensure compliance with Title VII. Affirmative action plans have been criticized by those who argue that this is reverse discrimination. *Johnson v. Transportation Agency, Santa Clara County* discusses one company's voluntary affirmative action policies.

14. One type of sexual harassment in a business setting involves an intolerable work environment or unwelcome sexual advances by a person in a position of power. It usually applies to women employees, although it can apply to men as well.

15. A major issue in the area of sexual harassment is whether agency law should apply to hold the principal liable for the agent's sexual harassment even if the principal is unaware of the situation. *Meritor Savings Bank v. Vinson* is a recent case that deals with the issue.

16. A second type of sexual harassment involves a hostile workplace environment. This occurs when sexually offensive actions by other employees make the workplace intolerable to a reasonable person. A recent trend is developing to change the measurement to a reasonable woman standard. The reasoning for this trend is discussed in *Ellison v. Brady*.

17. Although Title VII does not prohibit discrimination in employment on the basis of sexual orientation, some state and local governments may prohibit it. Note the examples of the California Labor Code and the San Francisco Ordinance. Managers need to be aware of differing policies especially if their firm has branch offices in different parts of the United States.

Selected Statutes

18. In addition to Title VII of the Civil Rights Act of 1964, there are other federal statutes which prohibit discrimination. They include the Americans with Disabilities Act, the Age Discrimination in Employment Act, and the Pregnancy Discrimination Act.

19. The Americans with Disabilities Act was passed by Congress in 1990. It corrected the limitations of the Rehabilitation Act and prohibits discrimination against the handicapped not only in employment but in many other areas. As a result, virtually no business is unaffected by the enactment of this statute. Businesses may not discriminate against any individuals who have a physical or mental impairment which substantially limits their major life activities. In fact businesses have a duty to reasonably accommodate any such handicapped persons. Because this act is relatively recent the requirements of reasonable accommodation are unclear. However in addition to creating a cost to businesses, there is an opportunity for businesses to create market opportunities.

20. The ADA prohibits discrimination in employment if a disabled person can perform the essential functions of the job. This may include a reasonable accommodation by the employer, but does not include an unreasonable hardship on the employer to accommodate the disabled employee.

21. The Age Discrimination in Employment Act was passed in 1967. This protection begins at the age of forty and has no upper limit after the end of 1993. The purpose of the act was to focus on the abilities, not the age, of the worker. If the act is violated, a worker's remedies include back pay and reinstatement if possible. If reinstatement is not possible, a monetary award is granted.

22. There are two exceptions to the Age Discrimination in Employment Act. The first is the bona fide occupational qualification. The second is the high policy maker exception which only affects top executives who have held their positions for at least two years. In order to open up advancement for others, these executives can be forced to retire at age sixty-five.

23. The Pregnancy Discrimination Act in 1978 was an amendment to Title VII. It was passed to protect pregnant women from discrimination.

MAJOR POINTS OF CASES

Bradwell v. The State of Illinois (p. 509)

This historic case is relevant in showing the need for inclusion of women under the Civil Rights Act of 1964. In this instance, a woman was denied the right to practice law.

The Court's reasoning was that a woman's nature made her unfit for duties outside domestic life. The Court cited as an example an existing law that prohibited married women from making contracts. In discussing unmarried women, the Court admitted that there were exceptions to the general rule but implied that they were not fulfilling their destinies.

Ulane v. Eastern Airlines, Inc. (p. 512)

The plaintiff, a licensed pilot, was hired by the defendant but was fired after undergoing a sex-change operation from male to female. The plaintiff sued under Title VII, alleging discrimination because of her sex. The lower court found for the defendant.

The appellate court reversed the decision, holding that Title VII's prohibition on sex discrimination does not include transsexuals. In reaching this decision, the court determined that the plain meaning of the statute only applies to women being discriminated against because they are women. A further rationale was the court's observation that congressional attempts to amend Title VII to include "affectational or orientation" had failed. In order for transsexuals to be protected under Title VII, Congress would have to amend the statute.

Price Waterhouse v. Hopkins (p. 515)

Hopkins was nominated as a candidate for partnership in the Price Waterhouse firm. After discussion among the current partners as to the appropriateness of her personality, her candidacy was deferred until the following year. Hopkins sued, alleging that she was discriminated against on the basis of sex.

The Supreme Court agreed. It stated that there are two important aspects of Title VII. The first is that an employer may not take gender into account and the second is the preservation of the employer's freedom of choice based on nondiscriminatory factors. In this case Hopkins, and other females, were judged on their behavior based on the stereotyping of female behavior in general.

Bradley v. Pizzaco of Nebraska, Inc. d/b/a Domino's Pizza (p. 518)

Bradley, a black man, was fired by Domino's Pizza because he refused to follow their policy forbidding employees to wear beards. Based on the fact that over fifty percent of black males suffer from a skin disease that is aggravated by shaving, Bradley sued Domino's. His claim was that their no-beard policy had a disparate impact on black males. Domino's argued that since the EEOC had failed to show that other black males had been affected by their policy, the agency had failed to demonstrate a pattern of discrimination. The trial court held that the EEOC had failed to make a prima facie case.

The appellate court reversed the decision. Title VII prohibits employment practices which have a disparate impact unless the practice is legitimately related to the job. There is no requirement that disparate claims must always show that others in the affected group were not hired or fired because of the policy. This is because it can be concluded that a company policy such as this might discourage those affected from applying for employment. The EEOC's

156

medical evidence supports Bradley's claim that Domino's no-beard policy discriminates against black males.

American Federation of State, County, and
Municipal Employees v. State of Washington (p. 521)

The state of Washington commissioned a study to determine whether wage disparity existed between jobs held primarily by men and jobs held primarily by women. Job disparity was found, with women generally earning less than men. The state enacted legislation providing for compensation to be based on comparable worth over a ten-year period.

The plaintiff brought suit for immediate implementation of the plan, charging that the state discriminated under the Civil Rights Act because of the lower wages received by women. The lower court agreed.

The appellate court reversed the decision. Market rate compensation is not in violation of the Civil Rights Act. There is nothing in the language or legislative history to indicate that Congress intended to abolish fundamental economic principles such as supply and demand. In addition, the comparable worth of the employee is only one factor of employment. The state of Washington may have chosen to enact the comparable worth plan, but it was not mandatory under Title VII of the Civil Rights Act of 1964.

Trans World Airlines v. Hardison (p. 523)

In this case, the Court was called upon to determine whether religious needs should take precedence over a company's collective bargaining contracts and seniority systems. The Court held that they should not.

The Court restated the validity of both the collective bargaining and seniority systems as an integral part of the rights of labor. Although religious discrimination is prohibited, destruction of these systems is not required to accommodate religious preferences. Accommodation should be made in other ways. In this case, the employer had attempted to compensate in reasonable ways and was justified in eventually firing the employee.

Diaz v. Pan American World Airways, Inc. (p. 525)

The issue in this case is whether limiting flight attendant employment to females only is a bona fide occupational qualification and thus exempt from action under the Civil Rights Act of 1964. The lower court held that it was a BFOQ because customers felt that their psychological needs were better served by women flight attendants.

The Supreme Court reversed the lower court decision. The Court held that the test that must be applied was the business necessity test. A BFOQ is valid only when the essence of the business is undermined by not exclusively hiring members of one sex. Because the primary business of airlines is safely transporting passengers, the sex of the flight attendant does not go to the essence of the business.

As to the customer preferences, the Court held that males were available with good psychological skills. The erasing of prejudices that only certain sexes have certain skills is one reason for the passage of the Civil Rights Act of 1964.

*Johnson v. Transportation Agency, Santa
Clara County* (p. 528)

This case deals with the claim that white, male workers are the new victims of discrimination. The defendant company instituted an affirmative action plan whose long-term goal was a work force reflecting the proportion of women in the area labor force. There was no quota, but the plan authorized consideration of sex as a factor in hiring and promotion. There were nine qualified applicants for a promotion. When the only qualified woman was promoted, the plaintiff sued, alleging that he had been discriminated against.

The Supreme Court looked at two issues. The first was whether consideration of sex in promotions was justified. The court held that it was because women were discriminated against in the past. In addition, sex was only one factor, as the applicant also had to be qualified.

The second issue was whether the affirmative action plan unnecessarily injured the male worker's chances for promotion. The Court held that because there was no quota under the plan, any qualified person could be promoted currently or in the future.

Therefore, the affirmative action plan, which was a gradual approach to eliminate imbalances in hiring and promotion, was judged to be nondiscriminatory and consistent with the law.

Meritor Savings Bank v. Vinson (p. 531)

The plaintiff was discharged for excessive use of sick leave. She filed suit against her supervisor and the bank claiming that during her four years of employment, she had been constantly sexually harassed by her supervisor. The lower court found for the bank because it had no knowledge of the alleged sexual harassment. The appellate court reversed, and the case was appealed to the Supreme Court.

There were four issues to be decided by the Supreme Court. The first was whether Title VII applies only to "tangible loss of an economic character" or includes "purely psychological aspects of the workplace environment." The Court held that the language of Title VII is not limited to tangible or economic discrimination. In addition, the EEOC guidelines establish, and are right in establishing, that sexual harassment leading to noneconomic injury can violate Title VII.

The second issue was whether the alleged voluntary consent of the plaintiff was a defense to a sexual harassment suit. The Court stated that the correct issue was whether the advances were unwelcome, not whether the plaintiff's conduct was voluntary or involuntary.

The third issue was whether the bank could be held liable if it was not aware of the situation. The Court declined to issue a definitive ruling that employees are automatically liable or that absence of notice is necessarily a defense. The Court looked to the intent of Title VII, which applies to employers, including agents of employers. The Court concluded that agency law principles should apply in sexual harassment cases.

The final issue before the Court was whether the plaintiff had a cause of action because the defendant bank had a policy against discrimination and a grievance procedure in place. The Court held that the plaintiff was not stopped from bringing this cause of action because the defendant's discrimination policy did not specifically state sexual harassment. As to the grievance procedure, the plaintiff would have been required to go to her supervisor first, which in this case was unreasonable.

Ellison v. Brady (p. 535)

Ellison and Gray worked together in the Treasury Department. After Gray asked Ellison out several times and was rebuffed, he sent her two cards and a letter stating his interest in her. Ellison was frightened by the tone of the writings and spoke to her supervisor who told Gray to leave Ellison alone. Gray transferred to another office, but filed and won union grievances. He was allowed to transfer back to Ellison's office on the condition he leave her alone. Ellison filed sexual harassment charges. The Treasury Department dismissed her complaint because it believed there were no patterns or practice of sexual harassment. On appeal, the EEOC affirmed the decision on the ground that the Treasury Department had taken adequate steps to prevent the continuance of Gray's conduct. Ellison appealed.

The appellate court held that Gray's actions created an abusive working environment. The court pointed to two things. The first was the frequency and intensity of Gray's actions. The second was consideration of the victim's perspective. The court stated that since women are more likely to be victims of rape and sexual assault, a reasonable woman standard should be implemented. The court felt that the traditional reasonable person standard was inadequate because it is male-biased and because men have different perceptions of what could be construed by women as sexual harrassment. The dissent argued that Title VII presupposes a legal term which can be applied to all persons. The creation of a reasonable woman standard would not address all potential victims and a gender neutral standard should be adopted.

SELF-TEST QUESTIONS

True/False

_____ 1.   The Civil Rights Act of 1964 is the only federal law that applies to employment discrimination. (p. 508)

_____ 2.   Traditionally discrimination against women was solely based on a concern that they should not be exploited in the workplace. (p. 509)

_____ 3.   The Equal Employment Opportunity Commission (EEOC) was created by the Equal Employment Opportunity Act and has the power to file suit against employers. (p. 511)

_____ 4.   Title VII eliminates employers' discretion in the selection of employees even if choices are based on foolish criteria. (p. 512)

_____ 5.   The term disparate is defined as treating a person differently based on the prohibited categories of Title VII. (p. 514)

_____ 6.   A practice that appears neutral on its face may violate Title VII by adversely affecting protected persons. (pp. 516-517)

_____ 7.   Title VII permits an employer to treat members of a protected class differently if the difference in treatment is pursuant to the terms of seniority system. (p. 520)

_____ 8. Today, the earning power of women equals that of men. (p. 520)

_____ 9. An employer is required to accommodate an employee's religious beliefs even if this creates an undue hardship on the conduct of the employer's business. (p. 522)

_____ 10. One criticism of affirmative action plans is the charge that white males are made the new victims of discrimination. (p. 527)

_____ 11. Since affirmative action plans involve racial or sexual discrimination in employment, only court-ordered plans that correct past discrimination are allowed. (p. 528)

_____ 12. The Civil Rights Act of 1991 requires the award of punitive damages in sexual harassment cases. (p. 531)

_____ 13. A new trend in sexual harassment is the "reasonable woman" standard. (p. 534)

_____ 14. Sex discrimination under federal law is tied to gender not orientation. (p. 537)

_____ 15. The Age Discrimination in Employment Act applies to all workers above the age of 40. (p. 543)

Multiple Choice

1. One of the major policy goals of the Civil Rights Act is to:
    a. provide a means of entry into the workplace for members of historically disadvantaged groups.
    b. provide equal pay for all workers in similar jobs.
    c. eliminate employers' freedom of selection based on past performance records.
    d. enable minorities and women to have preferential treatment through affirmative action programs. (pp. 510-511)

2. Which of the following is *not* true regarding the EEOC?
    a. It is a federal agency charged with enforcing Title VII.
    b. It has authority to file suits on behalf of aggrieved parties.
    c. In its fact finding role, it may gather information and ask the Congress to enact regulations.
    d. It was created by the Civil Rights Act of 1964. (p. 511)

3. Disparate treatment practices:
    a. must be obvious.
    b. can occur through stereotyping.
    c. do not apply to a person's religious beliefs.
    d. none of the above. (p. 514)

4. In the *Bradley* case where the black man was fired for not shaving off his beard, the court held that:
   a. for a disparate impact to be found, the EEOC had to show that more than one person had been fired under the policy.
   b. Domino's did not have the option to make an exception because Bradley did not tell them about his condition.
   c. Domino's had a legitimate employment goal because studies have shown the public perceives beards as unsanitary.
   d. the use of medical testing and studies was sufficient to show disparate impact.

   (pp. 518-519)

5. Past employment practices which discriminate:
   a. are considered "neutral" employment decision factors.
   b. have abolished the doctrine of seniority.
   c. have abolished the doctrine of comparable worth.
   d. require an intent to discriminate in order for an employee to bring suit.

   (pp. 519-520)

6. Comparable worth:
   a. compares the rate of pay among those holding the same type of jobs.
   b. compares the rate of pay between men and women in the same jobs.
   c. compares the worth of an employee's job with others in relation to the value to the company.
   d. compares jobs according to the workings of the market.

   (pp. 520-521)

7. Reasonable accommodation under Title VII only involves discrimination based on:
   a. sex.
   b. race.
   c. national origin.
   d. religion.

   (p. 522)

8. A bona fide occupational qualification (BFOQ):
   a. permits disparate treatment in business.
   b. has been widely construed by the courts.
   c. is relatively easy for an employer to establish.
   d. applies to sex and religion only.

   (p. 524)

9. Which of the following can *never* be a bona fide occupational qualification?
   a. religion.
   b. sex.
   c. national origin.
   d. race.

   (p. 525)

10. In the *Diaz* case where the airline fired the male flight attendant, the court held he should:
    a. not be reinstated because a poll showed passengers preferred female flight attendants.
    b. not be reinstated because a BFOQ applies in this situation.
    c. should be reinstated because he was a member of a minority group.
    d. should be reinstated because cabin service is not the primary function of an airline. (pp. 525-527)

11. Affirmative action plans:
    a. require decision making to be determined by neutral practices.
    b. are mandatory if the employer has a history of prior discrimination practices.
    c. are mandatory if there is a conspicuous imbalance in traditionally segregated job categories.
    d. illustrates a conflict between the goals of Title VII. (pp. 527-528)

12. Maria and Alex have both applied for the position of executive secretary to the president of Bischoff Inc. Maria has been a secretary to a woman in the sales department for seven years. She is known to be a competent secretary, but is not well liked by her co-workers as she tends to be rather snobbish. Alex has just graduated from a well-respected secretarial school with a 3.7 average but has had no previous experience in dealing with the pressures of the business world. In making this decision, the head of personnel:
    a. should choose Maria because male secretaries are still unusual in the business world due to public expectations.
    b. should choose Alex because he has no known personality defects.
    c. should not take the sex of the president into consideration even though the job involves some overnight travel.
    d. should be careful to apply job related criteria only to comply with federally mandated affirmative action policies. (pp. 527-528)

13. Sexual harassment:
    a. does not apply to white males because they are not in the protected group under the Civil Rights Act of 1964.
    b. holds employers strictly liable for any employee's practices in this area.
    c. goes beyond regular agency principles.
    d. can occur even if limited to jokes and comments which result in making the workplace intolerable. (p. 530-531)

14. In the *Vinson* case where the female accused her male supervisor of sexual harassment, the Court held:
    a. Vinson's supervisor was guilty of sexual harassment.
    b. Vinson had no economic injury and was thus prohibited from bringing suit.
    c. Vinson need not have gone through the bank's grievance procedure before reporting this to the EEOC.
    d. Vinson could not bring suit because she consented to her supervisor's advances. (pp. 531-534)

162

15. The Americans with Disabilities Act only:
    a. applies to employment.
    b. requires businesses to make a reasonable accommodation.
    c. applies to physical disabilities.
    d. applies to businesses with ties to the federal government.

(pp. 539-543)

Essay Questions

1. What are the two goals of Title VII? How do they conflict?

2. Discuss the two types of sexual harassment.

Chapter 19

Labor-Management Relations: The Regulation of Management

Labor unions have undergone historical periods of disfavor with the public in general and management in particular. In the early twentieth century, reflecting society's approval of labor unions, several acts were passed to aid labor unions.

This chapter discusses the history of labor unions. It also focuses upon legislation favorable to labor, with an emphasis on unfair labor practices by employers.

CHAPTER OBJECTIVES

After reading Chapter 19 of the text and studying the related materials in this chapter of the *Study Guide*, you will be able to fulfill the following objectives:

1. Understand the historical background of labor unions.

2. Identify the major acts passed to aid unionization and their concepts.

3. Recognize the powers and procedures of the NLRB.

4. Describe the prohibited unfair labor practices.

MAJOR POINTS TO REMEMBER

Historical Background

1. Early union goals were requirements that employers treat their employees in a more humane manner. These goals were not supported by either employers or the courts. Later goals were more specific, such as decent wages and an end to child labor. Employers and courts again opposed these goals. At first, courts sent union members to prison, and later they prohibited unionization through injunctions. Violent behavior by both management and labor erupted over these issues.

2. In the early twentieth century, legislators began to reflect society's acceptance of unions by passing several acts. The most important acts were:
   a. Norris-La Guardia Act (1932) -- This act limited the power of the federal courts to issue injunctions, outlawed yellow dog contracts, and limited the liability of unions in some instances.
   b. Wagner Act (1933) -- This act guaranteed employees the right to join or assist unions for the purpose of collective bargaining or making employment agreements. The act also created the National Labor Relations Board.

3. In the middle of the twentieth century, legislators passed acts that favored management in order to balance the power that unions then held. The most important of these were:
   a. Taft-Hartley Act (1947) -- This act outlawed a number of union practices. It will be fully discussed in Chapter 21.
   b. Landrum-Griffin Act (1959) -- This act required disclosure of information by unions. It also dealt with secondary boycotts and picketing. This act is also fully discussed in Chapter 21.

General Explanation of Collective Bargaining

4. The National Labor Relations Board, or NLRB, is an administrative agency empowered to resolve charges of unfair labor practices and to oversee union elections.

5. If an individual files a charge with the NLRB, an investigation is begun. If the claim is found to have some basis, the investigator tries to settle the case. If this effort is unsuccessful, a board determines whether to proceed with a hearing before an administrative law judge. The result may be appealed to the main board in Washington and again to the federal court of appeals. Note that the statute of limitations is restricted in these cases, in order to provide a quick resolution.

6. The National Labor Relations Act is applicable to most employers involved in interstate commerce. The parties must go before the NRLB before going to a court of appeals. A state may also enact laws, but if they conflict with federal law, the federal law preempts or governs. This is due to the supremacy clause in the Constitution, which declares that congressional acts are the law of the land.

7. The second power of the NLRB is to oversee union elections. Before any election can be held, the union must show support through authorization cards of at least 30 percent of the employees. A petition for an election is then filed. In the period between the filing and the actual election, employers must take great care that their activities are not unfair labor practices. If the employer's activities are judged unfair labor practices, the NLRB has the power to set aside the election if the union loses.

8. When the election is held, the union must receive a majority of the votes cast. Both the employer and the union supervise to insure that no unauthorized people vote. Only employees in that bargaining unit may vote. Certain people are not considered employees under the act. They include agricultural laborers, independent contractors, and supervisors.

9. There are three ways that a union becomes the representative of the employees in a bargaining unit. They are:
   a. Voluntary recognition -- An employer may recognize the union without an election.
   b. An election.
   c. Unfair labor practice charges -- If a union believes that an employer has committed a practice that would affect the outcome of an election, the union may take this complaint to the board. The board can certify the union as the representative of the employee.

10. After Continental Airlines, in a reorganization move, terminated all contracts with unions, Congress amended the law. Today if a business that is being reorganized wishes to terminate a labor agreement, the business must:
    a. Propose the necessary changes to an authorized representative.
    b. Supply enough information to allow the union to evaluate the proposal.
    c. Expect court approval *only* if the union has no good reason to reject the proposal and if it is right that the proposal be accepted.

Unfair Labor Practices by Employers

11. Employers are prohibited from interfering with employees' rights to self-organization or to join a union. For example, an employer generally may not limit the ability of unions to speak and distribute literature on company property if there is no alternative way of reaching the employees. Generally, employees are permitted to discuss unionization during nonworking hours in working or nonworking areas. They are permitted to distribute literature during nonworking hours in nonworking areas. *Lechmere v. N.L.R.B.* is a case in point.

12. A second unfair labor practice is for employers to threaten employees who vote for a union or to promise employees benefits if they do not vote for a union. Timing and custom are crucial in these matters. *NLRB v. Exchange Parts Co.* deals with the granting of benefits.

13. A third unfair labor practice is domination or support of a union to the extent that an employer controls it. For example, an employer cannot bargain with a union that represents less than a majority of the employees.

14. A fourth unfair labor practice is discrimination to discourage or encourage union membership. If an employee is dismissed, it must be for a legitimate reason unrelated to his or her support of the union. *Sure-Tan, Inc. v. NLRB* discusses this situation. If a plant is closed, it must be for a legitimate reason also. A lockout, in which the employer refuses to allow employees to return to work, is unlawful if not undertaken for economic or operational reasons.

15. A fifth unfair labor practice is discrimination against employees who file charges pursuant to the act or collect information.

16. A sixth unfair labor practice is refusal to bargain in good faith. Note that an agreement need not be reached, but mandatory subjects of bargaining such as wages or pensions must be discussed. An employer may not give his or her employees a benefit not bargained for with the union. However, if the union rejects a benefit, an employer may provide it if the bargaining had reached an impasse. In 1988, Congress passed an act requiring employers to provide written notice 60 days before closing a plant. *Southwest Forest Industries, Inc. v. NLRB* deals with the subject matter of mandatory bargaining. *NLRB v. General Electric Co.* deals with an employer's communication of bargaining information to employees.

17. The employer still retains his or her First Amendment right to freedom of speech. Arguments against unionization are legal, but no threats or promises can be made on the basis of the outcome of the election. *United Automobile, Aerospace and Agricultural Implement Workers of America v. NLRB* deals with this issue.

MAJOR POINTS OF CASES

Lechmere, Inc. v. N.L.R.B. (p. 556)

Nonemployee union organizers entered the Lechmere's parking lot used primarily by employees and placed handbills on the parked cars. When informed by the manager that Lechmere prohibited any kind of handbilling on its property, the organizers sued Lechmere for violating the National Labor Relations Act. The N.L.R.B. found for the organizers and Lechmere appealed.

The Supreme Court reversed the N.L.R.B.'s decision. Under the N.L.R.A. employers can prohibit distribution of union literature by nonemployee organizers unless the location of the business and the living quarters of the employees is so remote that it would otherwise be difficult to communicate with them. Because the union organizers failed to show any reason that it would be a hardship to communicate with employees in another fashion, Lechmere did not commit an unfair labor practice.

NLRB v. Exchange Parts Co. (p. 558)

In this case, the Court was called upon to decide if an employer's granting of benefits for the purpose of affecting a union election was prohibited by the National Labor Relations Act. The Court held that it was.

Even though the benefits are permanent in this case, the question arises about whether additional benefits might have been gained by the union. Any activity that influences the outcome of an election is prohibited.

Sure-Tan, Inc. v. NLRB (p. 561)

There are two issue in this case. The first is whether aliens without proper working papers are covered by the NLRA. The second issue is whether the employer's inquiry to the Immigration and Naturalization Service (INS) concerning the status of these employees was an unfair labor practice.

The Supreme Court held that undocumented aliens are employees under the NLRA. The rationale for this decision is that the act lists specific exclusions to the employee category. Aliens without working papers are not excluded from the statute.

As to the second issue, the Court held that the employer's request to the INS concerning the status of these workers was an unfair labor practice. This is so because the employer knew that the aliens had no proper working papers and contacted the INS in retaliation for these employees' labor activities. Note that a request for information from the INS that is *not* in retaliation for union activities is perfectly proper.

Southwest Forest Industries, Inc. v.
National Labor Relations Board (p. 564)

After a collective bargaining agreement between the employees and management ended, the employees went out on strike. The company sent a letter to its employees offering them different employment conditions than those discussed in meeting with the union representatives. The union filed an unfair labor practice charge.

The court held that in cases of expired contracts the employer must maintain the status quo until a new agreement is reached or until the parties have reached an impasse. It may then make new conditions if these conditions were understood by union. The company did not bargain in good faith with the union which is an unfair labor practice.

NLRB v. General Electric Co. (p. 565)

The issue in this case is whether the employer's take-it-or-leave-it offer, which was highly publicized to employees, was an unfair labor practice of not bargaining in good faith. The court held that it was.

The court prohibits making the best offer first and publicizing the offer because this indicates an absence of good faith by the employer.

United Automobile, Aerospace and Agricultural Implement
Workers of America v. National Labor Relations Board (p. 567)

Before a union representative election, Kawasaki's plant manager held a series of meetings with employees in which he stated that the plant's financial status was shaky. He stated it would be difficult for the plant to survive if the UAW's restriction on job classifications was implemented, but refused to directly answer the question of the plant's closing if such a restriction was implemented. The union alleged these statements were a violation of the law.

The court held that coercive threats were against labor law, but that statements based on objective financial facts were not. In this case, Kawasaki's predictions were based on economic necessity.

SELF-TEST QUESTIONS

True/False

_____ 1. Originally, courts favored the use of injunctions to force employees from acting collectively. (p. 549)

_____ 2. The Wagner Act defined and prohibited a number of unfair labor practices by both employers and unions. (pp. 550-551)

_____ 3. One of the major goals that Congress has sought through labor legislation is the balancing of bargaining power between labor and management in order to promote peaceful collective bargaining. (p. 551)

4. A union may gain recognition as the designated representative of the employees in a bargaining unit only through an election or an unfair labor practices proceedings. (p. 553)

_____ 5. The union must call for an election if an employer does not commit an unfair labor practice before the union's request for recognition. (p. 554)

_____ 6. In proving a violation of employees' rights to organize, a union must prove an employee's action coerced specific, named parties. (p. 555)

_____ 7. A company which prohibits the distribution of union literature must also prohibit the distribution of any other type of literature. (p. 557)

_____ 8. An employer who regularly grants increases at certain times of the year may continue to do so even if a union election is forthcoming. (p. 558)

_____ 9. An employer cannot fire an active member of union who violates a plant rule. (p. 560)

_____ 10. A company cannot violate the Wagner Act by encouraging union membership. (p. 562)

_____ 11. Any lockout where the employee refuses to allow the employees to work is illegal. (p. 562)

_____ 12. A new law on plant closings requires an employee to give written notice sixty days before a plant is to be closed. (p. 562)

_____ 13. The parties to a labor dispute must meet and confer, but they are not required to arrive at an agreement. (p. 563)

_____ 14. If a union goes on strike over a mandatory subject of bargaining, the workers are not protected. (p. 563)

_____ 15. All employer statements during an election that do not actually threaten reprisal for union activity are permissible under the provisions of the Taft-Hartley Act. (p. 566)

Multiple Choice

1. Historically, management's major weapon against union activity was the ex parte injunction granted on the basis of a motion by the employer without hearing evidence presented by the union. Management favored the use of this device because:
   a. it generally limited only harmful or dangerous union activity.
   b. it eased the tensions between unions and management.
   c. it often was all that was needed to break a union.
   d. it decreased incidents of violence by providing a "cooling off" period.

   (p. 549)

2. The first act to adopt the collective bargaining approach to labor relations was the:
   a. Clayton Act.
   b. Railway Labor Act.
   c. Norris-La Guardia Act.
   d. Wagner Act. (pp. 550-551)

3. Which is not true of the NLRB?
   a. It has both state and federal offices throughout the country.
   b. The regional offices are primarily responsible for conducting representation elections.
   c. The office of the general counsel prosecutes cases.
   d. Cases are taken before an administrative law judge and then may be appealed. (pp. 551-552)

4. In order to call for representation election, the union must demonstrate:
   a. the support of 30 percent or more of the employees in the bargaining unit.
   b. the support of a majority of the employees in the bargaining unit.
   c. the need for a collective-bargaining agent.
   d. both b and c. (p. 552)

5. XYZ Corporation and a union seeking to become the collective bargaining agent for some of XYZ's employees have a dispute concerning the composition of an appropriate bargaining unit. This determination will be made by:
   a. the employees.
   b. a union-management agreement.
   c. the NLRB.
   d. the court. (pp. 552-553)

6. The NLRB may certify a union without an election if:
   a. it recognizes the validity of the authorization cards.
   b. an employer commits an unlawful labor practice.
   c. the appropriate unit in which to conduct the election cannot be found.
   d. a and b. (pp. 554-555)

7. The International Brotherhood of Widgetworkers is attempting to organize the widget pressmen at Wonder Widget, Inc. The company wants to limit union contact with its employees as much as possible. In doing so it is *least* likely to commit an unfair labor practice by enforcing a rule that prohibits:
   a. employees from distributing literature in nonworking areas during nonworking time.
   b. employees from soliciting union support in working areas during nonworking time.
   c. employees from soliciting union support in nonworking areas during nonworking time.
   d. employees from distributing literature in working areas during nonworking time. (pp. 555-556)

8. In the *Exchange Parts Co.* case which dealt with the employer voluntarily granting benefits, the court held the action:
   a. violated labor law because it discriminated against union members.
   b. violated labor law because it possibly affected the outcome of the election.
   c. did not violate labor law because it was beneficial to most employees.
   d. did not violate labor law because the benefits were permanent and unconditional.
   (pp. 558-559)

9. A company cannot show support of a union by:
   a. cooperating with a union.
   b. assisting a union in any way.
   c. bargaining with a union which represents only a minority of its employees.
   d. none of the above are permissible. (pp. 559-560)

10. A union has petitioned the NLRB for a representation election, and a date for such an election has been set. Management would like to see the union's bid to become the employees' collective bargaining agent defeated. Management may legally:
    a. promise employees an additional ten cents per hour if the union is defeated.
    b. give employees a five cents per hour across-the-board raise.
    c. give employees a five cents per hour raise based on an annual productivity review.
    d. both b and c. (p. 560)

11. In the *Sure-Tan* case where the employer asked immigration officials to check the status of its employees, the Court held:
    a. this was not a violation of labor law because the provisions of the NLRA apply to undocumented alien employees.
    b. this was not a violation of labor law because the request was not the proximate cause of the employee's departure.
    c. this was a violation of labor law because labor law supersedes immigration law.
    d. this was a violation of labor law because the request was in retaliation for employees' protected union activity. (pp. 561-562)

12. A lockout is generally considered illegal when it is used:
    a. to oppose unionization or to force the employees to choose a particular union.
    b. to avoid operational problems that could result from a threatened strike.
    c. to time the closing of a plant so that the unusual economic losses could be avoided.
    d. by a multiemployer group in retaliation for a strike on only one member's plant. (p. 562)

13. The electricians' union and the management of Ace, Inc., have been engaged in contract negotiations for an extended period, during which the old contract expired. A number of issues, including merit pay, remain to be decided. Since this is a mandatory subject of bargaining, management may unilaterally institute a new merit pay plan:
    a. without offering it to the union.
    b. if it is still bargaining with the union on the issue.
    c. if the union has rejected the plan.
    d. if the union has rejected the plan and the parties have reached an impasse on the issue. (pp. 563-564)

14. Which of the following is *not* a failure on the part of management to bargain collectively?
    a. Management does not send representatives to the meetings who can bind the company.
    b. Management reaches an impasse with the union.
    c. Management refuses to bargain until an unfair labor practice charge is withdrawn.
    d. Management insistence upon new negotiations from the union.

    (p. 563)

15. In the *United Automobile* case where management hinted that a union victory might result in a plant closing, the court held:
    a. this statement was permissible because an upcoming union election does not restrict a manager's freedom of speech.
    b. this statement was permissible because it was based on economic necessity.
    c. this statement was impermissible because it could be construed as a threat against the employees if they supported the union.
    d. this statement was impermissible because it was too speculative.

    (pp. 567-568)

Essay Questions

1. Discuss the three ways in which a union may become the representative of the employees in the designated bargaining unit.

2. Discuss the unfair labor practice of domination or support of a union.

Chapter 20

Labor-Management Relations: The Regulation of Unions

The National Labor Relations Board oversees union activities as well as management activities.

This chapter deals with the unfair labor practices of unions as well as protected union rights such as the right to strike and the right to picket. In addition, the effects of unions on secondary employers are discussed.

CHAPTER OBJECTIVES

After reading Chapter 20 of the text and studying the related materials in this chapter of the *Study Guide*, you will be able to fulfill the following objectives:

1. Describe the prohibited unfair labor practices of unions.

2. Understand the rights and the limitations of protected union rights, including:
    a. The right to strike.
    b. The right to picket.

3. Recognize the rights and limitations of union activities that affect secondary employers.

MAJOR POINTS TO REMEMBER

Bargaining

1. An important function of the National Labor Relations Act is to protect against the unfair labor practices of unions. The practices by unions include:
    a. Refusal to bargain collectively with the employer.
    b. Demanding closed shop arguments.
    c. Unfair representation.
    d. Coercing employees.
    e. Excessive or discriminatory fees.
    f. Featherbedding.

2. A union that has been certified by the board cannot refuse to bargain with an employer. It must meet at reasonable times and act in good faith to come to an agreement.

3. A union cannot demand a closed shop agreement or one that stipulates that only union members be hired. In some states, it is legal for a union to demand a union shop or an agency shop. A union shop is one in which employees must join the union after a certain

period of employment. An agency shop is one in which employees who don't wish to join a union must pay union fees, because they are receiving benefits that unions confer upon an employee. If the state involved has a right-to-work law, neither a union shop nor an agency shop is allowable.

Duty of Fair Representation

4. A union cannot represent only those who voted in favor of unionization. All members of the bargaining unit must be fairly represented.

Unfair Labor Practices

5. A union cannot coerce the employees in their choice of union representation, *Revco D.S. Inc. (D.C.) v. NLRB* is a case in point.

6. A union cannot charge excessive or discriminatory fees.

7. A union cannot require an employer to pay for work that is not performed. This practice is known as *featherbedding*.

Protected Concerted Activities

8. Two major concerted or collective employee activities are the right to strike and picketing. The National Labor Relations Act protects both activities, if they are done lawfully. Employees have the right to refrain from concerted activities, as shown in *Pattern Makers' League of North America v. NLRB*. The courts take a broad view of concerted activities as shown by a Supreme Court decision that even if only one employee protests a violation of the collective bargaining agreement, this consists of concerted activity.

The Right to Strike

9. There are two types of strikes. An economic strike is one to obtain better working conditions or wages. An unfair labor practice is one to protest an employer's unfair labor practice. Note the economic risk to workers in economic strikes as in the Hormel strike.

10. There are several situations in which employees do *not* have the right to strike. These are cases where:
    a. The means or ends of the strike are unlawful.
    b. There is a no-strike clause in the contract.
    c. An employer is being forced to assign work to certain workers.
    d. The strike threatens the economy of the country.
    e. Employees are prohibited from striking.

11. If the strike is unlawful, courts may issue an injunction prohibiting the strike. If the strike threatens the country's economy, the president may order a postponement of the strike while the issues are investigated. If no solution is forthcoming, the president may ask the court to issue an injunction. After an injunction is issued, the parties must make every attempt to settle with the assistance of the Federal Mediation and Conciliation Service.

174

12. An employer has the right to replace the employees who go out on strike. These replacements may be permanent in the event of an economic strike. In the case of an unfair labor practices strike, the employees must be rehired when vacancies occur unless they have found other, equal employment. *NLRB v. Mackay Radio & Telegraph Co.* and *National Labor Relations Board v. Curtin Matheson Scientific Inc.* deal with the reinstatement of employees following economic strikes.

Picketing

13. A second concerted activity that is protected under the National Labor Relations Act is nonviolent picketing. Although the First Amendment guarantees freedom of speech, this right is limited to state action. Whether speech at privately owned shopping malls, which are open to the public, is protected had created a quandary for the lower courts. The Supreme Court has held that under the National Labor Relations Act there must be an accommodation between the employees' rights to picket and the property rights of employers.

14. There are three types of picketing. *Organizational picketing* is designed to convince employees to join the union. *Recognition picketing* is designed to persuade employers to recognize the union. Neither can be done if another union has been recognized or an election has taken place within the last year. A union cannot picket for more than thirty days without filing a petition for an election. A third kind of picketing is *informational*. Its purpose is to inform the public that the employer does not have a union contract. This picketing may take place for an unlimited time until an election is held.

Secondary Pressure

15. Secondary pressure or a secondary boycott involves affecting an employer other than the one whom the employees are disputing. Secondary boycotts are illegal unless the employees of the second employer put pressure themselves on their employer to support the striking workers.

16. Oftentimes union members wish to inform the public of their strike against a certain employer. This is done through the use of leaflets and through the use of picket signs. Leafleting is protected speech under the First Amendment as long as it merely seeks to inform and does not lead to a work stoppage by any employees of secondary employers. *DeBartolo Corporation v. Florida Gulf Coast Building and Construction Trades Council* involves the right of employees to pass out leaflets.

17. Often picketing affects consumers as well as employees of a secondary employer. If strikers request consumers not to buy a particular product, this is a legal activity. If strikers request consumers not to patronize a store that stocks the product, this is unlawful, because it now affects a secondary employer. *NLRB v. Retail Store Employees Union, Local 1001* is a case in point.

18. A second type of secondary pressure that is illegal is a hot cargo agreement. These agreements decree that workers not be required to handle nonunion materials.

19. A third type of secondary pressure is the work preservation clause, which protects employment generally done by a particular union. These agreements are legal if the purpose is to affect the policies of the primary employer.

20. If a union violates the law by engaging in prohibited secondary activity, the union may be liable for damages or be accused of an unfair labor practice.

MAJOR POINTS OF CASES

Revco D.S. Inc. (D.C.) v. NLRB (p. 574)

Hanna, a member of the union organizing committee, offered to pay Crosby, an anti-union employee, $100 to vote for the union. Upon hearing this, the company refused to bargain with the union alleging an unfair labor practice.

The appellate court overturned the hearing officer's judgment that Hanna was only joking and not committing an unfair labor practice. The court could find no substantial evidence that this suggestion was a joke and upheld the company's refusal to bargain with the union.

Pattern Makers' League of North America v. NLRB (p. 575)

The issue raised in this case is whether a clause in the union constitution violated the Wagner Act. The clause stated that any union members who resigned from the union during a strike and returned to work had to pay a fine.

The Supreme Court held that this clause and the action of the union in firing certain employees did violate the Wagner Act. The Wagner Act establishes the right to voluntary unionism and the right to refrain from concerted activities, such as a strike.

NLRB v. Mackay Radio & Telegraph Co. (p. 579)

The question raised in this case is whether an employer's discrimination in rehiring only certain strikers was an unfair labor practice under the jurisdiction of the NLRB. The Court held that it was.

The Court's rationale is that any action that discourages union membership is an unfair labor practice. Management does not have to rehire employees if there is a valid reason. Here the employees were not rehired because they were prominent leaders of the strike. This is considered an invalid reason and an unfair labor practice.

National Labor Relations Board v. Curtin Matheson Scientific, Inc. (p. 581)

The issue in this case is whether the NLRB legally had to presume that striker replacements oppose the union. Curtin was refusing to bargain with the union arguing that it needed no evidence for a good faith belief that the majority of employees no longer supported the union. The rationale was that since many workers out on economic strike had been replaced by other workers, the NLRB should have made a presumption that these new workers would not support the union since one union goal would be to reestablish the striking workers in their jobs. This of course would displace the replacement workers.

176

The NLRB had determined that it would make no presumption, but would look at each case separately and retain the requirements that the employer show some objective evidence if it refused to bargain under this good faith belief.

The Supreme Court agreed with the NLRB position for two reasons. The first was that although unions may wish to reestablish their workers, their ability to do so depends on their bargaining power. The second reason is that the Board's ruling is consistent with its mandate of achieving industrial peace.

DeBartolo Corporation v. Florida Gulf Coast Building and Construction Trades Council (p. 587)

Union workers passed out handbills at a certain mall asking customers not to shop there until the corporation which owned the mall agreed that all construction would be performed by contractors who paid fair wages. DeBartolo, the corporation in question, alleged that this was an unfair labor practice by the union.

The Court stated the major issue in the case was whether the handbills coerced persons from doing business at the mall. The evidence showed that this was not the case. The handbills were informational and truthfully advised customers of the union position. In addition, the handbills did not suggest a secondary strike by mall employees. Therefore, the passing out of handbills was legal.

NLRB v. Retail Store Employees Union, Local 1001 (p. 589)

This case deals with the effects of picketing upon a secondary employer. The Court held that if the effect of the picketing threatens this neutral party with ruin, it is illegal, because this result is unfair.

In this case, the product picketed against was the only product carried by the secondary employer. Note that if a lesser business loss is involved, the picketing at the secondary site is not illegal.

SELF-TEST QUESTIONS

_____ 1.   It is an unfair labor practice for a union that is certified as the collective bargaining agent to refuse to bargain collectively with the employer. (p. 571)

_____ 2.   A contract clause stating that the employer agrees to hire only workers in good standing in the union is illegal in all fifty states today. (p. 572)

_____ 3.   An agency shop does not require employees to join a union, but requires them to pay union dues. (p. 572)

_____ 4.   A union is required to fairly represent all union members in a bargaining unit but has no duty to nonunion employees. (p. 573)

_____ 5.   A union may not expel an employee from the union if he or she refuses to pay excessive fees. (p. 575)

_____ 6.   Employees may not act in concert without the assistance of a union. (p. 576)

___ 7. The Norris-La Guardia Act prohibits federal courts from enjoining any strike other than one that imperils national health or safety. (p. 577)

___ 8. The Wagner Act prohibits a union from striking to force an employer to assign work to a certain group of workers unless the employer is failing to comply with a board order. (p. 577)

___ 9. Union members may not strike if the strike threatens to cripple the economy of the United States. (p. 578)

___ 10. In a national emergency suit, parties are under a duty to accept proposals of settlement made by the Federal Mediation and Conciliation Service. (pp. 578-579)

___ 11. If an employee engages in an economic strike, the employer may hire a permanent replacement. (p. 579)

___ 12. The First Amendment prohibits the government and private parties from restricting the freedom of speech granted to picketers. (pp. 583-584)

___ 13. When employees of a company refuse to cross the picket lines of another company, this is an illegal secondary boycott. (p. 586)

___ 14. Asking consumers not to buy a particular product is lawful, but asking them not to patronize the secondary employer is unlawful. (p. 588)

___ 15. If a union engages in illegal secondary activity, an employer's only legal recourse is to file an unfair labor practice charge with the NLRB. (p. 590)

Multiple Choice

1. In a union shop, the union:
   a. may cause union employees to be discharged if they fail to attend a union meeting.
   b. determines which employees are eligible for hiring.
   c. could force a discharge of an employee for failing to comply with a union rule.
   d. forces employees to join the union after they are hired.

   (p. 572)

2. XYZ Inc., and the pipefitters' union are negotiating a contract in a state that does not have a right-to-work law. One of the issues under discussion is employee membership in the bargaining unit. Under the Taft-Hartley Act, it is an unfair labor practice for the union to seek:
   a. an agency shop.
   b. a closed shop.
   c. a union shop.
   d. both a and b.

   (pp. 572-573)

3. Which of the following is *not* an unfair union practice?
   a. Restraining the employees from engaging in concerted activities.
   b. Forcing employees to pay initiation fees.
   c. Failing to represent a worker in the bargaining unit.
   d. Requiring an employer to pay for work not performed.

   (pp. 573-575)

4. In the *Pattern Makers League* case where the union fined members who resigned from the union during a strike and went back to work, the court held this action was:
   a. consistent with precedent set by other court decisions.
   b. consistent with the legislative history preceding the passage of the National Labor Relations Act.
   c. inconsistent with policies of voluntary unionism.
   d. inconsistent with the Congressional intent in passage of the Taft-Hartley Act.

   (pp. 575-576)

5. A group of employees may engage in protected concerted activities:
   a. only when they are represented by a union.
   b. only when they are members of a union.
   c. only when they are assisted by a union.
   d. only when they act together as a group.

   (pp. 575-576)

6. Employers may obtain an injunction forbidding workers to strike if:
   a. the employees engage in violence.
   b. the employees block access to the plant.
   c. there is a no-strike clause in the contract.
   d. all of the above.

   (p. 577)

7. When the president of the United States determines that a strike or lockout affecting an entire industry would impair the national health or safety, he may:
   a. appoint a board to settle the dispute.
   b. order the Federal Mediation and Conciliation Service to settle the dispute.
   c. order the attorney general to ask a federal court to enjoin the strike or lockout for eighty days.
   d. order the NLRB to prohibit the strike or lockout for eighty days.

   (pp. 578-579)

8. The major function of the Federal Mediation and Conciliation Service is to:
   a. assist the parties in settling labor disputes that threaten to cause a substantial interruption of commerce.
   b. assist the parties in settling labor disputes whenever the parties request it.
   c. render binding decisions in labor disputes that threaten to cause substantial interruption of commerce.
   d. render binding decisions in labor disputes when asked by the parties to do so.

   (pp. 578-579)

9. In the *Mackay* case where the employer rehired some of the strikers, the court held:
   a. the NLRB lacked jurisdiction in the case because the strike was illegal.
   b. the NLRB lacked jurisdiction because the employer had not committed an unfair labor practice.
   c. because the strike was an economic strike, the employer was bound to reinstate all the striking employees.
   d. the employer had the right to rehire only certain workers but couldn't base his choice on the amount of union activity of a worker.   (pp. 579-580)

10. Both the United States Constitution and the Wagner Act protect picketing, therefore, state courts:
    a. may not restrict picketing in any manner.
    b. may enjoin violent acts but may not enjoin future peaceful picketing.
    c. may enjoin all future picketing if acts of violence occur.
    d. may enjoin picketing if the court suspects that violence will occur.

                                                                    (pp. 583-584)

11. Strikers are picketing outside the Jones Mfg. Co. protesting an alleged unfair labor practice. Joe, a delivery truck driver from Smith Supplies, refuses to cross the picket lines. The strikers have exerted:
    a. lawful primary pressure.
    b. unlawful primary pressure.
    c. lawful secondary pressure.
    d. unlawful secondary pressure.   (p. 585)

12. Priti is a union member who is handing out leaflets in front of a department store. The leaflets ask people not to purchase electronic products sold in the store which are manufactured by the Beaudry Electronic Corp. The leaflets can:
    a. be handed to customers, but not employees of the department store.
    b. encourage employees to refuse to sell Beaudry products.
    c. inform customers of the dispute with Beaudry.
    d. perform all of the above functions.   (pp. 586-587)

13. In the *DeBartolo* case where the union was accused of an unfair labor practice for passing out handbills asking customers to boycott the mall, the court held:
    a. this was lawful because union members have unrestricted First Amendment rights when dealing with labor disputes.
    b. this was lawful because the union members had limited their leafleting to the specific mall in question.
    c. this was unlawful because customers felt coerced.
    d. this was unlawful because the legislative history of the act can be interpreted as forbidding this type of behavior.   (pp. 587-588)

14. The shoemakers' union is engaged in a labor dispute with a major shoe company. In order to enlist public support for its position, the union wants to picket in front of department stores that sell the company's shoes. The union will commit an unfair labor practice if:
    a.   it asks customers not to patronize the department stores.
    b.   it asks customers not to purchase the company's shoes.
    c.   it causes the department store to lose business because customers stop buying the company's shoes.
    d.   it pickets the department stores for any reasons. (p. 588)

15. If union members violate the law by engaging in unlawful secondary activity, their employer may sue for:
    a.   monetary damages.
    b.   punitive damages.
    c.   an unfair labor practice charge, but no monetary damages.
    d.   any of the above, but must select only one remedy. (p. 590)

Essay Questions

1.   What are the differences between a closed shop, a union shop, and an agency shop?

2.   What is the purpose of secondary pressure and why has it been outlawed?

Chapter 21

Regulation of Property Rights: Eminent Domain, Zoning, and Environmental Law

This chapter discusses government regulation of property. Eminent domain, zoning, and environmental law are all limitations on the rights of property owners. Eminent domain and zoning are state or local regulations stemming from the police power of the states to protect the health, safety and general welfare of their citizens. Although local, state, and federal regulations are all involved in regulating pollution, the text focuses upon some of the major federal environmental laws. These regulations impose costs on businesses, but also create new business opportunities for innovative managers. This area of the law is continually evolving as more effects of technology upon the environment are discovered.

CHAPTER OBJECTIVES

After reading Chapter 21 of the text and studying the related materials in this chapter of the *Study Guide*, you will be able to fulfill the following objectives:

1. Describe government regulation of individual's property rights, including:
    a.   Eminent domain.
    b.   Zoning law.

2. Define the environment and understand its major functions.

3. Define pollution and understand the reasons for its growth.

4. Describe the powers and limitations of local, state, and federal statutes and regulations.

5. Understand the purpose of the major environmental statutes.

MAJOR POINTS TO REMEMBER

Land Use Regulation: Eminent Domain and Zoning

1. *Eminent domain* is the right of the government to take private property from a landowner. The Fifth Amendment to the Constitution permits eminent domain but limits the government's power by requiring that the landowner be given just compensation and that the land taken be for public use.

2. The term "public use" includes land taken for the use of the public, such as for an interstate highway. It also includes land taken for the public benefit, but not necessarily for public use. An example of this is the government condemnation of a slum area which is cleaned up by the government and then sold to a private party for development.

3.   Although eminent domain most often occurs with real property, personal property can, at times, be taken by the government for public use or public advantage. *City of Oakland v. Oakland Raiders* is a case in point.

4.   Some northern cities have tried to intimidate industries by stating they would take the industry by eminent domain if the owners were planning to relocate. Thus, the owners would only receive market value for the industry as well as gaining a new competitor. To date, no such actions have occurred.

5.   Government also can control the use of land by zoning ordinances or land use planning rules. The rationale is to protect the rights of the community in the areas of health, safety, and general welfare. No compensation need be paid to the landowner unless it is considered inverse condemnation, or such a severe regulation that the government is effectively taking the land.

6.   Since the legal environment today provides for greater regulation of property rights than in the past, zoning regulations have increased in scope and power. A recent issue in the area of land use concerns the prohibition of households of more than two unrelated parties as the *Village of Belle Terre v. Boraas* case illustrates.

7.   In some instances, the regulation of property may have an effect on individual freedoms. Whether a community can use zoning to regulate the location of businesses which show pornographic materials is the issue in *City of Renton v. Playtime Theatres, Inc.* while *Framingham Clinic, Inc. v. Board of Selectmen* deals with the right of a community to limit the availability of medical facilities where abortions are performed.

What Is the Environment?

8.   The *environment* is defined as all the physical elements of the world except human beings. The functions of the environment include:
    a.   Providing a place for existence.
    b.   Providing resources.
    c.   Providing intangible qualities, such as beauty.
    Environmental regulations attempt to protect these functions of the environment. Note the success of Japan in this area.

9.   *Pollution* is the human-caused diminished capacity of the environment to perform its function. It is not a recent phenomenon, but its effects became more serious in the 1960s because of:
    a.   High population densities.
    b.   Consumption of more resources.
    c.   New business practices.
    d.   Lack of legal and economic discouragement to pollute.

10.   Acid rain is a pollutant that remains unaffected by current environmental regulations. The cause of acid rain has not been determined with certainty, and new clean air regulations would cost billions of dollars.

11. Concerns with the quality of the environment is a world wide concern. However, a manager should be aware that the policies of other countries are not necessarily identical to those in the United States.

Legal Control of Environmental Pollution

12. Local, state, and federal regulations each attempt to control pollution. Local regulations may consist of zoning, land-use planning, and specific ordinances. Local regulations are limited to the local area and thus cannot affect the activities of surrounding areas. State regulations apply to the entire state and oftentimes local and state regulations work together. These regulations are in the form of legislation, administrative agency actions, and court decisions.

13. Each state has a body of common law. One doctrine that has been applied to problems of pollution is trespass. This is an intentional tort that involves unauthorized entry onto another's property. It has been held to include pollution. A second common law doctrine that is sometimes applied to pollution problems is the tort of nuisance. This is an act that disturbs the landowner's enjoyment of his or her property. Pollution also fits into this category. The common law remedies for these two doctrines are monetary damages or an injunction.

14. Federal regulations are the most far-reaching, for they apply to the entire country. There are two categories of federal environmental law. The first requires full disclosure of the effects of federal activities upon the environment. The second consists of laws that limit pollution. Violations of these regulations generally result in the assessment of fines. However, there is a strengthening of criminal sanctions being administered against corporate officers. In addition, prosecution can occur under non-environmental statutes such as mail and wire fraud, conspiracy and RICO. The National Environmental Policy Act of 1969, or NEPA, requires full disclosure of federal activity that affects the environment. *Breckinridge v. Rumsfeld* is a case that deals with this concept.

15. The second type of federal environmental law contains statutes and regulations aimed at limiting pollution. These have led to two categories of problems.

16. The first problem area is the ability of the EPA or OSHA to determine the level of acceptable pollution. Once an appropriate level of pollution is determined, it is difficult to allocate responsibility among the various polluters. The EPA recently has extended its definition of pollution sources to include plantwide pollution. The concept is known as the "bubble concept" and is discussed in *Chevron v. Natural Resources Defense Council, Inc.* The second problem area is the estimation of the cost to business balanced by the benefit or costs to society. Often it is difficult to analyze intangible benefits to society.

17. Two acts that raise the cost-benefit problem are the Clean Air Act and the Water Pollution Control Act. Companies have argued that these acts are not only costly but also technically unwieldy. *Union Electric Co. v. Environmental Protection Agency* is a case that presents this viewpoint.

18. The Clean Air Act of 1990 has taken an experimental approach to the high cost of government regulation of pollution. Under this plan businesses must reduce their emissions of sulphur dioxide by fifty percent. Each plant will have an allowance for each ton of acceptable emissions. These allowances can be sold to other businesses and/or investors. This plan raises incentives to businesses to stop polluting as well as cuts the number of government employees needed to oversee compliance.

MAJOR POINTS OF CASES

City of Oakland v. Oakland Raiders (p. 597)

The issue in this case is whether a city can use the doctrine of eminent domain to prevent a football team from moving to another city.

The defendants tried to persuade the court that eminent domain does not apply to intangible property and that this taking does not meet the constitutional requirements of "public use."

The court disagreed with both arguments. In answer to the first argument, the court stated that in neither the federal nor state constitution is any exclusion granted for intangible property.

In answer to the second argument, the court stated that "public use" can include recreation and enjoyment. Thus the court upheld the city's right to acquire the team through eminent domain. The dissent and concurrence stated that this decision greatly expanded government intervention in property rights and that a business should have the right to relocate without government interference.

Village of Belle Terre v. Boraas (p. 602)

A zoning ordinance that permitted only single-family homes composed of no more than two unrelated persons was challenged as unconstitutional.

The Court held that the ordinance was constitutional. The rationale was that no "fundamental" rights guaranteed by the Constitution were violated. In fact, the ordinance promoted the goals of health, safety, and the general welfare of the citizens.

City of Renton v. Playtime Theatres, Inc. (p. 603)

The zoning ordinance in this case required that adult motion picture theaters be located in a certain area of the city. The theater owners brought suit, claiming a violation of their First Amendment rights under the Constitution.

The Supreme Court held that this ordinance was "content-neutral" and served to deal with the secondary effects of such theaters in surrounding neighborhoods. Secondary effects include the prevention of crime and protecting property values. Therefore the ordinance was justified.

The dissent disagreed on several grounds. First the ordinance did not apply to other adult entertainment, such as adult book stores. Second, the ordinance was amended with the inclusion of the phrase "secondary effect" after the lawsuit began. The dissent maintained that the sole purpose of the ordinance was to control the content of the films shown in adult movie theaters and was unconstitutional.

Framingham Clinic, Inc. v. Board of Selectmen (p. 604)

In this case, a zoning bylaw that prohibited abortion clinics in the town was challenged. The court held that the bylaw was invalid. The rationale was that since the case of *Roe v. Wade*, an abortion is a constitutionally protected right. If the clinic were allowed to be banned, it would force women to travel to other clinics for a fundamental right.

Breckinridge v. Rumsfeld (p. 611)

The questions raised in this case are the meaning of the term human environment and whether an environmental impact statement is required under the NEPA. The court held that human environment does not include short-term economic disruptions, as in the case of closing military bases. Therefore there was no requirement for an environmental impact statement in this instance, because the scope of the act does not include social problems.

Chevron v. Natural Resources Defense Council, Inc. (p. 614)

Congress passed legislation requiring nonattainment states to establish a permit program to regulate "new or modified major stationary sources." The EPA interpreted the term source as allowing an industry to treat all pollution-emitting devices as if they were within a single entity. This concept is called the "bubble concept."

The Supreme Court reviewed the action of the EPA in order to determine if it was reasonable. Two questions had to be answered. The first was whether this interpretation violated the clear intent of the statute. The Court held that it did not.

The second question was whether the agency's interpretation was permissible. The Court held that it was. There is no specific definition of stationary source in the statute, and the fact that the EPA had varied interpretations of this term over the years indicated the flexibility of this agency. It is difficult to deal with the problems of regulating pollution, and the EPA's scheme was within the goals of the Act.

Union Electric Co. v. Environmental Protection Agency (p. 617)

The issue in this case is whether it was proper for the Court to review claims of economic or technological infeasibility under the Clean Air Act. The Court held that it was not proper.

Under the act, each state was responsible for setting its own requirements for clean air, subject to the approval of the act's administrator. The Court held that if a state sets a certain standard, the implication is that industry must conform. If it cannot, the implication is that the state is willing to lose this industry in order to protect the environment.

SELF-TEST QUESTIONS

True/False

____ 1. Eminent domain is a device to protect the individual from government power. (pp. 596-597)

_____ 2. Zoning regulations limit one landowner's property rights while recognizing the property rights of other landowners. (pp. 600-601)

_____ 3. The trend today is for communities to use land-use regulations as a means of controlling the quality of life. (pp. 601-602)

_____ 4. Environmental law is very narrow in its application and effect. (p. 605)

_____ 5. The environment consists of all the physical elements of the world. (p. 606)

_____ 6. Although pollution itself is not a modern phenomenon, its extent and consequences only recently have become an area of legal concern. (p. 608)

_____ 7. Environmental policy goals in the United States are consistent with those of other countries. (pp. 608-609)

_____ 8. State legislatures have the power to enact statutes regulating private business activities that cause pollution problems. (p. 610)

_____ 9. One aspect of environmental law is full disclosure of major activities affecting the environment by all state governments. (p. 611)

_____ 10. An environmental impact statement eliminates causes and sources of pollution. (p. 611)

_____ 11. The Environmental Protection Agency is the only governmental unit empowered to enforce environmental regulations. (p. 613)

_____ 12. The "bubble concept" provides that an individual piece of a company's equipment may be exempt from pollution standards in certain instances. (p. 613)

_____ 13. By an Act of Congress, administrative agencies are now required to issue environmental regulations only if the costs of compliance are less than the potential benefits to society. (p. 616)

_____ 14. Some environmental regulations set standards above the current technological limits of an industry. (p. 617)

_____ 15. The courts usually grant judicial relief from pollution regulations to companies on the grounds of economic infeasibility. (p. 617)

Multiple Choice

1. Eminent domain:
   a. is a right of the government found in the 14th Amendment of the Constitution.
   b. is a taking of property for public or private use.
   c. applies to real property only.
   d. is always accompanied by just compensation. (pp. 596-597)

2. In the *City of Oakland* case where the city tried to use the doctrine of eminent domain to keep a football team from moving to another city, the court held:
   a. eminent domain applies to real property only.
   b. eminent domain applies to tangible, but not intangible personal property.
   c. public use can include recreation and enjoyment.
   d. business should have the right to relocate without government interference.

   (pp. 597-599)

3. The major goal of zoning regulations is:
   a. the shifting of land use control from the individual property owner to other community residents.
   b. wise and efficient land use that balances the rights of the landowners and the community.
   c. to limit the compensation that local governments must pay for condemnation.
   d. to protect the landowner from arbitrary government condemnations.

   (pp. 600-602)

4. In the *City of Renton* case, which dealt with the right of a city to restrict pornographic films, the court held:
   a. the city could not restrict the location of films because this is discrimination.
   b. the city could not restrict the location of the films because other forms of adult entertainment were allowed in all areas.
   c. the city could not restrict the location of the films because the ordinance violates the First Amendment.
   d. the city could restrict the location of the films.   (pp. 603-604)

5. Environmental regulation is *least* concerned with:
   a. economic effects.
   b. intangible qualities of nature.
   c. the survival of human life.
   d. the preservation and management of resources.   (p. 607)

6. Pollution:
   a. is defined as emitting particles in the air or dumping waste into water.
   b. occurs at each stage of the production cycle.
   c. had traditionally been strictly regulated by the courts.
   d. was caused primarily by the rise in population.   (pp. 607-608)

7. In Japan:
   a. the traditional mediation approach is used in settling pollution disputes.
   b. injured parties rely on statistical correlation for causation as they do in American lawsuits.
   c. funding is provided by Japanese companies to make compensation payments to victims of pollution.
   d. a statute comparable to the National Environmental Policy Act was passed to restrict pollution.   (p. 609)

8. Local regulations may not:
   a. enact regulations for soil tests.
   b. enact preventative ordinances.
   c. preserve aesthetic features of local areas.
   d. govern air pollution. (pp. 609-610)

9. The town of Mayberry wants to protect its environment and the quality of life that its citizens enjoy. To do this, Mayberry may pass an ordinance:
   a. restricting the nighttime use of its airport.
   b. levying a fine on businesses outside the city limits that dump sewage in a river that runs through the town.
   c. limiting the density of new residential developments.
   d. both b and c. (pp. 609-610)

10. The major source of pollution control is:
   a. local government regulation.
   b. county government regulation.
   c. state government regulation.
   d. federal government regulation. (pp. 609-611)

11. The National Environmental Policy Act of 1969 (NEPA) requires:
   a. the federal government to guarantee the legal right to a clean and unpolluted environment.
   b. the preparation of an environmental impact statement whenever a federal activity has a major effect on the government.
   c. the federal government to take certain legal actions to eliminate causes and sources of pollution.
   d. both a and c. (p. 611)

12. In the *Breckinridge* case where the issue was whether an environmental impact statement was required for the closing of army bases, the court held:
   a. it was required because there is a long term impact on the community.
   b. it was required because the National Environmental Policy Act goes beyond the mere physical environment.
   c. it was not required because there was no economic impact on the physical environment.
   d. it was not required because the Congressional intent was not to reach social problems of this type. (pp. 611-612)

13. Which of the following is *not* a problem stemming from the government regulation of pollution?
   a. The ability of the government to determine the "correct" level of pollution.
   b. The difficulty of business employing a cost-benefit analysis.
   c. The effect of an inflexible set of standards.
   d. The financial effect of pollution regulations on business.
   (pp. 612-615)

14. Critics of the Environmental Protection Agency maintain:
    a. it is too lax in its enforcement.
    b. criminal sanctions are never imposed upon businesses.
    c. it implements unrealistic pollution standards.
    d. the agency is too expensive to maintain.   (pp. 612-615)

15. A cost-benefit analysis:
    a. is an economic tool used to determine the efficient allocation of funds.
    b. is required to be used by administrative agencies dealing with environmental problems.
    c. can never include intangible factors.
    d. a and b only.   (pp. 615-616)

Essay Questions

1. What are the similarities and differences between eminent domain and zoning?

2. What are the two goals of federal environmental law and how are they implemented?

Chapter 22

Federal Securities Regulation

A free market requires capital from nongovernment sources. A major source of private capital is the securities market, where publicly traded securities are bought and sold by both large and small investors.

The issuance, purchase, and sale of securities are regulated by both the state and the federal governments. This chapter focuses on federal regulation through the Federal Securities Acts of 1933 and 1934.

CHAPTER OBJECTIVES

After reading Chapter 22 of the text and studying the related materials in this chapter of the *Study Guide*, you will be able to fulfill the following objectives:

1.   Identify the types of securities covered under the 1933 and 1934 acts.

2.   Understand the objectives and scope of the 1933 act.

3.   Understand the objectives and scope of the 1934 act.

MAJOR POINTS TO REMEMBER

Historical Background of the Federal Securities Laws

1.   Interest in controlling private capital markets began before the stock market crash. The first regulations were enacted by some states in the early twentieth century. These laws were called *blue sky laws* and were ineffective because of their limited jurisdictions.

2.   The Securities Act of 1933 and Securities Act of 1934 were enacted to federally regulate securities. Note that the intent was not to provide insurance nor to protect investors from all mishaps that could occur from investing in the stock market.

Objectives of the 1933 and 1934 Acts

3.   The Federal Securities Acts of 1933 and 1934 have two major objectives. The first is to provide investors and financial advisors with adequate information about securities. The second objective is to provide a fair market and ensure investor confidence by raising the ethical standards of conduct in the buying and selling of securities.

4.   There are two concerns with the objectives of the federal securities acts. The first is whether individual investors are really benefitting from the costly disclosure information

provided by companies. The second concern is whether policing a market for fairness can be predictable for securities traders.

Federal Securities Law

5. The Securities and Exchange Commission is the administrative agency that oversees the federal securities laws that regulate the issuance, purchase, and sale of securities. The acts of 1933 and 1934 define *securities* very broadly. Besides stocks and bonds, investment contracts are considered securities. To determine if the federal securities laws apply, three activities must be present in a security or investment contract:
   a. Money is paid from one person to another.
   b. There is a common enterprise to earn profits.
   c. The profits arise primarily from the efforts of the parties other than the investor.
   This three-part test is applied in *Miller v. Central Chinchilla Group, Inc.*

6. The federal act that applies to the initial issuance of securities is the 1933 act. Note that selected issuers are exempt from this act. The purpose of the act is to require full disclosure about all material or important information through the filing of a registration statement. Note that fraud under this act does not require intent. A defense to this act is available to people other than the issuers of the securities. It is called the *due diligence defense* and is used when representatives of the issuers claim to have used due diligence to ascertain that the statements made by the issuers were true. *Escott v. Bar-Chris Construction Corp.* is a case in which this defense is used.

7. The federal act that applies to secondary purchases or sales of securities is the 1934 Act. The purpose of this act is to prevent deceptive practices or fraud. Note that intent is required as part of the burden of proof under this act and enormous fines may be assessed as the *Boesky* example illustrates.
   a. The trader must knowingly use material information which has not been disclosed to the public.
   b. The trader must have a fiduciary duty to the company.

8. One illegal activity under the 1933 act is insider trading which has the potential for enormous profits. Although corporate insiders are most likely to know confidential corporate information, insiders trading violations can apply to outsiders as well. Notice the importance of the fiduciary duty element in *In the Matter of Cady, Roberts & Co.* and *Dirks v. Securities and Exchange Commission*.

9. Both the 1933 and 1934 Acts inflict costs on businesses. With international securities markets gaining prominence, their less costly regulations may make them more desirable to American businesses. A second potential problem is the loss of influence of these American regulations.

MAJOR POINTS OF CASES

Miller v. Central Chinchilla Group, Inc. (p. 625)

The issue in this case is whether the contracts for the sale of chinchillas are investment contracts (securities) subject to the 1933 and 1934 federal securities laws.

The court held that they were. The plaintiffs had invested money in a common enterprise to earn profits. The investors were led to believe that their efforts were to be minimal and that the profits would come primarily from the defendant's efforts to secure additional investors. Thus, all three requirements for the applicability of security laws were present.

Escott v. BarChris Construction Corp. (p. 629)

This case focuses upon the due diligence defense to a charge of an antitrust violation under the 1933 act. This defense is available to any people associated with the initial issuance of stock, *except* the issuer.

In this case, three parties are accused of fraud. Each must establish due diligence.

The court discusses each party and his responsibility. The controller was responsible for his section of expertise and did not show due diligence in ascertaining whether that section or the accountant's section was correct. He is liable for fraud in both sections.

The outside director was found not liable on the accountant's section, as he reasonably believed it to be correct. However, he did not perform a reasonable investigation about the rest of the registration statement and did not establish due diligence for it.

The accountant was liable for the section written by him. He did not take some of the required accounting steps.

Note that because the firm was bankrupt and held no assets, creditors were eager to hold other parties liable.

In the Matter of Cady, Roberts & Co. (p. 639)

Gintel was a stockholder who was buying and selling Curtiss-Wright stock for his customers. Cowdin, a director of Curtiss-Wright, informed Gintel of the amount of a stock dividend to be paid by the company. The information had not yet been made public when Gintel acted on this information for the benefit of his customers and himself. He was accused of insider trading, but defended himself by stating he had a fiduciary duty to his clients.

The SEC found that Gintel had been guilty of insider trading. The rules against fraud in the 1934 Act use the phrase "any person." Although persons with confidential knowledge of corporate actions are generally those who are inside the corporation, "any person" includes outsiders as well. As to Gintel's fiduciary duty, the SEC held that he had a duty to Curtiss-Wright because of his relationship with Cowdin.

Dirks v. Securities and Exchange Commission (p. 641)

This case is a further attempt by the Court to define liability for inside information. The question in this case is whether all people receiving inside information are barred from acting upon it. The court held that they are not.

Dirks was a stock analyst for institutional investors. Neither he nor his company traded shares in Equity Funding. When he received a tip that Equity Funding's assets were overvalued because of corporate fraud, he investigated. Upon finding this charge to be true, Dirks disclosed his finding to clients and other investors. The SEC conducted a hearing on Dirks's behavior and found that as a tipper, he should have either publicly disclosed the information or refrained from trading. Dirks was censured by the SEC. He appealed to the Court of Appeals who entered judgment against him. Dirks then appealed to the Supreme Court.

The court stated that a duty to disclose stems from the relationship between parties. If a tipper receives the tip from one who has breached a fiduciary relationship with the corporation, the tipper assumes the same duty and cannot act on this inside information. Whether the tip is a breach of the insider's fiduciary duty depends on whether the insider will personally benefit.

In this case neither the insider who tipped Dirks, nor Dirks himself gained personally from the tip. Their only desire was to expose the fraud. Therefore Dirks had no duty to refrain from using the inside information.

SELF-TEST QUESTIONS

True/False

_____ 1.   Securities laws primarily protect big business, since few individuals invest directly or indirectly in the stock market. (p. 622)

_____ 2.   The 1933 act and the 1934 act were created because the blue sky laws were generally ineffective. (p. 623)

_____ 3.   One result of the securities laws is a higher standard of ethics in buying and selling securities. (pp. 624-625)

_____ 4.   A scheme to sell self-improvement lessons would not be considered a security under either the 1933 act or the 1934 act. (p. 625)

_____ 5.   The term *securities*, as used in the 1933 and 1934 acts, has been defined by the courts to include only stocks, bonds, and other traditional investments. (p. 625)

_____ 6.   The primary focus of the full disclosure policy is building investor confidence in the marketplace. (p. 626)

_____ 7.   The major purpose for registration under the 1933 act is to allow the SEC to judge the soundness of a proposed investment. (p. 627)

_____ 8.   The prospectus is a written summary of the registration statement which is viewed only by the SEC. (p. 627)

_____ 9.   Any misstatement of fact is fraud under the 1933 act, but not under the 1934 act. (pp. 627-628)

_____ 10.   The due diligence defense applies the standard of reasonable care of a prudent person. (p. 628)

_____ 11. The standard of reasonableness imposed by the due diligence defense is the amount of care required of a prudent person in the management of his or her own property. (p. 628)

_____ 12. The Act of 1934 is the key statute concerning insider trading. (p. 635)

_____ 13. Section 10(b) of the 1934 act makes it unlawful to use deception in connection with the sale of securities. (p. 635)

_____ 14. Only officers, directors, or employees of the issuing corporation are subject to the insider trading restrictions of Section 10 and Rule 10b-5 of the 1934 act. (p. 636)

_____ 15. A call option is a requirement to report anyone suspected of insider trading to the SEC. (p. 637)

Multiple Choice

1. The issuance, purchase, and sale of securities is subject to strict federal governmental regulations because:
   a. the majority of American investors are direct investors.
   b. most securities are privately traded.
   c. there are no state regulatory laws.
   d. it is a major source of private capital for business.
   (p. 622)

2. One major purpose of the federal securities laws is:
   a. to protect investors from worthless investments.
   b. to protect investors from unfair and manipulative practices.
   c. to provide insurance against large and unexpected fluctuations in the securities markets.
   d. to provide government approval of securities that are considered safe investments. (p. 624)

3. Which of the following is part of the Supreme Court test to determine if the investment is covered by securities laws?
   a. Whether there is fraud involved.
   b. Whether there is a common enterprise.
   c. Whether the investors are led to believe there will be a quick return on their investment.
   d. Whether profits arise primarily from the action of the investors.
   (p. 625)

4. Which of the following is *not* true concerning the 1933 Act?
   a. It deals with initial issuance of securities.
   b. Only governmental securities are exempt.
   c. It is also known as the truth-in-securities act.
   d. The filings must be registered with the Securities and Exchange Commission.

   (pp. 626-627)

5. MNO, Inc., wishes to raise additional capital in order to expand its plant and equipment. It would like to issue new securities as simply as possible without the need to register them under the 1933 act. MNO, Inc., could accomplish this through:
   a. the sale of common stock to the public.
   b. the sale of debentures to the public.
   c. the sale of common stock to a pension fund.
   d. none of the above (all new issues must be registered).

   (pp. 626-628)

6. Critics of the 1933 Act allege:
   a. the cost of preparing and filing exceeds the benefit to the public.
   b. the public can receive the information elsewhere.
   c. most investors don't need the information required under the Act.
   d. all of the above.

   (p. 627)

7. Fraud under the 1933 Act:
   a. is a more narrow concept than the general legal concept.
   b. only applies to material statements.
   c. allows the holder of the security to bring a legal action against the SEC.
   d. limits the liability to only the issues of the securities.

   (pp. 627-628)

8. In the *Escott* case, all four people listed below were found liable for fraud. Which one could *not* attempt to avoid liability under the due diligence defense?
   a. The issuer of the stock.
   b. The controller who was unaware of some of the inaccuracies, but who signed the registration statement.
   c. The outside director who became a board member on the eve of the financing.
   d. The young accountant who did not live up to the standards of the accounting profession.

   (pp. 629-635)

9. The primary focus of the 1934 Act:
   a. is upon secondary purchases of securities.
   b. established the SEC.
   c. abolished blue sky laws.
   d. originally was intended to create a system of insurance to protect bad investments.

   (p. 635)

10. Both the 1933 and 1934 acts contain provisions concerning fraud in securities transactions. Which of the following statements concerning these provisions is correct?
   a. Scienter is required for a violation of the 1934 act.
   b. Scienter is required for a violation of the 1933 act.
   c. Scienter is required for a violation of either the 1933 act or the 1934 act.
   d. Negligence, but not scienter, is required for a violation of either the 1933 act or the 1934 act. (p. 635)

11. Insider trading:
   a. applies only to those having special knowledge and employed by the corporation in question.
   b. applies to any corporate material which is unknown to the public.
   c. requires persons having inside knowledge to refrain from ever trading upon this knowledge.
   d. has recently been the subject of legislation which greatly enhanced the penalties. (pp. 636-639)

12. Which of the following activities is *least* likely to violate Section 10 and Rule 10b-5 of the 1934 act?
   a. A director who knows that earnings will be lower than expected for the quarter and who sells shares of stock in the corporation.
   b. A close friend of the company's president who learns from the president that the company has made a major technological breakthrough and purchases shares of the corporation's stock.
   c. A securities analyst who learns that a corporation is planning to enter a new market and passes the information on to investors who purchase the corporation's stock.
   d. A financial writer who owns a large number of shares who writes an overly favorable article on the company and then sells his shares at a profit. (pp. 636-639)

13. *In the Matter of Cady, Roberts & Co.*, which dealt with a broker who was accused of acting upon inside information, the court held.:
   a. since the broker was self-employed, he could not be guilty of inside information.
   b. the broker would have breached his fiduciary duty to his clients if he had not given them the inside information.
   c. he had a duty to reveal this knowledge to the public at large.
   d. his principal was also liable because the broker acted within the scope of his employment. (pp. 639-641)

14. In the *Dirks* case which dealt with the broker who exposed a fraud, the court held:
   a. he should have publicly disclosed the information because he held stock in the corporation.
   b. he should have publicly disclosed the information because he had a seat on the stock exchange.
   c. he need not have publicly disclosed the information because he personally did not benefit.
   d. he need not have publicly disclosed the information because he did not illegally obtain it. (pp. 641-643)

15. Which is *not* true about the fact that there are major foreign securities markets vying for business?
    a. These operations without securities regulations are becoming more attractive to American businesses.
    b. These markets impose new costs on American businesses.
    c. These markets strengthen the effectiveness of American securities regulations.
    d. These markets are formulating their own securities regulations based loosely on the 1933 and 1934 Acts. (p. 643)

Essay Question

1. What are the major differences between the 1933 and the 1934 Federal Securities Acts?

2. Discuss insider trading and the rationale for prohibiting it.

Chapter 23

Introduction to Antitrust

The antitrust laws in the country were a response to the big business trusts in the late 1880s. These laws have been amended and expanded so that they are still relevant in today's business world.

The major goal of the antitrust acts is to promote competition. This chapter provides an overview of the background and objectives of the major antitrust laws.

CHAPTER OBJECTIVES

After reading Chapter 23 of the text and studying the related materials in this chapter of the *Study Guide*, you will be able to fulfill the following objectives:

1. Understand the rationale and objectives of the antitrust acts.

2. Recognize the major antitrust acts.

3. Identify the parties who may bring suit and the remedies that each party may obtain.

4. Identify the groups exempted from the antitrust laws and the rationale for these exemptions.

MAJOR POINTS TO REMEMBER

What Is the Meaning of Antitrust?

1. A common meaning of *trust* is a property right held by a trustee to manage for the beneficiary of the trust. The antitrust laws are not directed at this type of trust. Historically businesses developed large trusts that were run by a single board of trustees. Antitrust laws were developed to eliminate these big business trusts by prohibiting attempts to monopolize or restrain trade.

Forces that Produced the Antitrust Laws

2. The antitrust movement was begun by populists, farmers, and small business owners. They believed in equal opportunity and were troubled by the great concentration of wealth in the hands of a few big-business owners. Mass production had accelerated the growth of big business and, in addition to creating trusts, some businessmen were attempting to eliminate competition by favoring some customers and forcing competitors out of business by price cutting or by exerting pressure on suppliers.

Objectives of the Antitrust Laws

3. Because the language is deliberately vague in many of the antitrust laws, the courts have interpreted the following as goals of the acts:

a. To further competition.
b. To provide for fair competition.
c. To encourage efficiency.
d. To limit the size of business.

Overview of the Major Federal Antitrust Laws

4. The major federal antitrust laws are:
   a. The Sherman Act (1890) -- This act prohibits any person or company from entering into any contract, combination, or conspiracy with others to restrain trade or control the market. It also prohibits monopolization or any attempt to create a monopoly.
   b. The Clayton Act (1914) -- This act prohibits price discrimination, sales that prohibit dealings with the seller's competitor, certain types of mergers, and interlocking corporate directorates.
   c. The Federal Trade Commission Act (1914) -- This act prohibits unfair methods of competition. In 1938, it was amended to include unfair or deceptive acts or practices as well. This act also established the Federal Trade Commission to implement and supervise compliance with the act.

Enforcement of the Antitrust Laws

5. There are three major enforcers of the antitrust laws:
   a. The Department of Justice -- The Antitrust Division is empowered to bring criminal or civil suits under the Sherman Act. It is empowered to bring civil suits under the Clayton Act.
   b. The Federal Trade Commission -- This administrative agency is empowered to bring civil suits against businesses under certain sections of the Clayton Act. Note that this overlaps with the power of the Justice Department. The Federal Trade Commission also has the exclusive power to enforce Section 5 of the Federal Trade Commission Act by bringing civil suits against businesses.
   c. Private parties -- Individuals may bring civil suits under the Sherman Act or under the Clayton Act. Private parties may recover treble damages, or three times their actual damages. Private parties can also sue in equity court for an injunction that may prohibit certain activities by the business. A private party may not institute a criminal suit.

   Often a private party refrains from suit until the government has sued. They do so because if the government is successful in its suit, private parties need not again prove violation but need only prove that they were injured.

   In addition to individual suits, private parties can use class actions if an entire class of people is injured by an action. Private parties can also avail themselves of a parens patriae action where state attorney generals sue on behalf of state citizens.

Remedies

6. Private actions result in the remedies of money damages or an injunction. Private parties will recover three times their actual damages plus court costs and reasonable attorney's fees.

7. Government actions by the Justice Department or the Federal Trade Commission may pursue two remedies:
   a. Equitable actions -- This is a control of future behavior by such actions as an injunction that requires a business to change its actions. For example, an injunction may require a business to sell a company that it acquired.
   b. Criminal sanctions -- These are punishments for wrongful behavior. They are discretionary; the government may choose to pursue a criminal action over a civil action in some cases. The punishment can be a fine or a prison term. Recently this charge was changed from a misdemeanor to a felony. Before the change it was common for the accused to enter a plea of nolo contendere, or no contest. Note that this is not an admission of guilt. The advantage of this plea was that it avoided costly trials and adverse publicity. Because the crimes are now considered felonies, many businesses no longer plead nolo contendere.

8. If the government sues a business under a civil action it will also receive three times its actual damages. A business may enter a consent decree. This is not an admission of wrongdoing; the business merely agrees to cease performing certain activities. In this way, the expense of a trial and adverse publicity are avoided.

Exemptions from the Antitrust Laws

9. Several groups are generally exempted from antitrust laws:
   a. Labor -- The rationale is that labor is not an article of commerce. However, activities between a labor union and an employee are not expressly exempt. *Powell v. National Football League* deals with this topic.
   b. Agricultural cooperatives -- The rationale is that farmers' economic plight in general should exempt them from this type of government regulation. If any one member of the cooperative is not a farmer, this exemption does not apply.
   c. State action exemption -- The rationale is that traditionally, states have been empowered to pass laws in the same area as the federal government if these laws do not conflict. Remember, under the concept of federalism, the federal law supersedes the state law. An example of the state action exemption is given in *Southern Motor Carriers Rate Conference, Inc. v. United States*.
   d. Regulated industries -- The rationale is that if an industry is regulated, with the intent that these regulations take the place of the antitrust laws, these businesses should be exempt. In other words, certain types of businesses have their own specific antitrust laws. This does not mean that all businesses regulated by the government are exempt.

Political Action

10. Although the antitrust laws are intended to further competition, businesses are entitled to freedom of speech. A business may request or lobby for special treatment by Congress or a state legislature. The *Noerr* case established the right of a business to lobby for favorable antilegislative legislation even though the passage of this legislation would injure competition. The rationale is that the Sherman Act was passed to regulate business, not political, actions.

11. An exception to the *Noerr* doctrine is the sham exception. This applies antitrust regulations to the attempts of a business which misuses legal processes in order to

directly harm a competitor such as by bringing a lawsuit against a competitor without probable cause. The *Noerr* doctrine is examined further in *Campbell v. City of Chicago*.

Price Discrimination

12. Section 2(a) of the Clayton Act, as amended by the Robinson-Patman Act, makes it illegal to discriminate in price if the following elements are present:
    a. A sale of goods.
    b. A sale in interstate commerce.
    c. Evidence that price discrimination existed between different purchasers at the same time.
    d. Goods of like grade and quality.
    e. An injury to competition.

13. The purpose of the Robinson-Patman Act is to prevent a seller from obtaining an unfair competitive advantage by discriminating in price among its customers. Critics of the Robinson-Patman Act contend that it conflicts with the antitrust ideal of reducing prices through competition. Although this may be true, the act endeavors to stop the concentrations of power in big business, which is another ideal of the antitrust laws.

MAJOR POINTS OF CASES

Powell v. National Football League (p. 659)

This case deals with whether the first refusal/compensation system provision of the National Football League still applied when no new contract had been agreed upon and when the parties were at an impasse.

In order to qualify for the labor exemption the contract must meet three criteria. First the restraint on trade must only affect those under the agreement. Second the rule in question must be a mandatory subject of collective bargaining. Third the agreement must be a result of arms length bargaining. All three of these criteria had been met in the recently expired Collective Bargaining Agreement. The trial court held that once the parties had reached an impasse, the nonstatutory labor exemption to antitrust law expires.

The appellate court reversed this decision on the grounds that the trial court's decision penalized one of the parties during a lawful stage of the collective bargaining process. This conflicts with federal labor laws. The First Refusal/Compensation system had been agreed upon in two previous contracts. The nonstatutory labor exemption extends beyond impasse.

Southern Motor Carriers Rate Conference,
Inc. v. United States (p. 662)

The issue in this case is whether the plaintiff is immune from antitrust laws because of the state action doctrine. There is a two-part test to determine when a state can regulate private parties. First, there must be state policy intended to regulate the private parties. Second, there must be active state supervision.

The Supreme Court found that both these tests were met in this case. Three of the four states involved expressly permit private motor common carriers to submit collective rates. The fourth state has shown its intent to do so by approving of the practice. In addition, all four

202

states actively supervised the rate-making activities. Therefore, the plaintiff was immune from the antitrust laws.

Campbell v. City of Chicago (p. 666)

The issue in this case was whether the Yellow Cab and Checker Taxi's lobbying which resulted in a city ordinance was passed which was immune from antitrust laws under the *Noerr* doctrine. This ordinance harmed their competitors.

The plaintiff argued that the lobbying effort should fall under the shown exception to the *Noerr* doctrine because it was really a ruse to interfere directly with the competitor's business.

The court held the lobbying efforts were protected under the *Noerr* doctrine because antitrust law does not apply to political actions such as lobbying. The decision which reduced competition did not come directly from the cab company, but by the City of Chicago.

SELF-TEST QUESTIONS

True/False

_____ 1.   The major purpose of the antitrust laws is to promote competition. (p. 646)

_____ 2.   Courts give great weight to the Populist goal of limitation on the size of business. (p. 651)

_____ 3.   The Sherman Act forbids restraints of trade and price discrimination. (p. 652)

_____ 4.   The antitrust laws are enforced both by the Department of Justice and the Federal Trade Commission. (p. 653)

_____ 5.   Once the government has successfully prosecuted a company for violation of the antitrust laws, no private action may follow.   (pp. 653-654)

_____ 6.   A parens patriae action is an antitrust suit brought by the attorney general of a state on behalf of the people of that state. (p. 654)

_____ 7.   The purpose of an equitable action under the antitrust laws is to control future behavior. (p. 656)

_____ 8.   Violations of the Sherman Act and the Clayton Act are subject to both civil and criminal sanctions. (p. 656)

_____ 9.   The law allows treble damages in suits by private parties not only to compensate the injured party, but also to punish the defendant. (p. 657)

_____ 10.   A consent decree can be used as a company's evidence of guilt by a private party bringing an antitrust suit. (pp. 657-658)

_____ 11.   Many labor union activities are exempt from antitrust laws because human labor is not considered a commodity. (p. 658)

_____ 12.   In general, the state action exemption allows states to pass statutes that result in legal restraint of trade. (p. 661)

_____ 13.   A business in a regulated industry cannot violate the federal antitrust laws as long as it is complying with the legitimate orders of its regulatory agency. (p. 663)

_____ 14.   The *Noerr* doctrine indicates that legitimate attempts to influence any branch of government are exempt from the antitrust laws. (pp. 664-665)

_____ 15.   One of the major purposes of the Robinson-Patman Act was to protect small businesses. (pp. 667-668)

Multiple Choice

1.   Which of the following was *not* one of the forces which led to the passage of antitrust legislation?
      a.   Concern over concentration of wealth.
      b.   Belief in laissez-faire economics.
      c.   The rights of individualism.
      d.   Expansion of the railway system.   (pp. 647-648)

2.   As a result of the vague language of the Sherman Act:
      a.   courts have had to rely heavily on legislative intent in order to interpret the act.
      b.   the language was interpreted in a more favorable fashion to small businesses.
      c.   showed Congressional intent to ensure vigorous enforcement.
      d.   forced the courts to develop a body of antitrust law.
                                                              (pp. 649-650)

3.   Monopolies and attempted monopolies are outlawed by the:
      a.   Sherman Act.
      b.   Clayton Act.
      c.   FTC Act.
      d.   Robinson-Patman Act.   (pp. 652-653)

4.   Unfair methods of competition are prohibited by the:
      a.   Sherman Act.
      b.   Clayton Act.
      c.   FTC Act.
      d.   Robinson-Patman Act.   (pp. 652-653)

5.   The Antitrust Division of the Justice Department has broad enforcement powers under the antitrust laws; however, it *cannot* enforce:
      a.   the criminal provision of the Sherman Act.
      b.   the civil provisions of the Sherman Act.
      c.   the Clayton Act.
      d.   the FTC Act.   (p. 653)

6. Acme Corp. is suing Wonder Widgets, Inc. for treble damages under the Sherman Act. Wonder has already been found guilty of the same violation in a criminal proceeding brought by the United States. In order to win its case, Acme Corp. must prove:
   a. a violation, injury, and the extent of its damages.
   b. only injury and the extent of its damages.
   c. only injury.
   d. only the extent of its damages.   (pp. 653-654)

7. A plea of nolo contendere to charges brought by the Justice Department is often considered advantageous because:
   a. it may not be used as prima facie evidence of liability in a subsequent private civil suit.
   b. it completely bars a subsequent private civil suit for treble damages.
   c. it will limit the punishment of an individual defendant to a fine rather than a prison sentence.
   d. it significantly reduces the penalty that the judge can impose upon the corporate defendant.   (pp. 656-657)

8. Which of the following statements concerning consent decrees is correct?
   a. A consent decree is a technical admission of wrongdoing and liability.
   b. A consent decree can only be entered into before the case goes to trial.
   c. A consent decree cannot be used as proof of an antitrust violation in a subsequent suit for damages.
   d. A consent decree does not require court approval.
                                                                    (pp. 657-658)

9. In the *Powell* case where the football players challenged the first refusal/compensation system provision, the court held:
   a. the labor exemption did not apply because the old contract had expired.
   b. the labor exemption did apply because it goes beyond an impasse stage in collective bargaining.
   c. the labor exemption would apply only if the parties came to an agreement within a reasonable time.
   d. sports teams are not considered labor under the original intent of antitrust law.   (pp. 659-660)

10. Agricultural cooperatives are exempted from antitrust law because:
    a. Congress wanted to originally restrain mainly big trusts.
    b. farmers are not considered businesspersons.
    c. farmers do not deal with large businesses.
    d. all of the above.   (pp. 660-661)

11. The state action exemption to antitrust laws exist because:
    a. the purpose of the antitrust laws is to restrain individual action.
    b. the purpose of the antitrust laws is to restrain state action.
    c. the federal government is sovereign to the state government.
    d. both b and c.   (p. 661)

12. The *Noerr* doctrine allows businesses to attempt to influence governmental activities unless:
   a. the public interest is harmed.
   b. they ask for special treatment.
   c. they institute bad faith lawsuits against competitors.
   d. they directly or indirectly harm competitors.   (pp. 664-665)

13. A company's actions in attempting to influence government action violate the antitrust laws:
   a. when it seeks anticompetitive legislation of value only to its own business.
   b. when it seeks anticompetitive legislation that is actually harmful to its competitors.
   c. when it seeks judicial, legislative, or administrative relief with actual anticompetitive intent.
   d. when it seeks judicial, legislative, or administrative relief in bad faith as a mere sham to cover up an attempt to actively harm a competitor.   (pp. 664-666)

14. In the *Campbell* case, where the cab companies lobbied to have an ordinance passed in their favor, the court held this action:
   a. violated antitrust law because it resulted in unfair competition.
   b. violated antitrust law because it was merely a sham.
   c. did not violate antitrust law because the cab companies have a right to pursue political action on their behalf.
   d. did not violate antitrust law because antitrust law only covers federal and state, not municipal, law.   (p. 666)

15. The Robinson-Patman Act:
   a. prohibits all price discrimination.
   b. covers only sales of tangible and intangible property.
   c. only applies to interstate commerce.
   d. repealed some earlier antitrust laws which conflicted with it.
                                                                        (pp. 667-668)

Essay Questions

1. What three parties can bring actions to enforce federal antitrust laws? What remedies does each have?

2. What is the *Noerr* doctrine? What are the exceptions to it, if any?

Chapter 24

Antitrust Law

There are three important acts that promote the antitrust goal of protecting and furthering competition. These are the Sherman Act, the Clayton Act, and the Federal Trade Commission Act.

This chapter discusses each act and its major impact upon business. Each act is deliberately vague, and the courts have been called on to define some of their terminology. Significant court decisions are reviewed.

CHAPTER OBJECTIVES

After reading Chapter 24 of the text and studying the related materials in this chapter of the *Study Guide*, you will be able to fulfill the following objectives:

1. Understand the concept of a monopoly and the relevant tests used by the courts in determining the legality of monopolies.

2. Understand the concept of restraint of trade and the relevant tests used by the courts in determining the legality of such restraints.

3. Define the Per Se Rule and recognize per se violations, including:
   a. Horizontal Market Divisions.
   b. Price fixing.
   c. Retail price maintenance.
   d. Group boycotts.
   e. Tying contracts.

4. Understand the concept of unfair or deceptive acts under the Federal Trade Commission Act.

5. Understand the concept of the different types of mergers and the relevant tests used by the courts in determining their legality.

MAJOR POINTS TO REMEMBER

Monopolies

1. A *monopoly* is the attempt of a firm to control prices or exclude competition in a particular geographic and product market. Certain monopolies are violations of Section 2 of the Sherman Act. To determine the anticompetitive effects, courts consider the geographic and product markets of the firm in question. If a firm is not in a position to influence prices or exclude competition, the firm has not unlawfully monopolized a market.

2. Some monopolies are excluded from the sanctions of the antitrust laws. Utilities, holders of copyrights and patents, and unique products are examples.

3. *Standard Oil*, an early antitrust case, set forth two elements for liability under the Sherman Act. The first is that the company must have acted maliciously in acquiring the monopoly. This element has been discarded by modern courts. The second element in the Standard Oil case is still followed today. It is the element of unreasonableness. This is known as the Rule of Reason which states that only unreasonable restraints of trade and unreasonable attempts to monopolize violate the Sherman Act. Courts look to the relevant product market and the relevant geographic market to determine reasonableness.

4. *Alcoa*, a second historic case, established the thrust upon defense. This applies if a company has a monopoly through no action of its own, but by the actions of other businesses in the relevant product and geographic markets. If a monopoly is thrust upon a company in this way, there is no violation of the Sherman Act. Note the football monopoly example.

5. Determining the relevant product market has proved difficult for the courts. In response to this difficulty, the Supreme Court defined *relevant product market* as all products "reasonably interchangeable." Note that by this broadening of the definition, fewer firms would be liable under Section 2 of the Sherman Act. In addition, the geographic market is usually interpreted by the courts as the nation. *Flip Side Productions, Inc. v. Jam Productions, Inc.* gives an example of an analysis of the geographic market.

6. The test for monopoly power was further expanded by the Supreme Court in a holding that announced a two-part test:
   a. The firm must possess monopoly power in the relevant market.
   b. The firm must have willfully acquired the monopoly, as opposed to arriving at a monopoly by accidental growth. The modern trend is to permit aggressive competition based on efficiency. *Aspen Skiing Co. v. Aspen Highlands Skiing Corp.* discusses this point.

Attempts to Monopolize

7. Section 2 of the Sherman Act also makes attempts to monopolize illegal. Courts require proof of an intent to monopolize to establish an unlawful attempt to monopolize.

Restraint of Trade

8. Section 1 of the Sherman Act makes restraint of trade illegal. It must be proved that there is a contract, combination, or conspiracy that results in an unreasonable restraint or interference with trade.

9. The traditional interpretation of Section 1 by the courts was that all restraints of trade are illegal. The modern approach is to follow the rule of reason doctrine and declare only unreasonable restraints of trade illegal. Under the Per Se Rule some restraints of trade are held to be per se, or automatically, unreasonable. They are:
   a. Horizontal Market Division.

     b.   Price fixing.

     c.   Some retail price maintenance agreements.

     d.   Group boycotts.

     e.   Tying contracts.

10. An example of a per se violation is a horizontal market division which is an agreement between competitors at the same level of the market to divide up territories to limit competition. *Palmer v. BRG of Georgia, Inc.* is a case in point.

11. Price fixing occurs when a firm enters into a contract, a combination (association), or a conspiracy (agreement) with one or more firms to set prices. Even setting a maximum price at which a product may be sold is illegal. *United States v. Socony-Vacuum Oil Co.* is a case which raises the question of the liability of those who attempt to set prices but who lack the actual power to do so. Note that in most cases, the defense of price fixing to combat ruinous competition has been rejected by the courts.

12. If a Section 1 price-fixing case is not per se illegal, courts analyze it under the Rule of Reason. The courts look to the purposes of the restraint of trade and determine whether the same results could be bought about in a way that does not impair competition. If so, the firm has violated Section 1 by not using the available alternative.

Resale Price Maintenance

13. A second category of per se violation under Section 1 of the Sherman Act is resale price maintenance. This is an agreement between parties in which the first party, selling to the second party, requires the second party to resell at a certain price. Courts have held some of these vertical price-fixing requirements illegal:

     a.   Manufacturer-customer -- When a manufacturer requires a customer to resell at a certain price, the courts hold this to be illegal.

     b.   Lessor-lessee -- When an owner of a business requires that the person leasing the business to resell at a certain price, the courts hold this to be illegal.

     c.   Patent holder-agent -- When a holder of a patent requires his or her agent to resell at a certain price, the courts hold this to be illegal.

The evolving doctrine is discussed in *California Retail Liquor Dealers Association v. Midcal Aluminum, Inc.*

14. At one time attempts by firms to control resale prices were legal if states had passed a law permitting fair trade agreements that set resale prices for all customers. This exemption was later repealed. Firms may still use the Colgate doctrine, which provides that manufacturers may announce to all customers that they will not sell to retailers who resell at a price different from the one that the manufacturer has set.

Group Boycotts

15. A third category of per se violation under Section 1 of the Sherman Act is group boycotts. A single business may decline to do business with a party, but businesses acting together cannot boycott a party or parties. It is also illegal for businesses to act together and demand that others not deal with a certain party or parties.

Tying Contracts

16. A fourth category of per se violation under Sections 1 and 3 of the Sherman Act is a tying contract. In this type of contract, a merchant agrees to sell certain goods to the buyer only if he or she agrees to purchase other goods as well. The following elements have been held to be necessary for an illegal tying contract:
    a. The seller must possess economic power over the tying product.
    b. A substantial amount of commerce in the tied product must be involved. This is the issue in *Baxley-DeLamar Monuments v. American Cemetery Association*.
    Note that there is also a defense of protecting the goodwill of the tying product or that the tying product is unique.

Section 5 of the Federal Trade Commission Act

17. The Federal Trade Commission is empowered to declare invalid certain other trade practices. Section 5 of the Federal Trade Commission Act declares "unfair methods of competition" to be illegal. The Wheeler-Lea Amendment later expanded this to include "unfair or deceptive acts or practices in commerce."

18. Only the Federal Trade Commission is empowered to enforce Section 5. It has the power to issue cease and desist orders, conduct administrative hearings, and issue trade regulations.

Mergers

19. A *merger* is the joining together of two companies in which one company becomes absorbed in the other and ceases to exist as a separate entity. There are three types of mergers. A *horizontal merger* is a joining of two companies that previously competed with each other. A *vertical merger* is a joining of two companies that previously had a supplier-customer relationship. All other types of mergers are *conglomerate mergers*.

20. The Clayton Act was enacted in response to public concern that the economic power of a few big businesses might seriously undermine democracy. Section 7 of the Clayton Act is designed to forbid horizontal and vertical mergers if they may substantially lessen competition or tend to create a monopoly. This law applies to acquisitions of a business through purchases of stock or the assets of a business.

21. In determining whether Section 7 of the Clayton Act is to be applied, courts use the relevant product market test and the relevant geographic market test. After the amendment of the act, courts began to consider other factors in regard to horizontal and vertical mergers. These factors include:
    a. Ease of entry into the market.
    b. Relative vigor of other firms.
    c. Peculiar characteristics of each firm.
    d. Demand for the industry's products.

MAJOR POINTS OF CASES

Flip Side Productions, Inc. v.
Jam Productions, Inc. (p. 676)

The issue in this case was whether the defendant's exclusive leasing of the Horizen facilities for music concerts violated the Sherman Act.

The court held that it did not. In the greater Chicago area, there were other arenas suitable for musical concerts competing for business. Thus the Horizen was not an "essential facility" for the plaintiffs and they failed to establish an antitrust injury.

Aspen Skiing Co. v. Aspen Highlands
Skiing Corp. (p. 677)

In 1962, skiers could purchase a special all-Aspen ticket that allowed them to ski in any of the resorts. Ski Co., the owners of one of the resorts, purchased a second resort in 1964 and opened a third in 1967. At that time, Ski Co. discontinued selling the all-Aspen ticket, promoted its own three-area ticket, and refused to sell the other resort lift tickets for the all-Aspen ticket. Highlands, the only other competitor, sued, claiming a violation of the Sherman Act.

The Supreme Court upheld the lower court's judgment that Ski Co. had violated Section 2 of the Sherman Act. The elements under this act are that a monopoly has been established and that exclusionary means are being used to hinder competition. Ski Co. did not contest the first element. As to the second, the Supreme Court found that consumers were adversely affected by the loss of the four-area ticket. In addition, Ski Co. was losing money, and so there was no justifiable business practice in refusing to cooperate with Highlands. In fact, the major purpose seemed to be to reduce competition.

Palmer v. BRG of Georgia, Inc. (p. 683)

HBJ, the country's largest provider of bar review courses, and BRG entered into an agreement whereby HBJ allowed BRG to run bar reviews under the HBJ trade name in the state of Georgia. In return, BRG agreed not to run bar review courses in other parts of the country. Palmer sued claiming this agreement raised the price of the BRG bar exam and that the agreement was a *per se* violation of Section 1 of the Sherman Act.

The Supreme Court held for the plaintiff. Referring to an earlier case the Court reiterated its ruling that competitors who had not previously competed in a certain area could not make agreements not to allocate territories. In this case, the ruling was extended to include competitors like HBJ and BRG who had previously competed.

United States v. Socony-Vacuum Oil Co. (p. 684)

This case focuses upon the question of whether a combination or conspiracy that set reasonable prices in order to avoid ruinous competition violated the Sherman Act. The Court held that it did.

The Court stated that the Sherman Act prohibits price fixing. It is illegal per se and the purpose and the amount of the price fixing are immaterial.

California Retail Liquor Dealers
Association v. Midcal Aluminum, Inc. (p. 690)

There are several issues involved in this case. The first is whether retailers may sell wine below a stipulated price in the region. The court held that they may. The Miller-Tydings Act had allowed resale price maintenance by the states; this act has been repealed.

The second issue is whether the state involvement in this case is enough for this activity to come within the state action exemption. The Court held that it was not. California met the first requirement by providing a clear purpose for the resale price maintenance. However, the state did not fulfill the second requirement because it did not supervise the enactment.

Baxley-DeLamar Monuments v.
American Cemetery Association (p. 696)

Baxley-DeLamar alleged that American Cemetery Association members conspired to tie the sale of grave lots with the purchase and installation of grave memorials. The district court allowed a motion to dismiss since only 57% of the market was controlled. Baxley-DeLamar appealed.

The appellate court held that the lower court had erred in granting the motion to dismiss. Economic power over the tying product may be established either by market share or the uniqueness of the product. All land is considered unique under the law and this is especially true of cemetery lots since oftentimes family members want to be buried together. The combination of market share and uniqueness in this case show the economic power of the defendants.

SELF-TEST QUESTIONS

True/False

____ 1. All companies that have monopolistic power within a given geographic and product market are in violation of the Sherman Act. (pp. 671-672)

____ 2. In determining the relevant product market, the court will consider the availability of reasonably interchangeable products. (pp. 674-675)

____ 3. In monopoly cases, the defendant is accused of interfering with free trade. (pp. 679-680)

____ 4. Because the word unreasonable is present in the Sherman Act, the court developed the Rule of Reason test. (pp. 681-682)

____ 5. The Per Se Rule outlaws business behavior without looking at the effects of a business's conduct. (p. 682)

____ 6. Price fixing is not a violation of the Sherman Act unless the defendant has a large share of market power. (p. 684)

____ 7. An agreement between competitors that merely attempts to stabilize prices is permissible under the Sherman Act. (p. 684)

_____ 8.   Resale price maintenance is a form of vertical price fixing.
            (p. 688)

_____ 9.   One defense to price fixing is the protection of dealers from price cutters.
            (p. 691)

_____ 10.   Courts are generally quite willing to accept an increased dealer service theory as
            a valid defense to an otherwise illegal vertical price-fixing agreement. (p. 692)

_____ 11.   Although it is clearly illegal for businesses to agree not to deal with a particular
            party, they may collectively demand that others not deal with a party without
            violating the antitrust laws. (pp. 692-693)

_____ 12.   Group boycotts are illegal per se. (pp. 693-694)

_____ 13.   In order for a tying agreement to be illegal, the plaintiff must prove that the
            defendant has economic power over the tying product and that a substantial
            amount of commerce in the tied product is involved.   (pp. 694-695)

_____ 14.   The FTC has the power to invalidate trade practices that conflict with the basic
            policies of the Sherman and Clayton Acts even though the practices do not
            actually violate these laws. (p. 697)

_____ 15.   A conglomerate merger is one in which neither competitors nor a customer and
            a supplier are involved. (p. 698)

Multiple Choice

1. Roger's Red Hots operates the only hot-dog concession at a large, metropolitan sports
    complex. Other concessions sell popcorn, candy, and cold drinks, and there are
    numerous fast-food outlets within several blocks of the complex. Roger's is most likely
    to be considered a monopoly if:
    a.   the geographic market is defined as the sports complex and the product market
          is defined as sandwiches.
    b.   the geographic market is defined as the sports complex and the product market
          is defined as fast foods and snacks.
    c.   the geographic market is defined as the neighborhood and the product market is
          defined as sandwiches.
    d.   the geographic market is defined as the neighborhood and the product market is
          defined as fast foods and snacks.   (pp. 671-672)

2. In order for a firm to be guilty of having an illegal monopoly, it must:
    a.   actually have engaged in improper or wrongful acts.
    b.   have a very large share of the relevant product and geographic markets.
    c.   willfully have acquired the monopoly.
    d.   both b and c.   (pp. 671-672)

3. In the *Aspen* case, where Ski Co. was accused of violating the Sherman Act, the Court held that Ski Co. was guilty because:
   a. it excluded a rival for efficiency reasons.
   b. it has a general duty to engage in a joint marketing program with competitors.
   c. it adversely affected consumers.
   d. any major change in the characters of the market is a violation of the Sherman Act. (pp. 677-679)

4. To be in violation of an attempt to monopolize, a business must be found guilty of all the following, *except*:
   a. a significant market share.
   b. interference with free trade.
   c. an intent to monopolize.
   d. engaging in conduct likely to lead to a monopoly. (pp. 679-680)

5. In judging a restraint of trade case, the court looks carefully at:
   a. geographic markets.
   b. product markets.
   c. unreasonable restraints to trade.
   d. all of the above. (pp. 680-681)

6. The Per Se Rule:
   a. outlaws clear cut violations of the Sherman Act.
   b. examines whether certain actions have an unreasonable effect on competition.
   c. considers the intent of the business.
   d. created exceptions to the Sherman Act for restraints which are beneficial to the public. (p. 682)

7. An allegation of price fixing can be defended by:
   a. the reasonable price defense.
   b. the lack of market power defense.
   c. the ruinous competition defense.
   d. none of the above. (pp. 684-686)

8. Midget Motors, Inc., and Zoom-Zoom Car Co., two manufacturers of toy racing cars, have been charged with price fixing under Section 1 of the Sherman Act. In such a case, their best defense would be to argue that:
   a. they had no agreement to set prices.
   b. the prices set were reasonable.
   c. the agreement actually enhanced competition.
   d. they lacked sufficient market power to fix prices.
   (pp. 684-686)

9. Which of the following vertical price-fixing agreements is *most* likely to be per se illegal?
   a. A manufacturer sets up its own retail outlets and specifies minimum retail prices.
   b. The owner of a business requires a lessee to resell a product at a set price.
   c. A manufacturer requires a wholesaler to sell at a set price.
   d. A patent holder requires his agents to sell his product above the set minimum price. (pp. 688-689)

214

10. In the *California Retail Dealers* case which dealt with the selling of wine below a stipulated price, the Court held the *California* plan:
    a.   violated the Sherman Act.
    b.   had established antitrust immunity because it had state supervision.
    c.   had established antitrust immunity because it was beneficial to consumers.
    d.   had established antitrust immunity because it did not adversely affect competitors. (pp. 690-691)

11. The *Colgate* doctrine:
    a.   greatly influenced antitrust decisions historically but has been overruled today.
    b.   was enacted during the depression to set new economic measures.
    c.   created an exception to the resale price maintenance rule.
    d.   can only be applied when a business is selling directly to consumers. (pp. 692-693)

12. Group boycotts involve two or more businesses which act in concert and agree to:
    a.   sell their goods in certain geographic areas only.
    b.   refuse to deal with certain businesses.
    c.   deprive competitors of a needed resource.
    d.   b and c. (pp. 693-694)

13. In the *Baxley-DeLamar* case where the trial court held the defendant did not have enough economic power for an unlawful tying conspiracy, the appellate court held:
    a.   the size of the market share was irrelevant because a conspiracy between a large number of companies was present.
    b.   a 57% market share does not demonstrate serious economic power.
    c.   the size of the market share along with the uniqueness of the product gave it sufficient market power for an unlawful tying conspiracy.
    d.   the issue the trial court should have addressed is whether the defendant dealt fraudulently with those in mourning. (pp. 696-697)

14. Goody Gadgets Distribution Corporation sells various types of kitchen tools and gadgets. It is acquiring Three Minute, Inc., a small manufacturer of egg timers. The combination is an example of:
    a.   a horizontal merger.
    b.   a vertical merger.
    c.   a conglomerate merger.
    d.   an unclassified merger. (p. 698)

15. Section 7 of the Clayton Act is the primary source of law in the area of mergers. This section was clarified by the Celler-Kefauver Amendment, which:
    a.   defined the point at which a merger has an anticompetitive effect.
    b.   limited application of the section to horizontal mergers.
    c.   extended the section to cover asset acquisitions as well as stock acquisitions.
    d.   limited the section to mergers with a probable anticompetitive effect. (pp. 698-699)

Essay Questions

1. Why did the legislature write the Sherman, Clayton, and Federal Trade Commission Acts in such vague language?

2. Distinguish between the Rule of Reason and Per Se violations as they apply to antitrust law.

Chapter 25

The International Legal Environment of Business

This chapter presents an overview of the international legal environment in which companies that are importers and exporters must function.

The first section of the chapter discusses international agreements dealing with documentary credits, GATT, and tariffs. The second section focuses upon contract clauses, government immunities, and the different options for developing a sales organization abroad.

CHAPTER OBJECTIVES

After reading Chapter 25 of the text and studying the related materials of this chapter of the *Study Guide*, you will be able to fulfill the following objectives:

1. Understand the purposes of the major agreements between countries:
   a. Documentary credits
   b. GATT
   c. Domestic content laws

2. Understand the contractual protections that a company may have when dealing with a foreign company.

3. Understand the problems that a company may have with government immunity of a foreign country.

4. Describe the options of a company that wishes to develop a sales organization abroad.

MAJOR POINTS TO REMEMBER

Problems Associated with Selling Goods in an International Environment

1. A major agreement among banks in 156 countries is the Uniform Customs and Practices for Documentary Credits. A *documentary credit* is a conditional bank payment instrument. The buyer of goods requests his or her bank to pay the seller or seller's bank when certain conditions are met. These conditions are the bank's receipt of certain documents relating to the goods, such as a transport document or an insurance certificate. The bank then pays on demand or at some specified future time.

2. Documentary credits offer both the buyer and the seller convenience because each deals with his or her local bank. In addition, both the buyer and seller have the security that the goods will conform and the payment will be made. *Sztejn v. J. Henry Schroder Banking Corporation* deals with documentary credits.

3. A second major agreement in international law is the General Agreement on Tariffs and Trade (GATT). Ninety countries are members of this organization and have agreed to trade with each other on the same terms. GATT regulates trade by monitoring thousands of products. The purpose of GATT is to reduce tariffs and nontariff trade barriers.

4. There are two types of tariffs or import duties. The first are specific tariffs, which are assessed in monetary units per the quality of goods. The second are ad valorem tariffs which are assessed by multiplying a certain percentage times the value of the goods. *James S. Baker (Imports) v. United States* illustrates the importance of certain classifications.

5. Currently, nontariff trade barriers are the main obstacle to free trade. Examples of NTBs are:
    a. Quota--Only a certain amount of a good is allowed to enter a certain country during a certain period.
    b. Domestic content laws--Require that a certain percentage of a good's value be produced in the domestic economy.
    c. Voluntary restraint agreements--Informal, nonbinding controls on a foreign producer.
    d. Direct investment restriction--Requirement that a portion of a business be domestically owned or the exclusion of foreigners from certain industries.

Activities by American Companies
Overseas

6. In international contracts, the parties often insert a choice of law clause to determine the country whose law will govern the contract. A choice of forum clause determines the location of the court or the arbitration proceeding. Note the contrast between the American practice of detailed contracts and the Asian practice of vague contracts. Note also the problems which arise with the complexity of language, even among people from different English speaking countries.

7. Another type of clause common in international contracts is an arbitration clause. This specifies that any disputes relating to the contract will be settled out of court by an arbitrator. These clauses should be carefully drafted to include specifics so that there won't be litigation about the meaning of the arbitration clause. Courts worldwide usually enforce arbitration clauses, as evidenced in *Mitsubishi Motors Corporation v. Soler Chrysler-Plymouth, Inc.*

8. Joint ventures often take a corporate form and carry on one-time projects, ongoing enterprises, or high-risk projects. Each partner in the joint venture has attributes that assist the other. For example, in a less developed country, the foreign partner may have the expertise and the local partner may have the raw materials. Control is a major issue in these ventures.

9.   Obtaining U.S. jurisdiction over foreign governments and their agents is sometimes difficult. The Sovereign Immunity Doctrine gave foreign countries complete immunity. The Foreign Sovereign Immunities Act (FSIA) modified this doctrine by distinguishing between government acts and private or commercial acts. Under the FSIA, only government acts are immune, as in the Mexicana air crash example, unless one of the following exceptions applies:

    a.   The government gives an express or implied waiver of immunity.

    b.   The government engages in commercial activities that either occur in the U.S. or have a direct impact on the U.S. The issue of direct impact is explored in *Martin v. Republic of South Africa*.

    c.   The government takes property rights in violation of international law. The property, or that taken in exchange for the property, is either present in the U.S. in connection with a commercial activity, or the property is owned or operated by an agency of the foreign country engaged in a commercial activity with the U.S.

    Note that obtaining jurisdiction does not mean that the plaintiff can easily receive money damages because a foreign country is generally immune from court-ordered attachments and executions.

10.   The Act of State Doctrine originally granted total immunity to acts of foreign government. Today it is a defense to a foreign government's action against a foreign investor if the action is in the public interest. An exception to this rule is a commercial obligation. *International Association of Machinists v. OPEC* focuses on the Act of State Doctrine.

11.   Sometimes the president of the United States will engage in the settlement of disputes to prevent political tensions with foreign countries. Often a country's religious beliefs and cultures come into play. *United States v. Alavarez-Machain* is a case where the court dealt with a treaty made by the president.

Developing a Sales Organization Abroad

12.   American firms that wish to sell goods abroad have several options. They can have a branch office or plant, traveling sales representatives, or foreign distributors. To avoid taxes as a "permanent establishment," many American firms use agents and/or distributors. Note that agents receive higher protection from foreign governments but pose higher risks. Therefore, any agency agreement should be carefully drafted.

13.   American firms also can license the use of their processes. However, the exporting of certain technologies or know-how is restricted by the U.S. government. Antitrust issues are also involved in licensing arrangements.

MAJOR POINTS OF CASES

Sztejn v. J. Henry Schroder Banking Corporation (p. 708)

This case raises the question of whether a bank can be held liable for payment on an irrevocable letter of credit. The court held that liability ensues in this case because the bank received notice of fraudulent documents before making payment.

Normally a bank is not expected to investigate dealings between the buyer and seller. If a bank pays unknowingly on fraudulent documents, the bank can use the due diligence defense if appropriate. Here, the bank had notice of fraud before payment and is therefore liable.

James S. Baker (Imports) v. United States (p. 709)

This case focuses upon the proper classification of lawn rakes in order to determine the appropriate duty to be paid by the importer. The Tariff Schedule lists rakes either under "horticulture" at 7.5 percent ad valorem or under "other" at 15 percent ad valorem.

The court looked to the congressional intent and the definition of *horticultural* and determined that lawn treatment is a horticultural activity. Therefore, the lower duty applies to lawn rakes.

Mitsubishi Motors Corporation v. Soler Chrysler-Plymouth, Inc. (p. 712)

The parties, Japanese and American companies, had a clause in their contract stating that all disputes would be settled by the Japan Commercial Arbitration Association. When an antitrust dispute arose, the American company refused to go to arbitration, fearing that U.S. antitrust laws would not be enforced. The Japanese company sued.

The Supreme Court held that the defendant must honor its contract. The Court stated that international arbitration should be effective under the Arbitration Act. The tribunal has to follow the intent of the parties and decide the dispute in accordance with the national law of the party bringing the claim. In addition, countries have the right to refuse to enforce the judgment if it is against the public policy of that country.

Martin v. Republic of South Africa (p. 715)

Martin, a black United States citizen, was injured in an automobile accident in South Africa where he was traveling with a dance group. He was discriminated against by a government owned ambulance and hospital which both refused to treat him. A second governmental hospital did treat him after more than a twenty-four hour wait and only after he was designated an honorary white. Upon his return home Martin sued the Republic of South Africa and the hospitals for his injuries.

The issue in the case was whether South Africa's behavior had "a direct effect in the United States" which is an exception to foreign government immunity under the Foreign Sovereign Immunities Act.

The court held South Africa was not liable as its acts did not constitute a direct effect in the United States. The court stated that it was following the precedent of all other courts which had dealt with the issue of personal injury claims affecting the United States.

International Association of Machinists v. OPEC (p. 717)

IAM filed suit against OPEC alleging that OPEC had fixed prices in violation of U.S. antitrust laws. The court held that the act of state doctrine barred it from hearing the case.

The act of state doctrine prohibits any U.S. court from judging the legality of the sovereign act of another country. The reasoning behind this rule is that a judgment might undermine U.S. international diplomacy. It is similar to the political question doctrine in domestic law which requires a court to defer to either the executive or legislative branch of government when these branches are better suited to resolve a politically sensitive question.

The court went on to say that the sovereign immunity doctrine is similar to the act of state doctrine in that they both show respect for the sovereignty of foreign countries. However the sovereign immunity doctrine allows the defendant country to refuse U.S. jurisdiction over their affairs. The act of state doctrine is one designed to avoid judicial action in sensitive areas.

United States v. Alavarez-Machain (p. 718)

Alavarez-Machain was a Mexican citizen and resident who was indicted for the kidnap and murder of a U.S. Drug Enforcement Administration agent. DEA officials abducted him from Mexico so that he could stand trial in the United States. Alavarez-Machain argued that his abduction was in violation of Article 9 of the extradition treaty between the United States and Mexico. The Court disagreed.

In its decision the Court first discussed the *Ker* precedent which held that an abduction from Peru was legal. The Court pointed out that Mexico was aware of this policy of the United States before it signed the extradition treaty.

As in the examination of a statute, the Court then studied the terms of the treaty. These terms made no mention of any restraint by either the United States or Mexico in abducting wanted people from each other's territories. In addition the history and practices under the treaty failed to show any objection to this practice. Therefore, the abduction of Alavarez-Machain was legal and the United States had jurisdiction to try him.

SELF-TEST QUESTIONS

True/False

_____ 1. The major purpose of a documentary credit is for the buyer's and seller's banks to act as mediators in the event of contractual disputes. (pp. 706-707)

_____ 2. GATT (The General Agreement on Tariffs and Trade) must be signed by any foreign country wishing to do business with an American company. (p. 709)

_____ 3. Nontariff trade barriers are a serious obstacle to free trade. (p. 710)

_____ 4. Nontariff trade barriers can include the stipulation that a certain percentage of a good's value be produced in the domestic economy. (p. 710)

_____ 5. European countries generally respect a choice of law clause in American contracts because freedom of contract is an important European ideal. (p. 711)

_____ 6. A choice of forum clause determines the location of the court or arbitration proceedings. (p. 711)

_____ 7. Arbitration agreements in international contracts are generally unenforceable outside the United States. (p. 712)

_____ 8. Joint ventures have become more popular in host countries because the foreign partner usually provides the necessary technology and management skills. (p. 714)

_____ 9. The Sovereign Immunity Doctrine protects foreign governments from attachments of property as well as from lawsuits. (p. 714)

_____ 10. The Act of State Doctrine can be a valid defense to a lawsuit. (p. 716)

_____ 11. The terms of a treaty between nations must be acted on in good faith, but is not binding. (p 718)

_____ 12. Settlement of disputes with foreign nations often involve political as well as financial considerations. (p. 720)

_____ 13. International laws tend to give more protection to a distributor of a product than an agent of a company. (p. 720)

_____ 14. Firms who do not wish to enter foreign markets can license the use of the processes. (p. 721)

_____ 15. U.S. citizens employed in foreign countries by U.S. employers are no longer protected by the Americans With Disabilities Act. (p. 722)

Multiple Choice

1. American multinational businesses must observe:
    a. laws of foreign governments.
    b. international laws.
    c. American laws.
    d. all of the above. (p. 705)

2. Which of the following is true concerning a documentary credit?
    a. It must be an unconditional document.
    b. The terms must be exact or the buyer may refuse shipment.
    c. The documentary credit cannot exist separately from the sales contract.
    d. Whenever the seller delivers the document, the buyer's bank must pay the seller or seller's bank. (p. 706)

3. In the *Sztejn* case, which dealt with whether a bank could be held liable on an irrevocable letter of credit, the court held:
   a. the bank was liable because it had notice of fraud before payment was requested.
   b. the bank was liable because it did not exercise due diligence.
   c. the bank was not liable because an irrevocable letter of credit may never be withdrawn.
   d. the bank was not liable because a bank need not become involved in controversies between the buyer and the seller. (pp. 708-709)

4. The General Agreement on Tariffs and Trade (GATT):
   a. has the ultimate goal of eliminating tariffs and nontrade tariff barriers.
   b. has less power than in the past because the number of nations which are involved is decreasing.
   c. is comprised of a number of nations who have agreed to trade with each other on the same terms.
   d. all of the above. (p. 709)

5. Tariffs:
   a. are taxes placed on imported goods.
   b. are taxes placed on imported and some domestic goods.
   c. classify products of all countries in one manner.
   d. classify dangerous products at a higher percentage rate. (p. 709)

6. Which of the following is *not* a nontariff trade barrier (NTB)?
   a. quotas.
   b. domestic content laws.
   c. countervailing duties.
   d. voluntary restraint agreements. (p. 710)

7. A choice of law clause in an international contract:
   a. usually is respected by all common law countries.
   b. determines the exact location of the court of forum.
   c. will require that any case heard in the United States be in a federal, not state, court.
   d. will be respected by all civil law countries only if it is felt to be relevant to the contract. (p. 711)

8. An arbitration clause in an international contract should contain the following:
   a. the location of the proceeding.
   b. a stipulation for at least three arbitrators.
   c. the right of discovery.
   d. both a and c. (pp. 711-712)

9. A joint venture between an investor and a government or business in a host country:
   a. can only be formed if the goal is to carry on an ongoing enterprise.
   b. benefits the host country because it allows the enterprise to qualify for participation in local export programs.
   c. usually involves major considerations about control.
   d. automatically provides for protection against expropriation of the investor's shares of the profit by the host government. (p. 714)

10. A foreign governmental act is *not* within the jurisdiction of the U.S. if:
    a. the government waives the right of immunity by implication.
    b. the government is engaging in political activities that affect the U.S.
    c. the government is engaging in commercial activities that affect the U.S.
    d. the government has legally taken property rights, and the property is present in the U.S. (p. 714)

11. In the *Martin* case, where the black alleged that his injury in South Africa had a direct effect on the U.S., the court held:
    a. Martin was correct because he was permanently disabled and this will affect his chances of employment in the U.S.
    b. Martin was correct because the government protects its citizens at all times, even when on foreign soil.
    c. Martin was incorrect because the injury happened in a foreign land and the Foreign Sovereign Immunity Act applies.
    d. Martin was incorrect because his personal injury was not considered to have a direct effect on the U.S. (pp. 715-716)

12. The Act of State Doctrine:
    a. grants blanket immunity to foreign governments.
    b. applies only if a commercial act takes place on foreign soil.
    c. contains an exception for cases where the government has a commercial obligation.
    d. applies to any action, public or private, which is in the interest of the foreign country. (p. 716)

13. In the *International* case where OPEC was alleged to have engaged in price fixing, the court declined to hear the case because:
    a. the act of state doctrine prohibits U.S. courts from hearing cases involving foreign countries.
    b. the act of state doctrine prohibits U.S. courts from hearing cases on foreign politically sensitive issues.
    c. the sovereign immunity doctrine prohibits U.S. courts from obtaining jurisdiction over foreign countries.
    d. the sovereign immunity doctrine prohibits U.S. courts from the disruption of U.S. diplomatic policy. (pp. 717-718)

14. The American Widget Company wishes to market widgets in India. The best way for the American Widget Company to avoid foreign income and employment taxes is to:
    a. open a branch office in India.
    b. open a production facility in India.
    c. employ American sales agents in India.
    d. employ Indian sales agents in India. (pp. 720-721)

15. A licensing agreement:
    a. is the most common form of direct American involvement overseas.
    b. can apply to sales of a product, but not use of a process.
    c. may involve U.S. antitrust issues.
    d. must be registered with the foreign government. (p. 721)

Essay Questions

1. Describe the major benefits of:
   a. documentary credits
   b. GATT
   c. tariffs and nontariff trade barriers

2. Discuss the options available to a United States firm wishing to sell its products or processes in other countries.

ANSWERS TO STUDY GUIDE SELF-TESTS

CHAPTER 1. INTRODUCTION TO THE LAW AND THE LEGAL ENVIRONMENT OF BUSINESS

True/False

1. False	6. True	11. True
2. True	7. False	12. False
3. True	8. True	13. False
4. True	9. False	14. False
5. False	10. True	15. True

Multiple Choice

1. a	6. c	11. a
2. a	7. b	12. c
3. d	8. c	13. d
4. c	9. b	14. b
5. d	10. d	15. a

Essay Questions

1. The two powerful groups which the law attempts to control are the government and corporations. The writers of the Constitution were concerned that the newly formed United States government did not become as powerful as the British government. Therefore the Constitution limits governmental power by dividing it into federal government and state government. In addition both federal and state government are divided into three branches: the executive, the legislature, and the judicial.

   During the Industrial Revolution there was a vast concentration of economic power in large corporations. The government legislated the Sherman Antitrust Act to limit the power of large corporations. Since then other groups such as labor and consumers have lobbied for laws which limit corporate (or any business) power even further.

2. There are no absolute rights in the law because rights frequently clash. The three cases in this chapter demonstrate this conflict of rights. In the first two cases, there was a clash between employer and employee rights, and in the third there was a clash between two individuals' rights to survival and another individual's right to live.

   Secondly, people do not see rights in the same way. What one person believes is art, another may believe is pornography.

   Lastly, the danger involved with the lack of absolute rights, is that at some point, persons may lose some of their rights. This is why court decisions attempt to balance conflicting rights very carefully.

ANSWERS TO STUDY GUIDE SELF-TESTS

CHAPTER 2.   INTRODUCTION TO THE COURTS

True/False

1. True	6. True	11. True
2. True	7. True	12. True
3. False	8. True	13. False
4. False	9. False	14. False
5. True	10. True	15. True

Multiple Choice

1. a	6. d	11. b
2. b	7. c	12. b
3. a	8. c	13. a
4. c	9. c	14. a
5. b	10. a	15. b

Essay Questions

1.   Federal courts are divided among geographic boundaries called circuits. Federal courts have more limited jurisdiction than state courts because they can only hear cases where there is a question of federal law or where there is diversity of citizenships (citizens from different states) and a monetary claim of $10,000 or more. There are also some specialized federal courts which deal exclusively with federal laws such as tax court or bankruptcy court.

   State courts have less of a limited jurisdiction than the federal courts. They may hear issues involving state law. Except for the federal courts of specialized jurisdiction, states may hear any of the types of cases that federal courts may hear. States have divisions of specialized jurisdiction such as a probate division which handles wills or a family law division which hears divorces and adoptions.

2.   An attorney may represent a guilty person for several reasons. First the attorney may not know that the person is guilty. Second, even if the attorney does know the person is guilty, it is up to the opposing attorney to prove that the person is guilty. Third, the attorney is not the judge of the accused; this function is to be performed by the jury, or the judge if no jury is present. Finally, as a safeguard, our legal system protects individual rights in that all accused parties are treated in the same manner.

ANSWERS TO STUDY GUIDE SELF-TESTS

CHAPTER 3. CIVIL LITIGATION AND ALTERNATIVE DISPUTE RESOLUTION

True/False

1. False	6. False	11. True
2. False	7. True	12. False
3. True	8. False	13. False
4. False	9. True	14. False
5. True	10. True	15. True

Multiple Choice

1. c	6. c	11. a
2. a	7. a	12. c
3. a	8. a	13. b
4. d	9. b	14. d
5. d	10. c	15. c

Essay Questions

1. In a trial court the plaintiff and the defendant are present. Evidence is presented, and witnesses are examined and cross examined. If appropriate, either side may request and be granted a jury. Issues of fact and law are decided.

    In an appellate court, the parties and witnesses are absent. The appeals court examines the record or partial record of the trial court in order to ascertain if any reversible errors are present. The attorneys from the trial submit written briefs discussing the case and may be called upon to make oral arguments. Only issues of law are decided at this level. The appellate court may affirm, reverse, or reverse and remand the trial court's decision.

2. The primary advantage of using alternative dispute resolution procedures is that they save time and money. Other advantages include the fact that when dealing with non-westerners, these types of proceedings are familiar to them and believed to be preferable to our court system. Alternative dispute resolution procedures are less adversarial in nature than the American court system. The goal is to reach a mutual satisfactory solution instead of having one imposed. In addition, the procedures are usually confidential and attract little, if any, publicity. Finally, in nonbinding alternative resolution procedures, either party still has the option of going to court.

ANSWERS TO STUDY GUIDE SELF-TESTS

CHAPTER 4. JUDICIAL REASONING AND DECISION MAKING

True/False

1. True	6. True	11. False
2. True	7. False	12. True
3. False	8. True	13. True
4. False	9. True	14. False
5. True	10. False	15. True

Multiple Choice

1. b	6. a	11. c
2. a	7. a	12. c
3. c	8. d	13. b
4. c	9. d	14. c
5. c	10. d	15. d

Essay Questions

1. Although a judge's personality is apparent to some extent in all of his or her decisions, it is most apparent in the "doing what is right" factor. In applying this factor to a case, a judge is relying heavily on the ethical beliefs he or she holds. The personality factor is also apparent in the balance of interest factor because a judge must consider the impact of the decision on other parties besides the ones in court. This requires a judgment based in part on the judge's own beliefs.

   The factors where the judge's beliefs are the least apparent are following the history or custom of the area and the use of social science data. In these cases, the beliefs of the community strongly affect the judge's ruling.

   Although the same reasoning would be applied to deferring to other branches of government, some judges strongly resist this, believing that the courts should decide all disputes coming before it. Others strongly believe that an elected body like the legislature or an administrative agency with greater expertise should make certain types of decisions. A judge's personality also affects whether to follow precedent or not based on whether he or she believes the time has come to amend the law.

2. The argument used to break precedent is that although the law must be predictable, it must also be flexible enough to change when appropriate. Lawyers argue for a change in precedent by arguing that a particular case is not the same as the precedential case. Dicta from previous cases is used to argue for change. Finally, looking at the laws of other states or districts is an argument for discarding outdated precedent and updating the law.

CHAPTER 5.   THE LEGISLATURE, LEGISLATION, AND THE EXECUTIVE
BRANCH

True/False

1. False	6. True	11. False
2. True	7. True	12. True
3. False	8. True	13. False
4. False	9. True	14. False
5. False	10. True	15. False

Multiple Choice

1. a	6. c	11. b
2. b	7. d	12. b
3. b	8. a	13. b
4. a	9. c	14. d
5. d	10. c	15. c

Essay Questions

1.   Statutes are enacted by the legislatures. Unless an area is limited by the Constitution, the legislators are able to investigate whether or not a statute is needed in a certain area. This is done through a legislative committee or subcommittee which has the power to call witnesses, request data, and prepare recommendations. The proposed law, or bill, is then voted upon by the entire body of legislators.

The common law is judge-made law. Courts must wait until disputes are brought before them, before acting. Courts do not have the authority to investigate whether a certain law should be passed. Courts also are generally bound by the doctrine of precedent. Occasionally, precedent is overturned, but this is the exception, rather than the usual practice.

2.   The executive branch of the government is limited by both the legislative and judicial branches. The legislative branch has the power to control funding for the executive programs. It may also shape legislative programs and refuse to approve executive appointments. The legislative branch's ultimate power is the right to impeach the executive.

The judicial branch has the power of judicial review which enables it to decide if an executive's actions are constitutional. Again note that cases must be brought before the judicial branch in order for it to act. However, courts generally refuse to challenge an executive action as the executive must voluntarily accept the court's judgment. Most issues of this sort are resolved outside the courts.

ANSWERS TO STUDY GUIDE SELF-TESTS

CHAPTER 6. CONSTITUTIONAL LAW AND BUSINESS

True/False

1. False	6. True	11. True
2. False	7. True	12. False
3. True	8. False	13. False
4. True	9. False	14. False
5. True	10. False	15. False

Multiple Choice

1. b	6. b	11. d
2. d	7. a	12. c
3. a	8. c	13. c
4. d	9. d	14. d
5. c	10. b	15. c

Essay Questions

1. The framers of the Constitution were primarily concerned about governmental power. They did not foresee the vast power that corporations would accumulate.

   As time has gone by, the courts have dealt with the concentrations of corporate power by interpreting the commerce clause quite broadly to include both interstate and intrastate activities. As the Katzenbach case demonstrates, the courts have even applied the commerce clause to protecting rights of parties against discrimination.

2. The courts have expanded the protection of freedom of speech of individuals to include businesses and professionals primarily because of the public's right to receive information. Advertisers often convey messages about health and cost in their advertisements. Even if they convey a political message, they have the same right as an individual to inform the public. Of course, the public has the right to disregard any of the information it chooses.

   As in the case of individuals, commercial speech may be limited to restrictions of a reasonable time, place, and manner. In addition, as an individual's protected speech, it must be concerned with lawful activity and not be deceptive.

CHAPTER 7. THE ADMINISTRATIVE AGENCY

True/False

1. False	6. True	11. True
2. False	7. False	12. True
3. True	8. False	13. False
4. True	9. False	14. True
5. False	10. True	15. False

Multiple Choice

1. d	6. d	11. a
2. c	7. b	12. b
3. c	8. a	13. d
4. a	9. c	14. a
5. c	10. d	15. b

Essay Questions

1. The powers of the administrative agency correspond to the functions of the three branches of government. Like the legislative branch, agencies have the power to make regulations. Like the executive branch, agencies may investigate whether regulations are necessary and whether the regulations have been followed. Like the judicial branch, agencies have the power to conduct hearings and to make law due to its decisions.

    The limitations on agency powers are primarily through the legislator's power to create or modify them, as well as financial control. The judicial branch limits the power of agencies by its power of judicial review. The Administrative Procedure Act sets standards and procedures agencies must follow, such as publication of rules in the Federal Register.

2. Both the trial and the hearing are open to the public, involve a complaint and answer by the parties, discovery procedures, and trial conferences. Evidence is presented in the same fashion, with the parties calling witnesses and cross-examining them. The trial has a judge and the agency hearing has a hearing examiner who functions in the same manner.

    The differences are that an agency hearing does not have a jury and so some rules of evidence are relaxed. In addition, more general evidence surrounding the events in question are admitted at an agency hearing.

CHAPTER 8. ETHICS: ITS RELATIONSHIP WITH THE LEGAL ENVIRONMENT AND BUSINESS DECISION MAKING

True/False

1. True	6. True	11. False
2. False	7. False	12. False
3. False	8. True	13. False
4. True	9. True	14. False
5. True	10. True	15. True

Multiple Choice

1. b	6. b	11. a
2. d	7. d	12. d
3. a	8. b	13. c
4. b	9. d	14. c
5. b	10. b	15. d

Essay Questions

1. The law encourages ethical behavior in several ways. First there are market and public expectations as shown in contract law. Promissory estoppel is one example.

    Secondly, there are government regulations, such as the antipollution laws, which penalize unethical behavior. If firms act ethically, they can prevent more laws or governmental regulations from being enacted as these rules would be unnecessary.

    Third there are laws which prohibit unethical behavior.

    A fourth way the law encourages ethical behavior is through its ability to be flexible enough to allow a judge or jury to base rulings on ethical values. An example of this given in the text are the finding that an "agreement in principle" is a contract, and the awarding of punitive damages.

2. Some critics may argue that considering the business entity is only self-interest. However if the ethical decision drives the business out of existence, then the business will be unable to act responsibly in the future. Secondly, a part of a firm's environment is the employees who work for the business. Protecting their jobs is important for the environment. Third, any investors in a company would soon cease to support the company with their investments if the business should show too great a monetary loss or went out of business.

CHAPTER 9.   THE LEGAL BASIS OF ENFORCEABLE BARGAINS: CONTRACTS - THE ESSENTIAL ELEMENTS

True/False

1. False	6. False	11. False
2. True	7. True	12. True
3. False	8. False	13. True
4. True	9. False	14. True
5. False	10. False	15. False

Multiple Choice

1. a	6. a	11. a
2. b	7. b	12. d
3. c	8. b	13. a
4. c	9. c	14. d
5. a	10. c	15. a

Essay Questions

1.   The process of bargaining involves bargaining position and deciding what strategies to employ during the bargaining process.

A person in a strong bargaining position is more likely to get the type of contract he or she desires. A person in a weak bargaining position may decide not to enter into a contract, or may decide to take what the other side offers in the hopes of getting a better contract in the future.

Strategies which can be employed during bargaining include hiring a third person to bargain on a party's behalf or using psychology to determine the needs of the other party. A person needs to determine his or her ethical beliefs about lying during bargaining. A win-win strategy is one where the bargainer allows the other party to come out of the negotiation a winner as well.

2.   An offer can be terminated by the offeror any time before acceptance by the offeree. There are three exceptions to this rule. One is when consideration has been given to keep the offer open. A second is when a merchant of goods has signed a writing promising to keep the offer open. The third is promissory estoppel when the courts stop a party from withdrawing an offer if the offeree has relied on the offer to his or her detriment.

ANSWERS TO STUDY GUIDE SELF-TESTS

CHAPTER 10. THE LEGAL BASIS OF ENFORCEABLE BARGAINS: CONTRACTS -
OTHER IMPORTANT CONSIDERATIONS

True/False

1. True	6. False	11. False
2. True	7. False	12. True
3. False	8. True	13. False
4. True	9. False	14. True
5. True	10. False	15. False

Multiple Choice

1. c	6. c	11. c
2. a	7. c	12. c
3. a	8. b	13. d
4. a	9. b	14. b
5. b	10. b	15. d

Essay Questions

1.   Courts will set aside a contract if there is a mistake, fraud, misrepresentation undue influence, or duress. If one of the parties to the contract has agreed to terms which contain an important mistake, the courts may set aside the contract. This unilateral mistake will only make the contract voidable if the other party knew or should have known of the mistake. If the mistake is bilateral, then the contract is also voidable. Fraud is the intentional misrepresentation of a material fact upon which the second party relied. Fraud only applies to facts about the past or present, not the future. A party's opinion is not considered fraud, unless that party is an expert in the subject matter of the agreement. Misrepresentation is similar to fraud except that misrepresentation does not require knowledge that the misrepresentation is false. Undue influence occurs when a party to a contract agrees to its terms because of the will of the other party. Duress is similar to undue influence with the additional element of extreme fear due to a threat.

2.   The two situations where a court may enforce a contract where none exists are quasi contract and promissory estoppel. In a quasi contract (also known as an implied in law contract) the party to the contract has no intent to contract, but has benefitted from the actions of the other party. If a contract is not implied by the court this party would be unjustly enriched at the expense of the other party.

       Promissory estoppel is a doctrine which enforces a promise for which no consideration is given. This only occurs in situations where the party who made the promise expected the other party to rely on this promise and when injustice would occur if the promise was not enforced.

CHAPTER 11. ASSESSING EXTERNAL COSTS OF DOING BUSINESS: TORT LIABILITY

True/False

1. True	6. False	11. False
2. True	7. False	12. True
3. False	8. True	13. True
4. True	9. False	14. False
5. False	10. True	15. True

Multiple Choice

1. c	6. c	11. b
2. a	7. d	12. d
3. d	8. b	13. a
4. d	9. b	14. d
5. a	10. c	15. b

Essay Questions

1.   The three principles which underlie the law of torts are victim compensation, allocation of risk and loss between the parties, and regulation of conduct. The goal of victim compensation is to "make the victim whole again." The victim must show that the defendant was responsible for the injuries by proving the four elements of a tort.

The second goal of alleviating the risk of the loss is closely related to the first goal. Victims do not have to bear the financial burden of an injury if another is at fault. However, if there is a defense against the victim, such as comparative negligence, the victim must absorb a portion of the financial burden.

The third goal is the regulation of conduct. This is a deterrent upon individuals to refrain from committing an intentional tort or to attempt to avoid negligent behavior. If persons or businesses know that they will be held financially liable, they tend to modify their behavior accordingly.

2.   Workers' compensation statutes were designed to save employers and employees the cost and time of litigation. Workers' compensation requires employers to contribute to a fund from which injured employees can draw in the event of an injury. The employee has no cause of action against the employer.

Workers' compensation has been criticized because the monetary awards are very low. With governmental and private assistance, employees today can afford to wait to be compensated until the case is won in court. Furthermore, since workplaces are safer now than in the past, allowing these cases to be litigated in the court system would not overburden the courts.

ANSWERS TO STUDY GUIDE SELF-TESTS

CHAPTER 12. PROPERTY RIGHTS

True/False

1. True	6. False	11. False
2. False	7. False	12. False
3. True	8. True	13. True
4. False	9. False	14. False
5. True	10. True	15. False

Multiple Choice

1. d	6. b	11. b
2. a	7. d	12. c
3. a	8. a	13. a
4. b	9. a	14. d
5. d	10. b	15. b

Essay Questions

1. Real property is land and anything firmly attached to it like a house or a tree. Tangible personal property is movable property which has a physical existence such as a lamp or a book. Fixtures are movable tangible personal property which are attached to real property. An example would be a ceiling fan which is installed in a room. Whether fixtures are a part of real property when it is sold is often an issue for the courts. They apply the three factors of the parties' intent, the possible damage if removed, and the appropriateness of the use. Intangible personal property is movable property which does not have a physical existence, but has very real value such as a copyright to a book.

2. Both property owners and individuals have rights, but these rights are limited by the rights of society in general. When an individual's rights conflict with a property owner's rights, the law favors the rights of the individual. This can be seen in movements to limit the concentrations of power in business through labor and antitrust legislation.

    When there is a conflict between the rights of property owners, the legal philosophy changes. The rights are considered mutual. Courts make decisions by balancing the economic and social importance of the conflicting uses of land. Courts have also held that certain values of owners, such as a view, are not rights of ownership.

ANSWERS TO STUDY GUIDE SELF-TESTS

CHAPTER 13. LEGAL ASPECTS OF BUSINESS ORGANIZATIONAL FORMS

True/False

1. True	6. False	11. False
2. False	7. True	12. False
3. True	8. True	13. True
4. True	9. True	14. True
5. False	10. False	15. False

Multiple Choice

1. b	6. d	11. b
2. c	7. c	12. c
3. b	8. d	13. a
4. c	9. d	14. b
5. a	10. a	15. a

Essay Questions

1. The four principles which affect a person's choice of a business organization are the principles of limited liability, profit sharing, management rights, and control. A person wishing total rights of control, management, and profit should select a sole proprietorship. The negative aspect of this choice is that the person will also have total liability for losses that the business or its insurance can't absorb. A person who chooses the partnership form of business shares the liability for business losses with other partners. He or she also shares profits, management rights, and control. A person who wants to limit his or her liability to the amount of the investment and have no responsibility for the management or control of the business should choose to be a limited partner in a limited partnership. He or she will still receive a percentage of the profits. A person wishing to limit his or her liability but who wishes some control in the business should invest in a corporation. The amount of control or management rights is determined by the amount of stock he or she holds. In a minority of states a person may wish to form a limited liability company which combines the advantages of the other four forms of business organizations. A member has limited liability, a right to a share of the profits, the right to management, and control of the business if he or she chooses.

2. Piercing the corporate veil is a doctrine used by the courts to remove the limited liability rights of corporate shareholders. This doctrine is applied only in certain situations. The first situation is when a corporation is found to be merely the alter ego of the shareholders. The second instance in which the doctrine applies is in cases where managers have mingled their personal property with corporate property to the extent that the corporation has no financial individuality. The third situation is one where members of the corporation have committed a fraud and justice requires that they be held personally liable.

ANSWERS TO STUDY GUIDE SELF-TESTS

CHAPTER 14. MEMBERS OF BUSINESS ORGANIZATIONS: REGULATION OF THEIR ACTIVITIES THROUGH AGENCY AND FIDUCIARY DUTY PRINCIPLES

True/False

1. False	6. True	11. True
2. False	7. False	12. False
3. True	8. False	13. False
4. False	9. False	14. True
5. True	10. False	15. True

Multiple Choice

1. b	6. b	11. c
2. a	7. a	12. a
3. b	8. a	13. c
4. b	9. d	14. d
5. d	10. d	15. c

Essay Questions

1. A principal-agent relationship is contractual. One of the major duties of the agent is to act on behalf of the principal. The second major duty of an agent is the fiduciary duties of care and loyalty. The major duty of the principal is to control the work activities of the agent.

    Agents may escape liability from their negligent torts by the doctrine of vicarious liability. Although the agent could be held liable, most injured third parties sue the principal because principals usually have more money than agents. Note that the tort must have been committed within the scope of the agent's employment for vicarious liability to apply. Agents have the power to bind the principal to a contract through actual authority, apparent authority, and ratification.

2. The fiduciary duty of care is the standard of care a prudent person would use when making decisions concerning the business. It is not required that persons make no mistakes, however, as this would be unrealistic. The business judgment rule is a defense if a party is accused of breaching this duty. The fiduciary duty of loyalty prohibits persons from taking advantage of their positions to influence the corporation for their own private gain.

    These fiduciary duties apply to agents in any type of business organization. In a partnership, partners are agents and principals to each other. In a limited partnership only the general partners are agents. In a corporation, directors and officers are agents to the corporation which is the principal. In limited liability enterprises, only members who are managers are agents to the enterprise which is the principal.

CHAPTER 15. WHITE-COLLAR AND BUSINESS CRIME: REGULATION OF
BUSINESS THROUGH THE CRIMINAL PROCESS

True/False

1. False	6. True	11. True
2. False	7. True	12. False
3. True	8. False	13. False
4. False	9. False	14. True
5. False	10. False	15. True

Multiple Choice

1. d	6. c	11. d
2. a	7. a	12. d
3. b	8. b	13. d
4. a	9. d	14. b
5. c	10. c	15. d

Essay Questions

1. In a civil case the plaintiff sues the defendant for money damages or an injunction. The purpose of a civil trial is to restore the plaintiff to his or her original position.

   In a criminal case, the state or federal government sues the defendant. The remedy is a fine or imprisonment. The purpose of criminal law is to punish the defendant. The procedure is different in a criminal case as well. There is an arraignment or appearance before a judge where the defendant enters his or her plea of guilty or not guilty. If the person pleads not guilty and has insufficient funds to hire an attorney, one is appointed by the court if he or she is subject to a prison sentence. There may be a preliminary hearing where the prosecutor must prove evidence exists connecting the defendant to the crime. In some cases a grand jury is used for this purpose instead of or in addition to a preliminary hearing. Another difference between civil and criminal proceedings is that a criminal defendant may plea bargain for a reduced sentence in return for admission of a lesser charge.

2. RICO is an act prohibiting the control or investment in any legal or illegal business by the use of money earned from two or more racketeering activities in a ten year period. The most common type of racketeering activity in white collar crime is mail or wire fraud.

   When the government brings charges, the penalties are the same as in all criminal cases - a fine and/or imprisonment. Under RICO these penalties are very severe. Private parties can also bring suit against a defendant under civil RICO. These penalties are three times the plaintiff's actual damages and in some cases, attorney fees.

CHAPTER 16. PRODUCTS LIABILITY

True/False

1. False	6. False	11. True
2. True	7. True	12. False
3. False	8. False	13. True
4. True	9. False	14. True
5. False	10. True	15. True

Multiple Choice

1. a	6. c	11. d
2. a	7. a	12. d
3. c	8. b	13. b
4. c	9. a	14. b
5. c	10. b	15. b

Essay Questions

1.   Warranties are promises given by the seller. They may be voluntarily made or imposed by law. An express warranty is voluntarily made by any seller. It can be made orally, in writing, pictorially, or by a sample or model.

Implied warranties are imposed by law. The implied warranty of merchantability is only imposed on a professional retailer or manufacturer. This warranty implies that the product is fit for ordinary purposes. The implied warranty of fitness for a particular purpose contains two requirements. First, the seller must know that the buyer is purchasing the goods for a specific purpose. Second, the buyer must rely on the seller's expertise.

Defenses to warranties are clear, conspicuous disclaimers, each of timely notice given to the seller and, in a few states, privity of contract must be established.

2.   A manufacturer has a duty to warn of the possible dangers of a product if the misuse of the product could make the product unreasonably dangerous. This duty is placed on the manufacturer because of its expertise concerning the product. The warning is usually given directly to consumers except in the case of prescription drugs in which the warning is conveyed to the prescribing physician.

There is no duty to warn of dangers which are obvious to the average person. However, since there have been cases litigating what is considered obvious, the best policy for a manufacturer is to include a warning.

CHAPTER 17. CONSUMER LAW

True/False

1. True	6. True	11. False
2. False	7. False	12. False
3. True	8. True	13. True
4. False	9. False	14. True
5. False	10. False	15. False

Multiple Choice

1. c	6. c	11. a
2. a	7. d	12. b
3. a	8. d	13. c
4. c	9. a	14. d
5. d	10. c	15. d

Essay Questions

1. The Holder-in-Due-Course Doctrine states that any party who buys a promissory note in good faith and without notice that there are contract defenses against it becomes a holder-in-due-course. This status gives the purchaser the right to sue for payment on the note whether or not there are valid contract defenses.

 The FTC modified this doctrine to disallow this rule to be used against consumers. Any party purchasing a consumer promissory note is on notice that any contract defenses which may arise could result in the legal nonpayment of the note.

2. Bankruptcy law has two major purposes. The first is to allow debtors a fresh start and the record is to allow for a fair distribution of the debtor's assets among his or her creditors.

 A Chapter 7 liquidation can be voluntary or involuntary. The debtor or his or her creditor(s) files a petition asking for relief. If granted, after a meeting with the creditors and the trustee in bankruptcy, all non-exempt property is liquidated and the debtor is discharged from his or her debt.

 A Chapter 11 reorganization can be voluntary or involuntary. A creditors' committee is formed to approve a reorganization plan by the debtor or anyone if the debtor does not file. If the plan is accepted, it governs the operation of the business.

 A Chapter 13 adjustment is only voluntary and the plan can only be submitted by the debtor. The plan is approved by the court and not the creditors. If approved the debtor is discharged after the completion of the plan.

CHAPTER 18. EMPLOYMENT DISCRIMINATION

True/False

1. False	6. True	11. False
2. False	7. True	12. False
3. True	8. False	13. True
4. False	9. False	14. True
5. True	10. True	15. False

Multiple Choice

1. a	6. c	11. d
2. c	7. d	12. c
3. b	8. a	13. d
4. d	9. b	14. c
5. a	10. d	15. b

Essay Questions

1. There are two goals of Title VII. The first is to provide equal opportunity for all workers to compete for jobs and promotions. The second is to provide protection groups, such as minorities and women, entry into certain types of jobs. The two goals conflict because the first goal is to eliminate discrimination of all kinds without regard to race, color, sex, religion, or natural origin. The second goal is intended to give preference to traditionally disadvantaged groups. Businesses have done this through voluntary affirmative action programs. White males are challenging these preferences as being reverse discrimination.

2. The first type of sexual harassment involves an intolerable workplace environment due to the unwelcome sexual advances of a person in power over the employee. The employee believes that he or she must give in to these sexual demands of this higher level employee to avoid being discriminated against for promotions or to keep from losing his or her job.

    The second type of sexual harassment involves a hostile workplace environment. This can occur through the actions of an employee on the same level. These actions do not only involve sexual advances, but rather actions such as sexual remarks or jokes which make the employee uncomfortable and affect his or her performance at work. Because these actions are generally directed at women, a trend is developing to make the standard for this type of harassment the reasonable woman standard.

CHAPTER 19. LABOR-MANAGEMENT RELATIONS: THE REGULATION OF MANAGEMENT

True/False

1. True	6. False	11. False
2. False	7. True	12. True
3. True	8. True	13. True
4. False	9. False	14. False
5. True	10. False	15. False

Multiple Choice

1. c	6. d	11. d
2. b	7. d	12. a
3. a	8. b	13. d
4. a	9. c	14. b
5. c	10. c	15. b

Essay Questions

1.   A union may become the representative of the employees in the designated bargaining unit in one of three ways. The first is through voluntary recognition of the union. If an employee is presented with authorization cards from the majority of the employees, management may decide that the results of a union election is a foregone conclusion and the union should be recognized without an election. The second way for a union to become the employee's representative is through an election with the majority of the voting employees supporting the union. The third way occurs when the employer has made a fair election impossible. The union can bring an unfair labor practice charge against the employer to the NLRB which will certify the union as the bargaining representative. This can only be done if a majority of the employees have signed authorization cards supporting the union.

2.   An employer who dominates or supports a union is guilty of an unfair labor practice act because employer support is believed to create a weak union or one which is under the control of management. An obvious example is recognition of a union which has less than majority support of the employees. Although it is oftentimes difficult to distinguish mere helpfulness from domination, the test is the extent of the support. The best course of action for an employer is to remain neutral.

ANSWERS TO STUDY GUIDE SELF-TESTS

CHAPTER 20   LABOR-MANAGEMENT RELATIONS: THE REGULATION
             OF UNIONS

True/False

1. True	6. False	11. True
2. True	7. False	12. False
3. True	8. False	13. False
4. False	9. True	14. True
5. True	10. False	15. False

Multiple Choice

1. d	6. c	11. b
2. b	7. a	12. c
3. b	8. d	13. a
4. d	9. b	14. a
5. d	10. a	15. c

Essay Questions

1. A closed shop is one where the employer agrees to hire only members in good standing of a union. The closed shop is illegal today because it discriminates in the hiring or retention of employees and promotes union membership.

   A union shop is one where an employee agrees to join the union after a certain period of employment. This is legal because, unlike the closed shop, it gives the employer freedom of choice in hiring. The rationale for requiring employees to join the union is that they are receiving the benefits a union provides and therefore must pay initiation fees and union dues, if not actively participate in union meetings.

   An agency shop is also legal. It requires employees to pay initiation fees and union dues because they are receiving the benefits a union provides. However, they do not have to become union members.

2. Secondary pressure is a boycott of an employer other than the one who employs the workers. It was hoped that applying pressure on a secondary employer would force the secondary employer to stop doing business with the primary employer and thus put pressure on the primary employer to accede to his or her employee's demands. This practice has been outlawed because Congress believed this type of activity was unfair to the secondary employer with whom the workers had no grievance. Primary pressure on the primary employer is all that is allowable under labor law today.

CHAPTER 21. REGULATION OF PROPERTY RIGHTS: EMINENT DOMAIN, ZONING, AND ENVIRONMENTAL LAW

True/False

1. True	6. True	11. False
2. True	7. False	12. True
3. True	8. True	13. False
4. False	9. False	14. True
5. False	10. False	15. False

Multiple Choice

1. d	6. b	11. b
2. c	7. c	12. d
3. b	8. d	13. b
4. d	9. c	14. c
5. a	10. d	15. a

Essay Questions

1.   Eminent domain and zoning are both examples of government control of private property. In both cases the use must be for the public good. Eminent domain occurs when the government purchases private property from the owner. This purchase must be for public use and the government must pay just compensation for the taking of the land. Zoning is a restriction by the government of how an individual's land can be used. The owner still owns the land, but is limited in his or her use of the land.

2.   There are two goals of federal environmental law. The first is full disclosure of any major federal activity having an impact on the environment. This is implemented by the National Environmental Policy Act which requires an environmental impact statement analyzing the effect of any federal activity upon the environment. The second goal of federal environmental law is to correct environmental problems such as air pollution, water pollution, toxic waste disposal, use of insecticides, and strip mining. These statutes are implemented mainly by the Environmental Protection Agency which has the power to assess fines and, in some cases bring criminal charges.

ANSWERS TO STUDY GUIDE SELF-TESTS

CHAPTER 22. FEDERAL SECURITIES REGULATION

True/False

1.	False	6.	False	11.	True
2.	True	7.	False	12.	True
3.	True	8.	False	13.	True
4.	False	9.	False	14.	False
5.	False	10.	True	15.	False

Multiple Choice

1.	d	6.	d	11.	d
2.	b	7.	c	12.	c
3.	b	8.	a	13.	d
4.	b	9.	a	14.	c
5.	c	10.	a	15.	a

Essay Questions

1. The 1933 Act applies to the initial issuance of securities. It is sometimes referred to as the truth-in-securities act because the major purpose of the 1933 Act is to require full disclosure of all material information. These filings are registered with the SEC and a summary of the filings is provided to interested investors. If a business does not disclose all material information, it is guilty of fraud, regardless of intent. A defense available to all but the issuer is the due diligence defense which alleges a reasonable effort was made to insure all the material statements were true.

    The 1934 Act covers the secondary purchase or sale of securities. Fraud is also an issue under this act, but intent must be proved. Insider trading activities come under this act.

2. Insider trading is the unlawful use of material inside information about a company. A person who uses this information for his or her benefit before the general public has the same information has violated this law. The insider does not have to be an employee of the corporation, but must have a fiduciary duty to the corporation.

    The purpose for the law against insider trading is to ensure that all investors have basically the same information before buying or selling stocks. This insures public confidence in the fairness of the securities market.

ANSWERS TO STUDY GUIDE SELF-TESTS

CHAPTER 23. INTRODUCTION TO ANTITRUST

True/False

1. True	6. True	11. True
2. False	7. True	12. True
3. False	8. False	13. False
4. True	9. True	14. True
5. False	10. False	15. True

Multiple Choice

1. b	6. b	11. a
2. d	7. a	12. c
3. a	8. c	13. d
4. c	9. b	14. c
5. d	10. a	15. c

Essay Questions

1. The three groups which can bring actions to enforce federal antitrust laws are the Department of Justice, the Federal Trade Commission, and private parties. The Justice Department and the FTC can bring a civil suit in which case the remedy is an injunction against the defendant. They can bring criminal actions in which case the punishment for this felony action is either a fine or a prison term.

    Private parties cannot institute a criminal suit. They may bring a civil suit for three times their actual damages. Or they may sue for an injunction against the defendant. Private parties can join together in a class action suit or have the attorney general of the state sue on their behalf under a parens patriae action.

2. The *Noerr* doctrine is based on the First Amendment which entitles persons, including businesses, freedom of speech. Under this doctrine businesses have the right to lobby for favorable treatment even if the passage of the bill would injure its competition. The reasoning for this doctrine is that antitrust law was enacted to regulate business, not political acts.

    An exception to the *Noerr* doctrine is the sham exception. This applies antitrust law against a business who is directly injuring a competitor such as bringing a frivolous lawsuit.

ANSWERS TO STUDY GUIDE SELF-TESTS

CHAPTER 24. ANTITRUST LAW

True/False

1. False	6. False	11. False
2. True	7. False	12. True
3. False	8. True	13. True
4. True	9. False	14. True
5. True	10. False	15. True

Multiple Choice

1. a	6. a	11. c
2. d	7. d	12. d
3. b	8. a	13. c
4. b	9. c	14. b
5. c	10. a	15. c

Essay Questions

1. The legislature deliberately wrote vague language into the Sherman, Clayton, and Federal Trade Commission Acts because it wanted the courts to formulate and refine antitrust law on a case by case basis. Antitrust law is very complex. For example, not all monopolies or mergers are bad. In some cases, they make for a more efficient market. For example it would be detrimental to have more than one utility service in a certain area.

    The courts have basically judged the legality of the fomulation of a monopoly or merger by the impact it has on the relevant geographic markets. If they do not injure competition or consumers, they are allowable.

2. When using the Rule of Reason, courts look at whether the action of the business has a harmful effect on competitors and/or consumers. The Rule of Reason is applied in cases involving attempts to monopolize, and restraint of trade cases.

    The Per Se Rule outlaws certain business practices on their face. If certain facts exist, a business is guilty of a violation of the Sherman Act regardless of the reasonableness of the action, the intent of the parties, or the amount of harm to competitors and/or consumers. The Per Se Rule is applied to cases involving price fixing, retail price maintenance, with customers and lessees and group boycotts. The Per Se Rule is applied to tying contracts unless the goodwill of the tying product is involved or it is unique.

ANSWERS TO STUDY GUIDE SELF-TESTS

CHAPTER 25. THE INTERNATIONAL LEGAL ENVIRONMENT OF BUSINESS

True/False

1. False	6. True	11. False
2. False	7. False	12. True
3. True	8. True	13. False
4. True	9. True	14. True
5. False	10. True	15. False

Multiple Choice

1. d	6. c	11. d
2. b	7. a	12. c
3. a	8. d	13. b
4. c	9. c	14. d
5. a	10. b	15. c

Essay Questions

1.   The major benefit of using documentary credits is to offer conveniences to both the buyer and the seller. This is done by two methods. First, the buyer and seller are able to use his or her own bank in handling the transaction. Second, the seller's bank reviews the document relating to the sale before paying the buyer.

   The major benefit of GATT is predictability. This comes from the security of knowing that all members of the organization's signatory countries will be trading with each other under the same set of rules.

   The major benefits of tariffs and nontariff trade barriers is the protection they give to domestic industries. Tariffs achieve this by levying a duty on imported products. Nontariff trade barriers achieve this protection by nonmonetary means such as quotas of goods which may be imported or by domestic content laws which stipulate that a certain percent of a good's value be produced domestically.

2.   A United States firm that wishes to do business in a foreign country has several options. The first is to set up its entire production there. The second is to set up a branch production facility or a branch office in the foreign country. The United States firm could also choose to license the use of its manufacturing process to business-persons in another country.

   Regardless of the choices made, a United States firm must be careful to follow United States laws on the export of technology or knowhow, and must follow United States antitrust law.

Motivation
for
Mission

Embracing God's
Vision for Your Community

Leader's Guide

Dwight Marable

For more information, please contact
Transforming Churches Network
1160 Vickery Ln. Ste #1, Cordova, TN 38016
901-757-9700
www.tcnprocess.com
terry@transformingchurchesnetwork.org

Table of Contents

Introduction

You may remember Indiana Jones in the movie *Raiders of the Lost Ark* and his exciting quest to find the Ark of the Covenant. This movie propelled Harrison Ford into a fabulous movie career that defined a genre of films for a generation. The Ark represented the ultimate religious icon, the very presence of God in the Old Testament and Jones was desperate to find it.

Just as the characters in this movie were searching for spiritual encounters, America is searching for spiritual realities today. The churched culture of the first half of the last century has come and gone, leaving Americans still searching for the "Ark" of happiness. Somehow the culture senses that the addictions of today do not lead to peace and health tomorrow. Spirituality that doesn't include church is on the rise.

Yet the church finds itself unable to give a clear message of how the love and forgiveness of Jesus Christ can end the angst in anxious hearts and minds. The well documented decline in the mainline denominations in our country have left church leaders across this country mystified and lost in their ability to stop the slide away from Christ. Baptisms of people who need to know Christ is almost at a standstill.

We must rethink our mission and how we are to fulfill it. Christ, in his "Great Commission," indicated that we are to go to them, not just invite them to join us. This series is designed to help you process your own role and opportunities in fulfilling the mission of Christ in our world today. When we engage with lost people with purpose and a heart of love, the personal passion of Christ for those who do not know Him revives our souls and energizes us for the task ahead.

Ways To Use This Resource

The six sessions found in this study guide can be used in various settings. They include the following:

• Small groups that meet in a home. These studies work very well for groups of all kinds.

• In an adult Sunday school class or Bible study. These can be done in small and large classes. If your class has more than 20 members, break members into small groups for the activities that require discussion.

• As a church-wide campaign emphasis. These six sessions can be studied as part of a church-wide program. The pastor can preach six sermons that correlate with the six sessions. And various groups can be organized, whether small groups that meet in homes or Sunday school classes that meet on the church campus. For a complete guide on how to organize such an effort, download the Church-wide Campaign Guide which can be found on the Transforming Churches Network website (www.tcnprocess.com).

Supplies Needed for These Studies

General Supplies
- DVD Player/VCR and TV
- Facilitator Guide
- Participant Guides
- Legal Pad
- Markers

Session 1: Lost in America
- Legal Pad
- Markers

Session 2: Why is the Church on Earth?
- Paper
- Pens/Markers
- Candy for Prizes
- Bibles

Session 3: CHANGE? You Gotta Be Kidding!
- Luther DVD or VHS - view clip at 1:46:29 - 1:55:22 (end of movie)
- DVD Player/VCR and TV
- Bibles

Session 4: The Search
- Legal Pad
- Markers
- Bibles
- Whiteboard or Flipchart

Session 5: The Power of a Team
- Bibles
- Legal Pad

Session 6: Where To From Here?
- Legal Pad
- Markers

Lost in America

Objective: *To take a candid look at what unchurched people think about the church today and to consider where our friends and acquaintances are in their faith journey.*

10-15
minutes

Discovery Activity

In groups of two or three ask everyone to share about a time when they got lost during the growing up years. After 4-5 minutes of interaction bring the group back together to talk about their stories.

Question #1: What kinds of emotions did the experience of being lost generate inside of you? (List the responses on a legal pad.)

Question #2: How does it feel to be lost without God in your life? If you've been a Christian since childhood, how do you think it would feel? (List these responses out also…you may want to note if the two lists overlap at all.)

15-20
minutes

Learning Activity

Allow everyone time to slowly read through the article "Unchurched Harry and Mary." After everyone has read, ask people to respond to the surprises and to the faith stages. What stood out to them? What was new information for them?

Draw Unchurched Harry and Mary

Next, pass out several colors of magic markers and a piece of paper to the original groupings with which you started this session. Instruct everyone that their assignment is to draw a picture of a typical person in the community that does not go to church. We will call them Unchurched Harry or Mary. Around the drawing of the person include descriptive phrases about things like:

Music taste	Stress level	Interests
Hobbies	Debt	Needs
Education	Satisfaction in life	Concerns
Work	Religious background	

Debrief

Debrief the exercise by walking around to the various drawings or ask each group to make a brief (30 second) presentation to the whole room. After the sharing is done, ask for a few comments or insights about the drawings. Transition from the drawings to the learning activity by indicating that the remainder of our session will focus on gaining a better understanding of people who do not go to church.

Unchurched Harry and Mary

There are lost, unchurched people all around us. If they continue without Christ until the end of their life on earth, they will spend eternity without Him (John 3:36, John 5:29).

Where should we start? How do we begin? A great starting place is a careful study of the world of the unchurched. To impact unchurched "Harry and Mary" we must understand how they think, feel and behave. In his book, *The Unchurched Next Door*, Thom Rainer discovered some very interesting things about people who do not have a church home. Here are ten surprises that Rainer and his team of researchers uncovered:

Surprise #1:   Most of the unchurched prefer to attend church on Sunday morning if they attend.

Surprise #2:   Females are likely to be either the most antagonistic or the most receptive to the Gospel.

Surprise #3:   Most of the unchurched feel guilty about not attending church.

Surprise #4:   82 percent of the unchurched are at least "somewhat likely" to attend church if they are invited.

Surprise #5:   Very few of the unchurched have had someone share with them how to become a Christian, and Christians have not been particularly influential in their lives.

Surprise #6:   Most of the unchurched have a positive view about pastors, ministers and the church.

Surprise #7:   Some types of "cold call" evangelism are effective, but many are not.

Surprise #8:   The unchurched would like to develop a real and sincere relationship with a Christian.

Surprise #9:   The attitudes of the unchurched are not correlated to where they live, their ethnic or racial background, or their gender.

Surprise #10: Many of the unchurched are far more concerned about the spiritual well-being of their children than of themselves.

Faith Stages

In addition to the surprising insights from their research, Rainer and his team also discovered that there were five distinct groupings of unchurched people in our culture today. Briefly, they are:

Group 5: The most resistant, even antagonistic to the church and to the Gospel. They are intensely skeptical of the Bible and the claims of Christianity. Many have had a wounding church experience from earlier in their lives. Their motto would be "Religion is okay for the weak-minded."

Group 4: Resistant to the Gospel but do not have an antagonistic attitude. Many have a belief in the afterlife which may or may not include heaven and hell. Christ is viewed as having an important role in history. They have used prayer as a safety net but don't know if anyone is really listening. Resistant to someone trying to convert them. Their motto would be "Just what is truth?"

Group 3: No apparent interest in the church but open to discussions. Believes in a heaven and hell. They have a positive view of Jesus and of most Christians, but what they believe about God is quite puzzling. Their motto would be "Church just isn't my thing."

Group 2: They may say all the right "spiritual" things but they have yet to make a personal step of faith. Often believe that one needs to work his or her way into heaven. Probably open to studying the Bible and to discussing its claims. Would be open to an invitation to visit a church. Their motto would be "Jesus is just alright with me."

Group 1: Highly receptive to hearing about the Gospel and engaging in spiritual conversations. Probably have been involved in a church at some point in their life. Feel bad about making excuses for not going to church more. Pray on a regular basis. Like Group 2's, they believe that one works their way to heaven. Their motto would be "What must I do to be saved?"

10-15 minutes

Practice Activity

Pair people up for this role playing exercise. It's everyone's opportunity to play Unchurched Harry or Mary. One person will role play one of the five unchurched profiles while the other person plays the role of a Christian trying to strike up a conversation. The person who is role playing is not to reveal which profile they are acting out. See if the "Christian" can guess who their person is at the end of the interview! Plan on giving each role play about 3-5 minutes and then reverse roles in each pairing so that the "Christian" now plays "Unchurched Harry or Mary."

Sample role playing questions:
1. Tell me a little bit about your religious background.
2. How would you describe your attitude toward the church?

3. What is your view of the typical Christian?
4. How do you believe someone will get to Heaven?
5. What do you think about Jesus Christ?
6. What is your biggest turn-off with Christians and churches?

Debrief

After the role-play is finished bring the whole group back together to debrief with these three questions:

Question #1: How did it feel to play an unchurched person?

Question #2: What dynamics did you observe in the role play?

Question #3: What can we learn from this experience?

Application Activity

5
minutes

Here is a homework assignment that will help you to apply what we've discovered today. In the next week (or before the next session), take a few minutes to talk to a friend that doesn't currently attend church very often. Simply explain that you are taking a class at your church and that you have the assignment to talk to someone about church and Christianity. Use the role-playing questions to guide your conversation.

Sample role playing questions:
1. Tell me a little bit about your religious background.
2. How would you describe your attitude toward the church?
3. What is your view of the typical Christian?
4. How do you believe someone will get to Heaven?
5. What do you think about Jesus Christ?
6. What is your biggest turn-off with Christians and churches?

Wrap-Up

Before closing out the session take some time in pairs or as a whole group to pray for these Friend Interviews and for God to help the church to become more effective in reaching into the community.

Why is the Church on Earth?

Objective: *For participants to carefully consider why the local church exists. A search of the scriptures will inform the discussion. Emphasis will be placed on how well both "we" and "me" are doing in the five purposes, and in particular the purpose of mission.*

Discovery Activity

Faith Stages

There will be three rounds for this team activity. Divide the group into even numbered teams of three or four players. Directions to the group:

"Each team will have one minute to brainstorm as many items as they can related to the category given. The goal is to list items that match the "master list" which will be read at the end of each round. The team with the most correct matches wins the competition."

Round #1: Things that help you see. After one minute has expired, read the list below to see how many correct matches each team has made.
1. Glasses
2. Telescope
3. Microscope
4. Binoculars

Round #2: Things that cut. After one minute has expired, read the list below to see how many correct matches each team has made.

1. Knife	5. Scissors
2. Axe	6. Hedge clippers
3. Hand saw	7. Whipper Snipper
4. Lawnmower	8. Chain saw

Round #3: Things that hit. After one minute has expired, read the list below to see how many correct matches each team has made.

1. Baseball bat	5. Golf club
2. Hammer	6. Fly swatter
3. Wrecking ball	7. Gun ("hit the target")
4. Tennis racquet	8. A wall ("hit the wall!")

Debrief

1. Find out which group had the most correct matches in the Name that Purpose game. Hand out a team prize.

2. The game is a way for us to begin thinking about the phrase purpose. Each of the categories was introduced with a purpose: i.e., things that help you see, things that cut, and things that hit. With the teams that you competed in, take a few minutes to share your responses to this statement:

    One of the things that gives me a sense of purpose in my life is _____ and here's why.

3. Bring the room back together and ask a few people to share briefly what their response to the statement was.

Learning Activity

30 minutes

To transition to the learning segment of the session, ask everyone to close their eyes for a moment and to "point north" with their finger. Ask everyone to open their eyes and to compare how everyone did.

The point to make is this: Having a purpose in life is like having a compass. Purpose is like knowing where "True North" is on a compass. Today, we're going to open up the Bible together to determine the purpose of the local church. In other words, we're going to wrestle with the question: "Why does the local church exist?"

Facilitator Instructions: In groups of two or three, look up the following passages. Try to find themes that will help us understand the purpose of the local church. Assign portions of the passages to different groups rather than have each group look up all twelve passages.

For this exercise we will use the five purposes that Rick Warren popularized in his book *The Purpose Driven Church* which are:

Fellowship, Worship, Discipleship, Mission, Ministry

Ask the groups to try to determine which of the five purposes their passages relate to (there could be more than one purpose). After 15-20 minutes bring everybody back together to report. Lead the group in a discussion about the themes that emerged from the passages. List them out on a legal pad. You'll have to keep it moving along so that you have time for the other pieces of the module.

Passage	Purpose of the Church
• Matthew 28:19-20	
• Acts 1:8	
• Acts 2:42-47	
• Romans 15: 6, 17-22	
• 2 Corinthians 4:1-6	
• Ephesians 2:1-9	
• Ephesians 4:11-16	
• Colossians 2:6-7	
• Colossians 3:12-16	
• Colossians 4:5,6	
• Hebrews 10:24-25	
• 1 Peter 2:1-5, 9-12	

Practice Activity

10-15
minutes

Personal and Church Assessment

Ask each person to do a bit of assessment regarding the themes that emerged from the scripture search activity. Instruct everyone to give themselves and the church a score on each of the themes using the following scoring:

(1) practiced rarely...
(3) practiced somewhat...
(5) practiced often

For Example:

	Me	Our church
Worship	3	4
Discipleship	2	3
Ministry	3	3
Fellowship	2	3
Mission	2	2

After everyone has a couple of minutes to assess themselves and the church have them pair up with one or two others to discuss their scores. Next, conduct a large group discussion where you ask people to reflect on these two questions:

Question #1: Which purpose are you most inconsistent at living out and why?

Question #2: Which purpose are we as a church most inconsistent at living out and why?

Key Point: Most churches around the U.S. struggle with reaching out into their community. Although there may be things a church can do to strengthen its other purposes, most churches agree that impacting non-Christians with the Gospel is the purpose that they most need to improve.

After making this point, drive it home by quoting an LCMS research finding by Alan Klaas. Ask a few people to respond to the quote after you read it.

A study of 4,371 lay people and 886 clergy in Lutheran congregations provided helpful insights into attitudes about outreach. Fifteen congregational activities were listed. Lay people and clergy picked the top six "purposes of a local congregation." Evangelism was not one of the top six selected by 99 percent of the laity and 94 percent of the clergy. A more general concept, "bringing in new members," did not appear among the top six purposes selected by 70 percent of laity and 58 percent of clergy. (*In Search of the Unchurched* by Alan C. Klaas)

Suggest to the group:
"With this in mind, this study is going to focus solely on understanding and strengthening the outreach potential of our congregation. In future segments we will learn more about God's heart for the world and His expectations for us to be involved in His mission."

5 minutes

Application Activity

"Interview a Friend" Homework Assignment

Here is a homework assignment that will help you to apply what we've discovered today. In the next week, (or before the next session) take a few minutes to talk to a friend that doesn't currently attend church. Simply explain that you are taking a class at your church and that you have the assignment to talk to someone who does not go to church.
Questions to ask:

1. What impressions do you have of church?

2. What are some of the reasons why more people don't go to church?

3. What are some of the needs in our community that a church could try to address?

Wrap-Up

Before closing out the session take some time in pairs or as a whole group to pray for these Friend Interviews and for God to help the church to become more effective in reaching into the community.

Change? You've Got to be Kidding Me!

Objective: *For participants to learn about the value and behavior shifts which are necessary to reach their unchurched friends and to determine personal action steps related to the shifts.*

15-20
minutes

Discovery Activity

Luther Video Clip

*Before moving into the activity, ask for volunteers to share about their "Friend Interview" that was given for homework in the previous session. After a few people have shared move on to the activity below.

Show a clip from the movie "Luther." (If your local video rental store does not carry this movie, you can order it online on www.Amazon.com or similar websites.) The scene starts at 1:46:29 and ends at 1:55:22 (the end of the movie).

Set the scene for the group: In this final scene from the movie "Luther," all that Martin Luther had been working toward comes to a head in Augsburg in 1530. The dynamics of a revolution were everywhere, but the fledgling movement teetered on the brink of extinction. Pay attention to the change dynamics at play as you watch this scene.

Question #1: What stood out to you as you watched this scene? What grabbed your heart?

Question #2: What values guided the attitudes and behavior of the various characters (Luther, the Emperor, the Princes)?

Question #3: What fed the change process?

Question #4: What does this teach us about change?

10-15
minutes

Learning Activity

After debriefing the movie, have everyone open up to the article about Value Shifts. Ask them to read through the article slowly and to think about themselves as they read about the shifts.

Value Shifts

Values show up in our behavior. Competing values drove the actions of Martin Luther and his followers. We can look at our checkbooks, our calendars and our lifestyles to gain insight into our deeply held values. Author Thom Rainer suggests that there are a number of shifts which Christians must embrace in order to reach out to people who need Christ. Carefully consider which shift or shifts God is challenging you with as you read through what Rainer suggests. These shifts are found in his work, *The Unchurched Next Door* (Chapter 9).

Shift #1 Lethargy to Vitality
Christians don't share their faith with others because they are not growing spiritually. Lack of spiritual growth inevitably leads to a sense of disinter-

est in talking to others about God. It's hard to talk about something that has become stale or mundane for you personally.

Shift #2 Inclusive to Exclusive
In the minds of many believers today there is a commonly held belief that one does not have to have a personal relationship with Christ as your Lord and Savior to make it into Heaven. God is perceived as a merciful God who will cut people slack in the end regardless of what they think of Christ. We have become so open-minded and tolerant of other viewpoints that we have moved away from a central teaching of the Bible.

Shift #3 Unreal Hell to Hell is Very Real
More and more believers deny the existence of hell. Rather, those who do not place their faith in Christ will simply cease to exist when they die. Evangelism becomes less of a priority when hell becomes unimportant.

Shift #4 Busy to Intentional
Most Christians lead such full and demanding lives that finding time for the unchurched becomes near impossible. Trimming calendars and becoming committed to building friendships with the unchurched takes effort.

Shift #5 Fearful to Confident
We are afraid to talk about spiritual things because we think that we will make others uncomfortable. Fear of being rejected or of not knowing what to say in a conversation grips the heart of many believers.

Shift #6 Disinterested to Inviting
One of the overwhelming findings of Rainer's research is that unchurched people will come to church with us if we would only invite them.

Once everyone has read through, take a few minutes to ask for people to respond to the article by answering the question: "What stood out to you about the six shifts?"

Next, transition the group to the Acts 11 passage to further reinforce what they've read and discussed.

Practice Activity

15-20 minutes

Ask everyone to spend time in Acts 11:1-18 with a partner. Give them a few minutes to work through the passage and the two reflection questions. Then take time as a whole group to discuss the reflection questions out loud together. After you've discussed the questions move on to the Practicing the Six Shifts exercise. Give everyone a moment to score themselves and the church. Then ask them to share their results with someone nearby and the reasons that they scored themselves the way that they did.

Question #1: What value and belief shifts did Peter and the other Jewish Christians go through in this passage?

Question #2: Why was this such a critical time in the growth and expansion of the young Christian church?

Practicing the Six Shifts

Score yourself and your church on the six shifts. Use a scale of 1-10 with the following guidelines:

For you:
  (1) Do not need to change / Already done…...
  (10) I REALLY must change

For the church:
  (1) Do not need to change / Already done....
  (10) We REALLY must change

Shift Needed	My Personal Score	Our Church Score
Shift #1 From Lethargy to Vitality		
Shift #2 Inclusive to Exclusive		
Shift #3 Unreal Hell to Hell is Very Real		
Shift #4 Busy to Intentional		
Shift #5 Fearful to Confident		
Shift #6 Disinterested to Inviting		

Application Activity

5-10
minutes

Close out the session with each person filling in the Me and the Shifts reflection exercise. Three to five minutes should be sufficient. If time allows, ask people to share what they've recorded and to pray for one another.

Me and the Shifts

Pick two of the shifts that were discussed today and write down a few specific action steps you can take to align your values with God's values.

Session 4

The Search

Objective: *To build a biblical foundation for the notion that God desires His church to grow and expand and to inspire participants to commit to furthering God's redemptive plan.*

15 minutes

Discovery Activity

Facilitator Instructions: Everyone has two minutes to go outside and find something that is growing or has grown. Please bring your item back into the room with you.

Once everyone is back in the room have them get into groups of three for some interaction. Ask each group to spend a couple of minutes brainstorming.

Question #1: What was necessary in the growth of the examples you brought back?

Question #2: After a couple of minutes, ask them to transition to this second question: What is involved in the growth of a local church? Let each group interpret what is meant by the term growth!

Debrief

Bring the whole group back together to discuss the second question. As people share, build a list on a legal pad of the various responses.

Key Point: There are a number of factors that contribute to the growth of a local church. In this session we will be taking a deeper look at one aspect of God's heart for growth: growth through reaching out into our communities.

20 minutes

Learning Activity

Ask everyone to turn to the article entitled "The Search" and to carefully read it. Encourage them to underline or highlight key points as they read. After everyone has read through the article ask them to pair up with someone near them to discuss the questions at the end of the article. If time allows, spend some time discussing the same questions as a whole group.

The Search

"How then can they call on the one they have not believed in? And how can they believe in the one whom they have not heard? And how can they hear without someone preaching to them? And how can they preach unless they are sent?" (Romans 10:14-15)

Paul doesn't leave us very much wiggle room in this verse. It is pretty clear that God has entrusted Christians with the responsibility to search for people who are lost without Christ and we are to share the good news of what Christ has done. However, in the twenty-first century we have a small problem. Listen to what author Kennon Callahan has to say:

The day of the local church is over. The day of the mission outpost has come. More precisely, the day of the churched-culture local church is over…What I am suggesting is that the way in which local churches have done business, conducted leadership, and developed administration is no longer functional in our time. Churches that cling to the old ways that worked so well in the churched culture will survive for a number of years. Their people will grow old together, and many of those churches will eventually die…the spirit of a mission outpost is one of mission, whereas the spirit of a churched-culture local church is one of maintenance. (*Effective Church Leadership*, p.22-23)

In 21st Century North America, we can no longer call ourselves a churched-culture. Many in our culture today are not turning to the church for answers or for help. We now have an entire generation that has grown up without setting foot in our churches. That is why Callahan argues that the day of the local church is over. The world that we live in will require churches to act and think differently. We can no longer assume that unchurched people will come to us. Instead we have to act and think like missionaries who are staffing what Callahan calls a mission outpost.

What are the qualities of a mission outpost?
• For starters, a mission outpost assumes by its very nature that it exists for others. It is a declaration that others need to be searched for and they need to be told and exposed to the life-transforming truth of the Gospel.

• A mission outpost is an expression of intentionality. Searching for the unchurched requires effort. As Paul says in Romans 10, how on earth can we expect people to hear about Christ unless we go out to them? As stated earlier, we don't have the luxury of people just walking in off of the streets like we did 20-40 years ago. That age of the church no longer exists. We live in a day that requires us to move out into the harvest… out into the fields.

• A mission outpost exists because it is placed in a mission field. Everyone who works on the mission outpost understands that the mission field is all around them. Make no mistake, North America is one of the largest mission fields in the world in the 21st Century.

• Maintaining the mission outpost is secondary to the goal of getting the message out and searching for hungry hearts. In other words, the management of the mission outpost is not nearly as important as spreading the news.

Jesus said to Peter that the gates of Hades would not prevent God from building His church. Later in Acts, he commissioned Peter and others to go into all the world to search for souls in the harvest. He wants His church to grow through the rescuing of lost sheep. Local churches which have become mission outposts are what's needed in a culture that is no longer "churched."

Question #1: What is one thing that stands out to you as you read this article?

Question #2: What is most troubling (or challenging) to you personally about the article?

Question #3: In your mind, what has contributed to the demise of the "churched-culture" for which Callahan argues? Do you agree or disagree with his assessment?

20 minutes

Practice Activity

Divide into groups of two or three to look into what the Bible says about God's heart for the unsaved and our responsibility. Ask each group to look up the passages and to note what the Bible teaches about reaching out. After 10-15 minutes bring the group back together and discuss each passage noting the findings on a whiteboard or flipchart.

Scripture Search Passages

Passage	Principles about Reaching Out
Matthew 28:18-20	
Mark 16:15-16	
Acts 1:8	
Romans 10:14-15	
Luke 15	

5 minutes

Application Activity

As a way to wrap up the session, ask people to write down a few names of people that they know who need Jesus. In smaller pairings, close out your time together by praying for the names that people have written down. Encourage people to pray for opportunities to talk about God and for God to create open hearts.

The Power of a Team

Objective: *To equip believers with a framework for understanding the role of doing church as a team rather than flying solo.*

10-15
minutes

Discovery Activity

Introduce the fact that geese fly together in a "V" formation. In smaller groupings, ask people to respond to the question next to the picture. Give them 2 or 3 minutes to think out loud.

What are some of the reasons that geese fly in this peculiar formation?

Next, take a few minutes to talk about some of the unique features of why geese fly in "V" formation. Encourage people to fill in the blanks as you read the information below.

Geese Facts

Geese take turns in the leadership position. When one goose gets tired, it rotates to the back of the formation and another goose flies to the lead position.

As each goose flaps its wings, it creates an "uplift" for the birds that are behind it. By flying in "V" position the birds are able to fly 70% farther than they could "flying solo."

Geese honk at one another while they are flying to offer encouragement to those flying in the front of the "V."

When a goose gets sick or injured, two geese will drop out of the formation and will follow their comrade down to the ground. They stay with the wounded bird until it dies or is strong enough to fly again. The "V" formation enables all of the birds to see the direction that the group is flying toward.

Next, (in the original groupings) ask people to respond to the sharing questions:

Question #1: Tell about a time when you did or did not experience "flying in a V." It could be at church, sports, in the workplace, family, etc.

Question #2: Bring the group back together and ask the room to reflect on the stories that they heard by asking this question: What themes or threads ran through the stories that were shared in your group?

10-15
minutes

Learning Activity

After you have had your discussion about the geese and the flying "V" draw everyone's attention to the article entitled "The Flying V." Encourage folks to read the article slowly and to underline key thoughts and phrases. After everyone has read the article, take a few minutes to discuss it by asking:

Question #1: What grabs your attention from this article?

Question #2: How does it challenge you personally?

Question #3: Which myth is the strongest in our church and why?

The Flying V

Lessons for the Church come in the most unusual places sometimes. Take geese for example. Who would have thought that geese could teach the Church a thing or two? In particular, the way geese fly is a tremendous illustration about the power of teamwork. It's been said that a team will outperform an individual every day of the week. God has designed us to "fly" in cooperation with others. We can accomplish so much more through the power of a team. So, let's take a look at a few myths which flying geese dispel in our churches.

Myth: The Pastor can do it alone.
In the West, we have constructed an oddly shaped "V" when it comes to the pattern in which we fly in our churches. In many congregations, the paid staff are the ones who do ministry while the rest of us stand on the ground and watch them fly. Our pastors have become superheroes who are capable of leaping tall buildings in a single bound, run faster than a locomotive, and can stop a bullet with their bare hands! We have built a model of "doing church" which suggests that the goose who is flying in the lead position is meant to always stay there. The reality is that the pastor can not fly alone, nor can he fly at the head of the "V" without assistance and shared leadership.

Myth: I'm not gifted.
Oh, yes you are! The New Testament clearly teaches that every believer is equipped by God with spiritual gifts that He expects to be used for the building of His Kingdom. God has graciously bestowed on each one of us unique ways that we can serve Him and others in a fulfilling way. Make no mistake about it; you are gifted! You are gifted by God to make an incredible contribution… one which will have eternal impact.

Myth: I can fly alone.
As the geese so amply illustrate, we need the "updraft" of others around us. Sure, we can try to fly solo, but the wind resistance is much more demanding. When we fly with others we have the support and encouragement we need to fly faster and farther. God has made it clear from many passages in the New Testament that each believer has a role to play in the "V." The apostle Paul likens the church to the human body and he suggests that each believer has a special part to play in how the body functions. You need the "V", and the people sitting around you in church need the "V."

20-25
minutes

Practice Activity

Assign participants into two's and three's. Give everyone 10-15 minutes to work through the various passages. Then, bring everyone back together to talk about the principles and ideas that each passage is reinforcing. Capture the comments of the group on a legal pad.

The Flying V in the New Testament

Look up each of these passages and record a few insights about how the church is meant to fly in a "V." In particular, what place do these passages have to say about the role of the pastor, the nature of teamwork, spiritual gifts and any other "flying geese" principles that you notice?

Passage	Flying "V" Principles
Romans 12:6-8	
1 Corinthians 12:1-10	
1 Peter 4:10-11	
Ephesians 4:11-16	

15
minutes

Application Activity

After you have had a thorough discussion on the four passages, allow everyone to have some individual time to reflect on what the flying "V" means for them personally. Once everyone has had 4-5 minutes to write down some thoughts, ask them to get into groups of three to share their reflections.

Debrief

Question #1: Which myth from the "Flying V" article is the most challenging for me personally and why?

Question #2: What specific action steps can I take to become a contributing "goose" in my church's "Flying V"?

Question #3: What is one thing that could get in the way of putting this into action?

Wrap-Up

Take a few minutes as you close out the session to celebrate new learning around the room. Ask everyone to stand and for a few people to share their response to this statement:

One highlight for me from today is _____.

Where To From Here?

Objective: *To discuss the implications that this study has upon our lives and to make plans regarding the next steps of living out God's vision for the lost.*

10-15 minutes

Discovery Activity

Facilitator Instructions: This session is a review of what the group learned over the last few weeks. In this opening activity, give people the time and space to reflect about their experiences.

Implications of Motivation for Mission

• What is the greatest learning you have taken away from the study?

• What was the most fun?

• What was the greatest benefit to you personally?

• What practical changes have you made in your life as a result of this study? What changes do you want to make in the future? Who will you partner with to give you support and accountability in making those changes?

10-15 minutes

Discussion Activity

Facilitator Instructions: Introduce this discussion by reading the passage and then explain how the church began as a Jerusalem-centered movement, something that was focused on the restoration of Israel. But the book of Acts reveals how the Holy Spirit propelled the church out from Jerusalem. One illustration of this is the key role played by the Antioch church in starting churches throughout the Roman Empire. (See Acts 13:1-3)

The Scattered Church

> But you will receive power when the Holy Spirit comes on you; and you will be my witnesses in Jerusalem, and in all Judea and Samaria, and to the ends of the earth. (Acts 1:8)

While Christianity began at the center as a Jerusalem movement, it did not remain a religion that required those on the outside to come to that center. It quickly became a movement that moved out to the fringes. It became a scattered church that spread throughout the world.

Discussion Questions:

1. Why is a scattered church view so crucial to the spreading of the Gospel?

2. What do you think might be some of the keys to a church moving out from the center?

Learning Activity

15-20
minutes

8 Hinge Factors that Open Doors to the Community

Facilitator Instructions: After the discussion about the scattered church, ask people what it might mean for the church to be scattered in the world today. The good thing is that we don't have to guess what this might mean for the church. We know the key practices or factors that churches must do in order to open doors to their communities.

Extensive research has been performed on churches to identify the key factors that contribute to a church opening its doors and engaging their communities with the Gospel of Jesus Christ. Eight factors open doors of a church and release the people of God go do what has been introduced over the last five sessions.

They are divided into two groups. The first four primarily apply to the pastor and also to key leaders of the church. It is important for everyone in the church to understand these factors. Often pastors feel that they cannot move out into mission because the people they care for have expectations of them that contradict these four factors. The people of God must align their expectations of their leaders with factors that will open doors.

The second set of four apply to four aspects of the way that the church at large operates. Here are the eight Hinge Factors.

Leadership Factors	Church Factors
Empowering God's People for Works of Service	Community Outreach
Personal Leadership	Focused Prayer
Visionary Leadership	Functional Board
Bridge-Building Leadership	Inspiring Worship

Briefly introduce the eight factors that are outlined on the next two pages. There is no need to gain a complete understanding of them. The point is to give people a picture of the focus the church must have in order to reach the community.

Four Leadership Hinge Factors

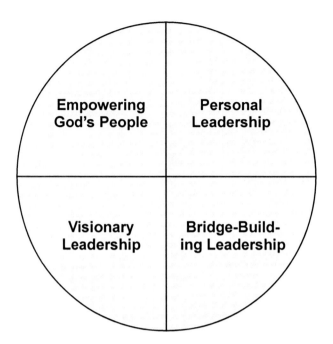

Empowering God's People for Works of Service
This hinge swings open as the pastor, key leaders and the entire church realize that the role of leaders is to empower people to serve, not to do all of the serving.

Personal Leadership
Leaders must manage their own lives, particularly in the areas of physical, mental, spiritual, and relational development.

Visionary Leadership
Vision must be in the driver's seat as the church ventures out into the community. Vision comes by seeking the heart of God and seeing where He is already working in the community.

Bridge-Building Leadership
Moving out into the community to reach the lost cannot be led from the church office. Pastors and other leaders must learn about the needs, the culture, and the people in your local community by actually meeting with them and building a relationship bridge that the Gospel can travel across.

Four Church Hinge Factors

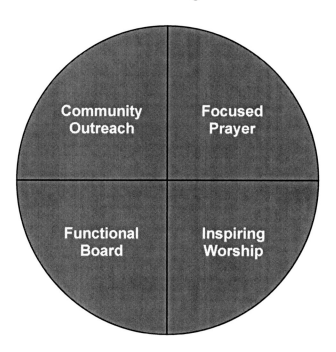

Community Outreach
The location of sowing the seeds of the Gospel in order to reap an eternal harvest happens in our local communities.

Focused Prayer
Prayer that opens doors incorporates intercession for those who need to know Christ. This occurs through things like prayer for the unchurched by name and prayer for the church's vision.

Functional Board
Church boards must support the Pastor's leadership role while providing protection for the congregation by setting healthy boundaries.

Inspiring Worship
Seekers attend church hoping to make friends and connect with God in a way that is meaningful to them. The key is to develop an approach to the worship experience that fits your context and accomplishes your agreed upon mission and vision.

10-15
minutes

Application Activity

Options for Next Steps

Facilitator Instructions: After going over the eight factors, ask people to think about the kinds of things that they might need in order to move into this vision. Break people into groups of three to discuss the opening question below. Then gather people after seven or eight minutes and talk about this question as a whole group.

After that discussion, introduce the three study options below. These are the next steps options for opening doors into the community.

Moving out into God's mission requires focus and intentional effort. These are the eight factors that must be the focus. As next steps in this focus, there are a few options that are crucial steps to take as your church moves forward to open doors to the community.

• Based on what you have learned, what kind of equipping do you need to take next steps?

Option A: Passion for Prayer: Seeking God to Open Doors To Your Community

This study correlates with the Hinge Factor of Focused Prayer. In these six sessions, you will study the Lord's Prayer and discuss ways to pray both individually and as a group so that you can make a greater impact upon the world around you. Topics include:

1. Connecting with Your Father
2. Hallowed Be Your Name
3. Your Kingdom Come
4. Daily Bread
5. Forgive Us Our Debts
6. Deliver Us From Evil

Option B: Reaching Your Community: Discovering Natural Ways to Share the Gospel

In this study you will be equipped to apply the Hinge Factor of Community Outreach. These six sessions will prepare you to reach out to your friends and neighbors. You will learn the basics of how to serve your community, how to develop good listening skills and how to share your testimony. Topics include:

1. Natural Evangelism
2. Improving Your Serve
3. Improving Your Serve (Together)
4. Friendships Through Listening
5. Friendships Through Curiosity
6. Natural Sharing

Option C: People of Passion

If you find that this study has energized you and instilled you with a passionate desire to get serious about this effort, then you might fit the bill for an experimental group called People of Passion. This is a small group of about seven people who will be focused on forging a new path for the church to open doors to the community. One way to gauge whether you want to participate in a People of Passion group is to reflect on the following questions:

Yes No

☐ ☐ Do you have a deep passion for Christ, to the point that you want others to know him and do whatever it takes to change your life so that God can work through you in this way?

☐ ☐ Do you have a deep passion for the church, one that is expressed in a love for the local church along with desire to see it flourish?

☐ ☐ Do you have a deep passion for your community, especially those who don't know Jesus and His love for them.

☐ ☐ Do you have ability to adjust your schedule to participate in a group that will require up to three hours of your time per week for about six months.

☐ ☐ Do you have the emotional energy at this time in your life to invest in the development of new ideas about how the church can open doors to the community?

☐ ☐ Do you like trying out new ideas and think about ways of doing things that don't fit the way things have been done in the past?

Discussion Questions:

• Are you interested in taking the next steps to open the doors of your church?

• What next step interests you the most?

• What kind of role would you like to play in this next step? Leader? Host? Member?

CPSIA information can be obtained at www.ICGtesting.com
Printed in the USA
LVOW09s1029080813

346691LV00003B/14/P